For Cc

MW01145909

The American Krag Rifle and Carbine

by
Joe Poyer

Edited by
Craig Riesch

Ammunition for the
U.S. Krag Rifle and Carbine
Ed Furler, Jr.

2nd Edition, Revised

North Cape Publications®, Inc.

The American Krag Rifle and Carbine

For Lt. Colonel William R. Mook, USAF, ret., preeminent Kragologist!

The author would like to thank all those who helped, directly or indirectly, with this project. He would especially like to mention Ken Catero; Ed Cote; Scott Duff, Scott Duff Publications; Nick Ferris; Jim Gronning, Gruning Precision Gunsmith; John Jordan; John McCabe, U.S. Park Service, Springfield Armory Museum; Roy Marcot, Old Fort Lowell Armory Press; Don Moore; J. Michael Metzgar and Ken Fladrich, Armory of Orange, Orange, CA; Tom Pearce; Ed Seiss, S&S Firearms; and Woody Travis for their help and support.

Also, special thanks to Jonathan Peck, and to John Gangel and Brian Maize of Little John's Auction Service, Orange, California, for making the Peck Collection of Krag rifles and carbines available to the author and editor for research and photography.

This publication is designed to provide authoritative and accurate information of the subject matter covered. However, it should be recognized that serial numbers and dates, as well as other information given within, are necessarily limited by the accuracy of source materials.

ISBN-13: 978-188239131-8
ISBN-10: 1-882391-31-4

North Cape Publications®, Inc. P.O. Box 1027, Tustin, California 92781
714 832-3621, Fax 714 832-5302
E-mail: ncape@ix.netcom.com
Internet Website http://www.northcapepubs.com

Printed by Delta Printing Solutions, Valencia, CA 91355

The American Krag Rifle and Carbine

Table of Contents

The American Krag Rifle and Carbine

The American Krag Rifle and Carbine

The American Krag Rifle and Carbine

The American Krag Rifle and Carbine

The American Krag Rifle and Carbine

The American Krag Rifle and Carbine

Tables

The American Krag Rifle and Carbine

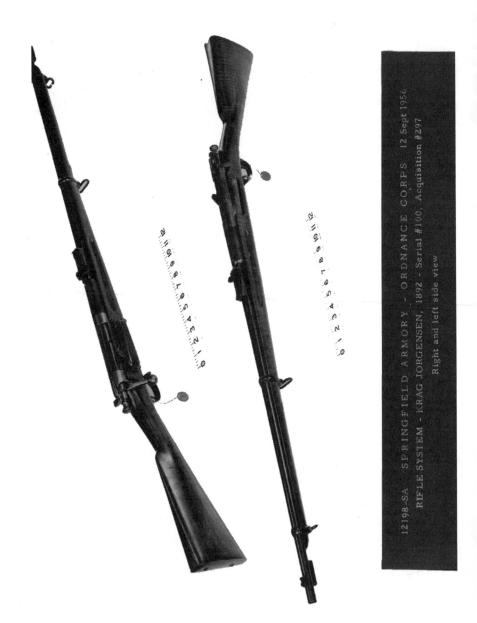

12198-SA   SPRINGFIELD ARMORY - ORDNANCE CORPS   12 Sept 1956
RIFLE SYSTEM - KRAG JORGENSEN, 1892 - Serial #100. Acquisition #297

Right and left side view

The American Krag Rifle and Carbine

Figs. 1 and 2 a-b. The Krag rifle shown on these two pages bears the serial number 100, and is a handmade rifle built in Norway under the direct supervision of Colonel Ole Hermann Johannes Krag and submitted to the U.S. Board on Magazine Arms in 1890. It is believed to be Test Rifle No. 5. The photograph on page X was taken in September 1956 at the Springfield Armory and was provided through the courtesy of the Springfield Armory National Historic Site. The photographs on this page were taken in September 2002 at the Springfield Armory by the author.

The American Krag Rifle and Carbine

Fig. 3. Trooper of the 4th Cavalry at Ft. Riley, Kansas, holds his new Model 1896 Krag Carbine. North Cape Publications collection.

The American Krag Rifle and Carbine

Fig. 4. 1st Cavalry troopers at Fort Robinson, Nebraska, in 1897 with their new Model 1896 Krag carbines and Model 1892 Colt revolvers.

The American Krag Rifle and Carbine

Fig. 5. "Doughboy" of the 4th Infantry holding a new Model 1892 Krag Rifle. Note how the front and rear rows of cartridges are staggered in his web belt.

The American Krag Rifle and Carbine

Fig. 6. 7th Cavalry trooper, mounted, outside the stable gate at Fort Grant, Arizona Territory, holds a Model 1898 Krag Carbine.

Fig. 7. Three Volunteer infantrymen in the Philippines (note stacked Model 1884 Springfield rifles) are visited by a regular with Krag Model 1896 Rifle (right).

Fig. 8. This unknown 25th Infantry soldier was photographed in 1907 with his Krag Model 1898 service rifle, possibly just before turning it in for the new U.S. Magazine Rifle, Caliber .30, Model of 1903.

The American Krag Rifle and Carbine

Fig. 9. Private Adelbert Card, Company F, 24th Infantry, U.S. Army, Manila, 1901. Pvt. Card is holding a Model 1892 rifle refurbished as a Model 1896. Photo courtesy of Lou Card.

Chapter 1
The American Krag Rifle and Carbine

The Krag was the first rifle produced at the Springfield Armory that was not called a "Springfield" either formally or informally. The reason was simply that the Krag was a foreign magazine-loading design selected by the U.S. Army Ordnance Department.

The rifle was designed by Colonel Ole Hermann Johannes Krag and Erik Jørgensen, both Norwegian citizens. Ole Krag, born in 1837, was a Norwegian Army Lieutenant of Infantry and later Artillery. In 1866, he was assigned to Norway's chief arms design and manufacturing facility, the Kongsberk Vapenfabrik (Kongsberg Arms Factory) as an inspection officer. He rose to superintendent of the factory in 1880 and fifteen years later, was promoted to the rank of Colonel and became Master General of Ordnance.

Erik Jørgensen, born in 1848, was trained as a gunsmith in Drammen, Norway. He became a military armorer in 1872 and was assigned to the Smaalenes *Jegerbataljon* in the Norwegian Army. He also operated a commercial gun shop in Fredrikstad, Norway, until 1882 when he was employed by the Kongsberg Arms Factory. Krag and Jørgensen collaborated on the design of a magazine system for a repeating rifle which used a rectangular box with a gate. A spring-loaded carrier and follower moved the cartridges from right to left in the box magazine and lifted them one by one into the bolt raceway as the action was worked. The bolt was designed with a long guide rib for smooth operation and locked into the receiver with a single lug.

Norway and Sweden were aligned in a confederation during the latter part of the 19th century but maintained separate military establishments. As in most countries in Europe in the late 1880s and early 1890s, Norway and Sweden were searching for new military rifles to replace their single-shot Remington "rolling blocks" and 10.15 mm Jarmann tubular magazine repeating rifles. In 1889, a Joint Commission was established to select a new rifle and cartridge.

The American Krag Rifle and Carbine

Fig. 1-1. Top to bottom: Krag Jørgensen Model 1892, 1896, and 1898 rifles. North Cape Publications and Craig Riesch collections.

The American Krag Rifle and Carbine

Denmark was also searching for a new rifle for its army and had conducted a long series of tests before selecting the Krag receiver and magazine system in 1889. To this, they added the shrouded barrel of the Model 1888 Mauser "Commission" rifle. The Danes also modified the magazine system so that the gate was hinged at the front to open forward rather than down and to the side as in the original design. The cartridge selected for the Danish Krag-Jørgensen was an 8 x 58 mm rimmed cartridge.

Between 1889 and 1893, the Norwegian and Swedish members of their Joint Commission managed to select a new cartridge, the 6.5 x 55 mm rimless, but could agree on little else. The Norwegians pressed for the adoption the Krag system but the Swedish members resisted. They were more interested in the Mauser system as it could be clip-loaded. In 1893, the members of the Joint Commission agreed to disagree. The Swedes adopted the Mauser and the Norwegians the Krag-Jørgensen, both in 6.5 x 55 mm.

The U.S. Krag-Jørgensen

Legend has it that the move to a small caliber, bolt-action repeating rifle by the U.S. Army was delayed by hidebound Ordnance officials who were afraid that troops would waste ammunition if given a repeater. While ammunition wastage was a consideration, it was only part of the problem.

The Army had adopted the Spencer repeating rifle and carbine in 1863. Unfortunately, its massive cast receiver did not allow it to be chambered for a more powerful cartridge. When it became clear that the Spencer could not be "upgraded," the Army began searching for a better repeating rifle.

The post–Civil War period was one of drastic military downsizing and totally inadequate budgets. Yet the Ordnance Department devoted a great deal of time and effort to the search for a repeating rifle that would withstand the rigors of military service. A Magazine Board was authorized in 1878 to hold a series of trials which selected the Winchester Hotchkiss for field testing. It was one of the

The American Krag Rifle and Carbine

first American-designed bolt-action repeaters but it proved too fragile for military service. Testing was repeated again with a second board in 1882 with another batch of repeating rifle designs, but with the same result.

Europe in the latter half of the 19th century was an armed camp with sporadic wars breaking out every few years as nations jockeyed for empires and economic dominance. Small-arms development was pushed hard. In 1885, a French chemist, Paul Marie Eugene Vieille, succeeded in developing *Poudre B,* a smokeless powder that was not only clean burning but more powerful than black gunpowder. The French Army, with memories of the Franco-Prussian War debacle of 1870–71 fresh in their minds, adopted a small-caliber, smokeless powder bolt-action rifle, the Lebel, in 1886. And the race was on.

The Board on Magazine Arms Selects the Krag

The U.S. Army Ordnance Department completed its review of all existing small-caliber, repeating military rifles in the same year. The Chief of Ordnance pinpointed the problem when he wrote in his report that the problem was not in finding a suitable design for a small-caliber, repeating rifle but that there did not then exist in the United States, a "suitable small-arms [smokeless] powder." He went on to state that ". . . all the elements entering into the problem [of the rifle] are ready the moment the powder is obtained." That statement was only a bit premature.

A Board on Magazine Arms consisting of five officers under the direction of Robert H. Hall, Lt. Colonel, 6th Infantry, was established by General Order No. 136 in New York City in November 1890 to review the latest examples of military rifles. They met the following month and for the next two years at the Army Building, they conducted tests on fifty-three different magazine arms.

Among the fifty-three rifles tested by the board were eleven types currently in use by other nations: the Austrian Mannlicher rifle and carbine (8 mm), Belgian Model 1889 Mauser (7.65 mm), British Lee-Speed (.303 in.), Danish Krag-Jørgensen (8 mm), German Mauser

The American Krag Rifle and Carbine

Model 1889 (7.65 mm), Japanese Murata (8 mm), Portuguese Kropatschek (8 mm), Romanian Mannlicher rifle (6.5 mm), Russian Model 1891 Mosin-Nagant rifle (7.62 mm) and the Swiss Schmidt-Rubin Model 1889 rifle (7.5 mm). The Board, with both a small caliber and a magazine cutoff as two of the main requirements for the new American military rifle in mind, selected the Krag-Jørgensen.

The Krag-Jørgensen design was built around a box magazine holding five loose cartridges. When the magazine was closed by means of a gate, the cartridges were lined up in proper order to be fed one by one into the breech each time the bolt was worked. A cutoff device, when activated, prevented cartridges in the magazine from being loaded so that the soldier could insert one cartridge at a time when the bolt was open.

Fig. 1-2. The Krag-Jørgensen box magazine held 5 cartridges. A sixth could be inserted in the breech. A cutoff device allowed the rifle to be used as a single-loader with the magazine held in reserve.

Six variations of the Krag chambered for two cartridges, the Model 1892, Caliber .30 Government cartridge (a.k.a. .30-40 Krag) and a rimless .30-caliber cartridge, both developed at Frankford Arsenal, were tested.

Each of the fifty-three rifles was fired 500 times without cleaning. They were then subjected to blowing sand, sprays of water and defective cartridges. Each rifle was rusted and fired twenty more times. The results were painstakingly documented by the Board and the tabulated results were submitted on August 19, 1892, to Brigadier General D.W. Flagler, Chief of Ordnance, who in turn sent them on to the

The American Krag Rifle and Carbine

Secretary of War, recommending the adoption of Rifle No. 5, the Danish version of the Krag-Jørgensen rifle.

The Rationale for the Magazine Cutoff

The Krag was selected over the many Mauser and other designs for its ruggedness, relatively simple construction and because it could be used as both a magazine loader and, by throwing a lever, a single-shot rifle with the magazine full of cartridges held in reserve. Keep in mind that since the American Revolution, the American soldier had been trained to fire single-shot muskets and rifles. The concept of expending too many rounds of ammunition in combat is a mystery to most people born and raised after World War I. When compared to the 60,000 rounds expended per casualty during the War in Vietnam, it seemed a very short-sided and hidebound policy.

But consider their reasoning.

One thousand .30-40 Government cartridges in the wooden shipping crate from Frankford Arsenal weighed 75 lbs and supplied twenty-five soldiers with a standard daily issue of forty rounds. A company of 120 men thus required 360 lbs of ammunition. A combat issue was one hundred rounds, and so a 75 lb crate supplied only ten men. A 120-man company required 900 lbs of ammunition *per day*. Even an understrength American division of 8,000 to 9,000 men in 1894 would have required 30–33.75 tons of ammunition per combat day!

Fig. 1-3. This 55-man company of California Volunteer Infantry with their Krags prior to embarking at San Francisco for the Philippines in 1902 would have required an issue of 165 pounds of ammunition per day for garrison duty or 412.5 pounds per day combat ration.

The American Krag Rifle and Carbine

Moving tons of ammunition was less a consideration in Europe where a well-developed railroad and road net in a relatively smaller area made transportation quite a bit easier. But in the vast open spaces of North America where the American Army expected to do its fighting, railheads were often great distances from forts and encampments. Horse-drawn wagons moved all supplies between railhead and post; there were few metaled roads, in fact, few roads at all, most being little more than rutted wagon tracks once past the Mississippi River. Transporting large quantities of ammunition, not to mention rations, animal feed, spare parts, clothing, bedding, tools and all the thousand and one items an army requires, by muscle power alone was a problem of tremendous importance.

The Protests

Even though the Board had done a thorough job in selecting the new rifle design, accusations were made (mostly by American inventors and designers, few of whom had submitted test rifles) that the Board had done a poor job. It was hinted strongly that because the board members were relatively low-ranking officers (two lieutenant colonels, a major and two captains), they lacked sufficient small-arms experience to choose a new rifle. In reality, three of the officers on the board were combat veterans and two were experienced ordnance officers.

A group of American inventors convinced Congress to persuade the Army to conduct new tests. This was done by the simple expedient of attaching to the budgetary authority of $400,000 to begin production, a restriction that it not be spent upon any foreign invention until all suitable American designs had been tested as well. The American designers were given 30 days to submit their rifles, and another examining board was convened on March 1, 1893. Thirteen American designs were examined and tested, none of which were found to be as suitable as the Krag. This finding was reported on May 16, 1893, and transmitted to the Secretary of War by Major General John M. Schofield on May 26, 1893, and the Krag-Jørgensen was confirmed as the Army's new rifle.

The American Krag Rifle and Carbine

PRODUCTION BEGINS

In June 1893, the Springfield Armory began tooling up for production. The first Krag rifle came off the line six months later on New Year's Day 1894.

Production ramped up slowly to the forty rifles a day that Colonel Alfred Mordecai, the commanding officer at Springfield Armory, had projected to the Chief of Ordnance. By September, production had reached sixty rifles per day. The objective was to produce sufficient rifles to arm all infantry regiments within a short space of time, followed by carbines for the cavalry.

Fig. 1-4. The Springfield Armory Water Shops in 1900.

The first three Model 1892 rifles went to the Frankford Arsenal and the Board on Smokeless Powder for testing. Other early rifles went to various Army installations for testing and development.

The next group to receive the new rifle were certain governors of the then forty-four states and six territories. State governors had

The American Krag Rifle and Carbine

quite a bit more influence on national politics at the end of the 19th century than they do today and so it was deemed politically expedient to acquaint them with such a radical departure in military firearms.

Complaints

The governor of Colorado received rifle serial #9. He lent his rifle to a writer for the magazine, *Shooting and Fishing*, who produced a critical article in which he reported that the rifle shot high (the effects of the sighting tables developed during the previous winter) and to the left (a characteristic of the Krag rifle for which no provision had been made for automatic correction in the rear sight) and the slide jumped forward. Needless to say, the article created a controversy of the kind that has dogged the introduction of every new small arm in the U.S. Army from the Model 1798 to the M16.

An interesting bit of information came to the author from his editor regarding the Model 1892 sight for rifle #9. Some years ago, the editor had examined the Colorado governor's rifle which was in a well-known collection at the time. The owner of the collection told him that when he received the rifle the slide was very loose. On disassembling it, the editor found that the slide catch's coil spring was cracked. Could this have been the reason the *Shooting and Fishing* writer reported that the slide jumped forward under recoil?

How Many Krags?

In 1894, the infantry totaled twenty-five regiments, all under strength, or less than 15,000 men including officers. The cavalry consisted of ten regiments (the 11th through 15th Cavalries were not organized until 1901). A reduction in the cavalry branch in 1890 had eliminated Companies L and M and reduced the total number of enlisted men in each company to 40. With officers and others, the Cavalry arm constituted somewhat less than 6,000 of the Army's authorized strength (never reached) of 25,000. Company L was reconstituted the next year in the 1st through 8th Cavalry regiments and enrolled only Native Americans from the area in which each troop was stationed. Although these units

The American Krag Rifle and Carbine

received high marks for skill and discipline, language difficulties as well as racism on both sides ended the experiment in 1897, and they were disbanded. As late as 1898, all but two cavalry units, one at Fort Myer, Virginia, and another at Fort Ethan Allen, Vermont, were stationed west of the Mississippi River in thirty-one posts.

But a series of problems plagued the new rifle and delayed its distribution. The front sight blade and rear sight leaf were changed to improve accuracy. Measurements by William R. Mook and Nick Ferris of numerous Model 1892 sights show no change in range graduations, supporting the contention that all were changed before issue.

An all-steel ramrod replaced the brass-tipped rods. Then it was discovered that because each rifle had been fired five times before being accepted, and not cleaned, the bores had rusted from the mercuric primers in the cartridges. Then the completion of bayonet scabbards was delayed. Finally, it was discovered that the cartridge primer was being pierced and the bolt faces were being eroded by the hot gases. The problem was not solved for another year until the primers were changed from copper to brass cups and the firing pin nose was shortened and its shape was changed slightly.

The 4th Infantry Regiment at Fort Sherman, Idaho, was the first to receive the new rifles in early October 1894. And they began a process that was repeated on post after post across the nation from New York to Hawaii, from Florida to Alaska. Each soldier turned in his .45-70 Springfield and was given a brand-new Krag coated in cosmoline. Stripping down to his undershirt, he took the new rifle out onto the parade ground where barrels of kerosene were waiting. After removing the stock, he opened the bolt and dunked the rifle into the barrel, swished it around and began the laborious process of cleaning off the smelly, greasy preservative.

In spite of the effort involved in readying the rifle for service, most soldiers were delighted to receive the new smokeless-powder magazine rifles. On posts where cavalry or mounted artillery units were also quartered, troopers wandered over to look at the new rifle

The American Krag Rifle and Carbine

with envy. The mounted units would not begin receiving the new Krag carbine until mid-1896.

The new rifles had reached every regular Army infantry unit (less than 15,000 men) by the end of 1896. All cavalry units were equipped with the Krag carbine the following year. The National Guard, which numbered some 100,000 men, never saw the Model 1892 in its original form. They soldiered on with the Model 1884 .45-70 Springfield rifle and carbine.

More Complaints

By 1894, the frontier had disappeared and the troops were rarely called upon to do any real soldiering. The winter of 1889–1890 had seen a final action against the Sioux, who, in a desperate attempt to regain their

Fig. 1-5. These two doughboys ham it up for the camera with their new Model 1892 Krag rifles and bayonets.

lands, had left the reservation for the Dakota Badlands. The troops were called out in a massive show of force and most of the Sioux returned to the reservation. But the old white vs. red animosity had first to play out in the Massacre at Wounded Knee.

The American Krag Rifle and Carbine

An antidote to the boredom of routine garrison duty and work parties, marksmanship training was very popular with the doughboys and troopers. [The term "doughboy" was commonly used from the 1880s on. — Ed.] A soldier could earn distinction in the form of medals (but not extra pay) for marksmanship qualification. Soldiers, officer and enlisted alike, had therefore looked forward to the new small-caliber, high-velocity smokeless-powder arms with a tremendous amount of anticipation.

Fig. 1-6. This Light Artillery trooper with his Krag carbine wears a marksmanship medal with six bars.

The annual small-arms qualification exercises were held every autumn. But the new Model 1892 rifles were issued so late in 1894 that those qualifications were fired for the last time with the .45-70 Springfields. This meant that the usual feedback that came from the entire Army shooting under controlled conditions was delayed until

The American Krag Rifle and Carbine

the following year. The few complaints that made their way to Springfield in the meantime were dismissed as the "usual carping." Even so, soldiers who failed to win their marksmanship badges, as well as others, made their dissatisfaction known and changes were made the following year that resulted in the Model 1896 rifle and carbine.

In spite of the problems with the new rifle, the Model 1892 rifle served long and hard with the regulars during the Spanish-American War and in the Philippines. In 1897 and again in 1900, Model 1892 rifles still in service were recalled and rebuilt as Model 1896 rifles with updated bolt assemblies and new cutoffs and safeties. They were equipped with the improved Model 1896 rear sight, and so they soldiered on.

Two more rifle and three carbine models followed the Model 1892 Krag, each improving on the last. The selection of a rear sight remained a problem but it stemmed from indecision regarding tactical use and not design. A shorter 26-inch barrel, tested in 1902–03, profoundly influenced the design of the next American service rifle, the Model 1903 Springfield.

The Krag was the first smokeless powder, small-caliber repeating magazine rifle adopted by the United States military, and a major technical advance over the single-shot, large-caliber, black-powder rifles and carbines that preceded it. As such, it was not a perfect rifle, but it tried hard and came close, and that's as much as you can ask of any pioneer.

THE U.S. KRAG IN SERVICE

While the Krag had a rather short military lifetime of only fifteen years with the regular Army, it packed a great deal of experience into those years. It served with the regular Army doughboys in Cuba and Puerto Rico and again in the dozens of campaigns throughout the Philippine Islands, where it was immortalized in the "Carabao Song" sung around campfires and in canteens:

"Damn, Damn, Damn the Filipinos,

14

The American Krag Rifle and Carbine

> Pockmarked, Kakiak ladrones!
> Underneath the starry flag
> Civilize them with a Krag
> And return us to our beloved homes!"

Cuba

Cuba had been a Spanish colony since the days of Christopher Columbus. The Spanish had long bled the country of its agricultural and mineral wealth and left the native population in deep poverty. American newspapers had begun agitating to clear the Spanish from Cuba as early as the 1870s. By the end of the last decade of the 19th century, Spain had been painted as the devil incarnate. Reports from Cuba by such well-known journalists as Richard Harding Davis and a young Winston S. Churchill only served to inflame the situation. Two events sent the two countries to war.

The first was a letter stolen by Cuban insurgents from the Havana main post office. Written in December 1897 by the Spanish Minister to the United States, Enrique Dupuy de Lôme, it characterized President McKinley as a ". . . weakling . . . and a bidder for the admiration of the crowd . . . a would-be politician . . . ." Dupuy de Lôme resigned promptly but the damage was done. On February 15, 1898, the U.S. battleship *Maine* exploded while at anchor in Havana harbor. Two hundred and sixty of her crew were killed. The cause was never established but most Americans attributed it to Spanish sabotage.

An ultimatum to Spain on March 27 demanding the right of the United States to act as an arbitrator between the Spanish government and the insurgents was dispatched. When Spain appeared to be looking for a way to comply without damaging the Spanish monarchy, Congress refused to negotiate. A joint resolution was passed by Congress on April 19 and it was signed by President McKinley the next day. War, in effect, had been declared.

By 1898, the regular Army's authorized strength (never met) was 28,000 men and officers. Not since the Civil War had the army been trained in greater than regimental strength. There was no mobi-

The American Krag Rifle and Carbine

Fig. 1-7. Lt. Colonel Theodore Roosevelt (center with suspenders) poses with members of the 1st Volunteer Cavalry, better known as the Rough Riders, on Kettle Hill. Photo courtesy of the Library of Congress.

lization plan and the greater part of the army was stationed in the West. The position of the National Guard was unclear. It was thought by many legal experts that the Federal government did not have the authority to mobilize the Guard for service outside the United States. To get around this, Congress authorized the raising of "Volunteer" units in which the Guard could serve if they wished.

The first military action was the attack on and the establishment of an American naval base at Guantánamo by U.S. Marines, followed by the bombardment of Spanish positions at the entrance to Santiago Bay. Major General William R. Shafter embarked his infantry force at Tampa for Cuba a few days later and it was a fiasco. No detailed planning of any kind had been conducted to load 17,000 men and equipment. Four days were needed to load and assemble the force

The American Krag Rifle and Carbine

and put to sea. On June 20, they reached Santiago and, thanks only to the fact that the Spanish did not oppose the landing, was it successful.

To reach Santiago, it was necessary to first capture the village of El Caney and the surrounding ridges known collectively as San Juan. Confusion resulted due to poor-to-nonexistent communications and the extremely hot weather. A column of U.S. troops moving to the front came under fire from American artillery when signals from an observation balloon were confused. The troops advanced — almost as a mob — rather than by units and field officers struggled to retain control. When they reached San Juan Hill and Kettle Hill, the Spanish defenders opened fire with their Mausers. The troops returned heavy fire from their Krags in the first real battle test of the new rifle as they rushed up, supported by a battery of Gatling guns. On July 1, 1898, Lt. Colonel Theodore Roosevelt led his 1st Volunteer Cavalry (now

Fig. 1-8. The 3rd Wisconsin Volunteer Infantry gets ready to charge the Spanish entrenchments at Coamo, outside San Juan, Puerto Rico. When troops entered the town they found it had already surrendered to war correspondent Richard Harding Davis! Library of Congress photo.

The American Krag Rifle and Carbine

dismounted) up Kettle Hill. The Rough Riders, as the 1st Volunteers were known, were the only non-Regulars in Cuba armed with Krag Model 1896 carbines. A few hours later, the village of El Caney fell after some confusion, and the way to Santiago lay open.

In Santiago itself, the Spanish were running low on ammunition and food. The Spanish fleet in the harbor was ordered to sail in the hope that it would draw off the U.S. Navy and force the U.S. Army to move on toward Havana. The Spanish Admiral, Pascual Cervera, objected strenuously, but obeyed. On the morning of July 3, the Spanish fleet dashed for the open sea. A running sea battle ended with the destruction of the Spanish flotilla. On July 17, Spanish forces at Santiago surrendered.

General Nelson Miles now moved a force of 3,000 men to Puerto Rico. Reinforced with more troops a few days later, the Americans met little resistance and the island was secured within a matter of days, ending the fighting.

The Philippines

On May 1, 1898, Commodore George Dewey sailed the American fleet into Manila harbor and decimated the Spanish naval fleet. On the first of July, 2,500 American troops arrived to occupy Manila. The Americans were determined to force the Spanish to surrender, but wanted only a minimum of aid from Filipino forces led by Emilio Aguinaldo, for fear of a bloodbath. The State Department in Washington was also trying to make up its mind what to do with the islands once the Spanish surrendered. They did not want to be obligated to Aguinaldo any more than necessary. With a great deal of tact and some skill, U.S. forces were interposed between the city walls and the investing insurgents.

When the Americans advanced to relieve the Spanish troops, insurgents rushed to join them and opened fire on the Spanish against orders. The Americans managed to persuade the insurgents to stop firing and withdraw and the Spanish finally surrendered. The surrender terms were signed on August 14, two days after the formal terms of surrender between Spain and the United States had ended the war.

The American Krag Rifle and Carbine

All through the winter, the uneasy truce between the U.S. forces and the Filipino insurgents endured as the U.S. government struggled with how to proceed. In February 1899, the Filipinos, tired of waiting, decided to occupy their own city. Major General Elwell S. Otis, commanding the American forces, had only 21,000 men on hand, many of whom were volunteers whose term of enlistment was running out. In effect then, he had only 12,000 troops against 40,000 insurgents who had occupied a ring of blockhouses surrounding Manila on three sides. Even so, General Otis did not hesitate. The battle that developed lasted for two days and cost the insurgents 3,000 dead and wounded and the Americans, 250. The insurgents withdrew into the countryside and began a guerrilla campaign.

Fig. 1-9. Emilio Aguinaldo y Famy, President of the Philippine Republic and Leader of the Insurrection. Library of Congress photo.

Ten new volunteer regiments were raised in the United States and 35,000 reinforcements were sent to the Philippines. In April 1900, General Otis began an offensive on Luzon against insurgent strongholds. Two columns, one under Major General Arthur MacArthur, drove up the island and by mid-May, had broken the back of the insurgency. In October, operations to lay a complicated operation to trap Aguinaldo began. They did not succeed as well as had been hoped, but Aguinaldo was forced to disperse his forces. Aguinaldo was finally captured in March 1901 in the southern part of Luzon.

The American Krag Rifle and Carbine

Between May 1900 and March 1901, the army fought more than one thousand separate engagements, many with heavy casualties. While the campaign to pacify the insurgents was completed by April 1902, fighting in the Philippines continued into the second decade of the 20th century. Moro tribesmen bitterly resented any outsiders and were determined to rid their lands of all foreigners. For years they carried on a guerrilla war against the Americans and fellow Filipinos. General John J. Pershing decisively defeated the Moros at Mt. Bagsak in 1913, but still the insurgency continues sporadically to this day. But those later battles were fought primarily by the Philippine Constabulary, and after independence in 1946, by the Philippine Army.

China

The Krag also saw hard service in China against armed bands who styled themselves the "Righteous Harmonious Fists," roughly translated into English as "Boxers." The Boxers were outraged at the arrogance of the Western powers who they felt, rightly so, were looting China and attempting to destroy their culture and religion.

When the Boxers surrounded and laid siege to the Legation compound at Peking in 1900 and threatened to execute all Westerners found inside, an international expeditionary force of concerned nations was organized. General Arthur MacArthur, then commanding in the Philippines, dispatched the 9th and 14th Infantry Regiments, elements of the 6th Cavalry and a battalion of Marines to China from the Philippines where all had seen hard service. Their worn Krags and other equipment were replaced in Manila before they sailed. The troops were outraged and demanded to keep their faithful rifles, many of which had been carried all the way from Cuba. But MacArthur wanted them to present a professional appearance to the rest of the Allied force which consisted of British, Japanese, German and Russian troops.

The Americans, as the most battle experienced, bore the brunt of the fighting and casualties, which may have led seventeen years later in France to General John Pershing's refusal to allow American troops to serve under foreign command.

The American Krag Rifle and Carbine

Fig. 1-10. The 14th Infantry marches along the outer walls of Peking on August 14, 1900. That day, they cleared the walls with fire from their Krags and lifted the siege of the Foreign Legations. U.S. Army Military History Institute photo.

The first attempt to march on Peking with a small force was repulsed. The 9th Infantry landed at the port city of Tagu to reinforce the garrison on July 13, 1900. They were quickly ordered to Tientsin by the British commander of the Allied force, Brigadier A.R.F. Dorward. A Russian attack had failed to breach the walled city, but the 9th Infantry took the first line of fortifications in a battle that lasted 15 hours. The Americans fought across open ground nearly two-thirds of a mile wide to the inner wall under accurate sniper fire which caused heavy losses, including the regimental commander, Colonel Liscomb. The city fell that night and the Boxers fled. A company of the Sixth Cavalry was detailed to hold the area and clear out the last of the Boxers and their supporters. The march on Peking resumed.

By August, more units had arrived from the United States to help swell the Allied forces to nearly 18,000. The march to Peking was made under constant harassing fire as well as lack of drinking water and supplies. But on August 14, the expeditionary force arrived before the Tung Pein gate in the walled city of Peking.

The American Krag Rifle and Carbine

Once again, Brigadier Dorward sent the Krag-armed American troops forward against walls swarming with heavily armed and determined Boxers. Accurate fire from the 14th Infantry's Krags cleared the walls while other American troops fought their way through a water gate. Elements of the 14th Infantry scaled the walls and swept the inner compound with rifle fire. Other American units turned their Krags on Boxers in surrounding settlements to kill or drive out snipers. When it was all over, a British column in clean uniforms and with unfired rifles were led by bagpipers through the gates, under the rifles of the 14th Infantry, to relieve the embattled legation.

On the following day, the Americans were sent again to break through the gates into the Imperial City itself. Backed by artillery and Gatling guns, the Boxers were decimated and the gates forced. On August 28, combat teams from each of the Allied nations occupied the Forbidden City, and looted the imperial palaces. The force was led by the Russians, followed by the Japanese, the British and finally, the smallest contingent, the Americans.

A tip to Krag collectors, always check the lightening holes cut into the Krag buttstock. They made excellent hiding places for looted gem stones and jewelry.

THE END OF THE LINE

The Krag was withdrawn from service in 1907 as the regular Army replaced it with the new U.S. Magazine Rifle, Caliber .30, Model of 1903. But that was not the end of the Krag's service to the United States. It continued to serve with the National Guard well into the next decade and when the United States entered World War I, it was called back to equip such special regular units as Railway Engineers. Six battalions of the Railway Engineers were equipped with some 7,600 Krags. Armories were also emptied to supply stateside training camps with Krag rifles to teach the new "National Army" how to march and shoot.

Following the Great War, the last of the military's Krags were sold off in the 1920s and 1930s and many became respectable hunting

22

and target rifles for new generations. An uncounted number of young hunters learned to shoot with a Krag carbine or rifle. Thousands of them brought down their first deer with a remodeled Krag, including the author.

CONVENTIONS

1. Following the editorial practice of North Cape Publications, Inc., major changes to parts are classified as "Types." For instance, "two kinds of lower barrel bands were developed and used. The first is designated as Type 1 and the second as Type 2," etc. This system is used for the convenience of collectors only and was never used by the U.S. Army's Ordnance Department.

2. The Krag was never referred to by the Ordnance Department or the military as a "Springfield" after the national armory in which it was built, as were rifles before and after. The design was the work of Colonel Ole Hermann Johannes Krag and Erik Jørgensen, both Norwegian citizens. Therefore the design is often referred to in this text as the Krag-Jørgensen, out of respect for their accomplishments.

3. At the National Armories, changes were implemented by work orders approved by the Ordnance Department. Following a practice established at the Springfield National Armory at the end of the eighteenth century, manufactured parts were used up first, when safety was not a concern, and before a new part was introduced. Especially after the reorganization of the Springfield Armory in 1894, parts were drawn from bins or racks and delivered to assemblers. The bins and racks were replenished at intervals, not when they were empty. Thus an "old" part could lie in the bottom of the bin or at the back of a rack for several weeks or even months, before being drawn out and used.

    With very few exceptions, changes to the Krag rifle and carbine cannot be pinpointed to a specific serial number. Thus most parts changes are described as taking place at "circa serial number XXX." Circa means "about." All "circa serial number XXX" ranges have been established according to observations made by the author, editor and other researchers. These last are credited when known.

4. All markings on a rifle part are shown in quotation marks, i.e., "MODEL 1898"; the quotation marks were not part of the marking unless so noted.

5. Serial numbers are shown divided by commas to make them more readable. Commas were not used in markings on the rifle or carbine.

6. When measurements are given from a point to a hole or other opening, that measurement is understood to be to the center of the hole or opening, unless otherwise noted.

7. All reference directions are given from the shooter's standpoint while looking toward the muzzle with the rifle shouldered. Thus right side refers to the side with the bolt handle, etc.

8. Line drawings of parts are often used in preference to photographs for clarity or to emphasize certain aspects. Occasionally, a drawing or part of a drawing is exaggerated to emphasize a point. Where exaggeration is used it is noted in the text and/or caption.

9. The American Krag rifle and carbine, despite their European origins, were designed and manufactured according to the English system of measurement. All dimensions are thus given in decimal inches, feet and yards. Non-North American readers can easily convert measurements from decimal inches to millimeters by multiplying by 25.4. Example: 2.3 inches x 25.4 = 58.42 millimeters or 5.84 centimeters. There are twelve inches in a foot and three feet in a yard.

10. Information may be repeated several times in the text at different points so the reader does not have to page back and forth.

Chapter 2
U.S. Krag Rifle and Carbine Part-by-Part

INTRODUCTION

The Krag-Jørgensen rifle and carbine as adopted in 1892 by the U.S. Army is a relatively simple rifle in terms of the number and variety of parts and models when compared to those that would follow. Basically, there were only three standard rifle models and three standard carbine models (a fourth if you count the Model 1892 carbine, which was apparently never put into production). The differences between the models are relatively slight. The majority of changes concerned improved production techniques or minor corrections in the placement of various parts. The most significant changes, and the most visible, had to do with the rear sight and the handguard. In all, six rifle and four carbine sights were placed on various models with handguards manufactured to fit.

Finally, even the exotic models like the Board of Ordnance and Fortifications Rifle and the .22 Gallery Practice Rifles all used standard parts with few exceptions, depending on the year in which they were assembled. Exceptions will be noted as we proceed.

BUTT PLATE ASSEMBLY

The butt plate for the Krag rifle and carbine was formed from mild steel and browned. It measured 4.80 inches long by 1.755 inches wide at its widest point. Its tang was bent at right angles to wrap around the top of the butt. The tang was 1.280 inches long. The same butt plate was used on both the rifle and carbine, and other variations depending on their period of manufacture, see Figure 2-1.

The butt plate had two holes for the butt plate screws. The screw hole in the tang was 0.218 inch in diameter, counterbored to 0.3 inch. It was 0.430 inch behind the point of the tang. The screw hole in the

The American Krag Rifle and Carbine

Fig. 2-1. Two different butt plates were used on the Krag rifle and carbine, without a trap on the early Model 1892s and with a trap on the later models.

plate was 0.310 inch in diameter and counterbored to 0.410 inch. It was located 1.45 inches above the toe. The outside of the plate was polished smooth before browning and the inside was not.

NOTE: The term "brown" or "browning" was used at the Springfield Armory to indicate what we today call "blue" or "bluing." The process involved rusting the steel part with a mixture of nitric and hydrochloric acid, then carding (polishing) the part to remove the reddish rust that was formed. After the desired depth of color was achieved, the part was boiled in water, which caused a chemical reaction that prevented further rusting. The process imparted a deep blue-black color. The amount of blue depended on how highly the part was polished.

Two types of butt plates were used on the Krag series of rifles and carbines. They are described in Table 2-1 and the following paragraphs.

The **Type 1** butt plate was used on the Model 1892 rifle in three variations. They did not have the opening for the butt plate cap.

From the start of production to August 1895, the **Type 1A** butt plate was used. It had a straight toe to fit the Type 1 Model 1892 stock. The plate was 0.08 inch thick, see Figure 2-2.

26

The American Krag Rifle and Carbine

Table 2-1 Krag Rifle and Carbine Butt Plates		
Type	**Characteristics**	**Models Used On**
1A	Straight toe, no trap, 0.08 inch thick	M1892 Rifle and Carbine
1B	Curved toe, no trap, 0.10 inch thick	M1892 Rifle M1896 Cadet
1C	Curved toe, no trap but unfinished lugs, 0.10 inch thick	M1892 Rifle
2	Curved toe, with trap, 0.10 inch thick	M1896 Rifle M1896 Carbine M1898 Rifle and Carbine M1899 Carbine Board of Ordnance & Fortifications Rifle "U.S. Magazine Carbine, caliber .30, Model of 1899, altered for Knife Bayonet and Sling," Gallery Practice Rifle, .22 cal.

After August 1895 the thickness of the butt plate **(Type 1B)** was increased by 0.04 inch, according to official documents. In fact, the butt plate thickness was only increased by 0.02 inch to 0.10 inch according to measurements of numerous examples. It was also curved inward at the toe to provide more protection for the wood of the butt. It did not have the trap for the cleaning kit, see Figure 2-3.

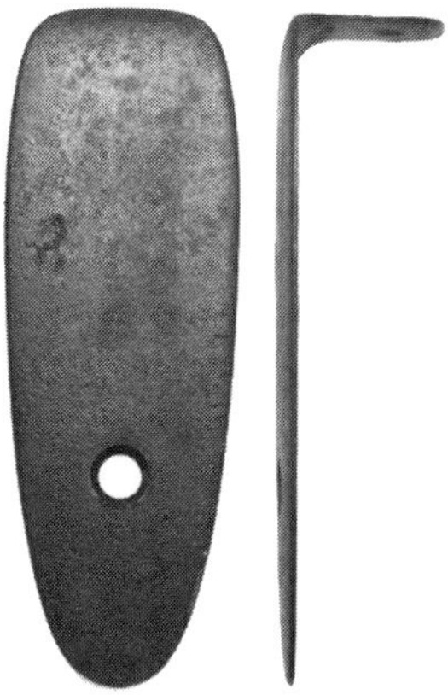

The Type 1B butt plate was also used on the 404 Model 1896 Krag Cadet Rifles

Fig. 2-2. The Type 1A butt plate had a straight toe and no trap.

The American Krag Rifle and Carbine

manufactured in late 1895 and early 1896 and issued to the U.S. Military Academy at West Point, New York. These rifles were withdrawn in 1900 and refurbished and reissued as standard infantry rifles. The butt plates were replaced with the Type 2 at that time.

Type 1C butt plate, circa serial # range 19,000 to 20,200, may have lugs for the butt plate cap that were not completely machined. They may also have been used as replacement parts.

Fig. 2-3. The toe on the Type 1B butt plate was curved but did not have a butt trap.

The **Type 2** butt plate was used from the start of Model 1896 production to the end of all Krag production. It was similar to the Type 1B butt plate but with the addition of a cap assembly for the cleaning kit, see Figure 2-4.

The hole for the cleaning kit was 1.62 inches in diameter and located in the center of the plate, 1.3 inches below the top of the tang. On the inside of the hole, two square lugs were machined at the bottom of the hole and pierced with a pin hole 0.130 inch in diameter to allow the cap to open and close. Two inches above the toe, a second lug was machined. It was round, tapered slightly toward the top and threaded to hold the cap spring in place.

Fig. 2-4. The Type 2 butt plate had a trap door for access to the cleaning kit and rods.

The American Krag Rifle and Carbine

Fig. 2-5. The Type 2 butt plate and cap were hand-fitted and stamped with a fitting number.

All but the earliest Type 2 butt plates and caps were stamped with an identical fitting number in small serif type, 0.09 inch high, see Figure 2-5.

BUTT PLATE SCREWS

Two types of lower butt plate screws and one type of upper butt plate screw were used for the Krag rifle and carbine.

Lower Butt Plate Screw

The lower butt plate wood screw was used on all previous U.S. rifle muskets and rifles from 1855 on. It had eight threads. Two types were used on the Krag rifle and carbine.

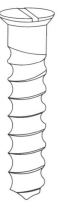

Fig. 2-7. Flat-head Type 2 butt plate screw.

The **Type 1** lower butt plate screw had a slightly domed head. The head projected above the surface of the butt plate; the domed head was found to cause the stock to crack by applying extra pressure when the command to "order arms" was given and the rifle or carbine was grounded sharply, see Figure 2-6. The Type 1 lower butt plate screw was 1.5 inches long. The slotted head was 0.45 inch in diameter.

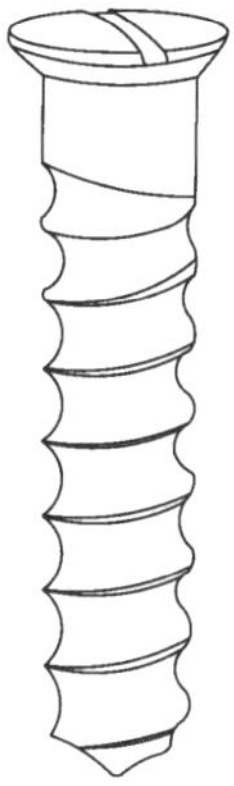

Fig. 2-6. The Type 1 butt plate screw had a slightly domed head.

The **Type 2** lower butt plate screw (Figure 2-7) had a flat head so that it sat flush or slightly below the countersink in the lower screw hole in the butt plate. Its head was 0.45 inch in diameter. It was introduced at circa serial #4,500.

29

The American Krag Rifle and Carbine

NOTE: Although the butt plate screw with the slightly domed head had been in continuous use on U.S. Army rifle muskets and rifles since the advent of the Model 1855 rifle musket, it had not previously caused the splitting problem as the compound curvature of the previous butt plates had kept it from making direct contact with the ground. The Type 2 screw was also used on the Model 1903 Springfield and Rock Island rifles.

Upper Butt Plate Screw

This screw was a smaller version of the lower butt plate screw. It was 0.885 inch long overall. Its slightly domed head was 0.3 inch in diameter and it had seven threads. It was unchanged throughout Krag production, see Figure 2-8.

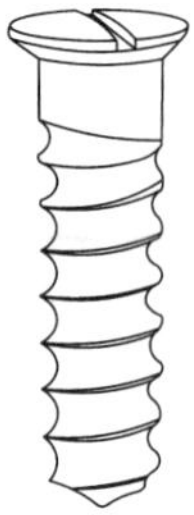

NOTE: The upper butt plate screw was in use from 1855 through the end of M1 Garand production in 1957, achieving at least 102 years of continuous production.

Fig. 2-8. Upper butt plate screw.

Butt Trap Cap

When the decision was made to eliminate the one-piece ramrod, a three-piece rod, similar to that used for the .45-70 Springfield carbine, was designed and produced that fit into a trap in the buttstock. A hole was cut into the Type 2 butt plate and a spring-loaded cap was designed to close it, see Figure 2-9.

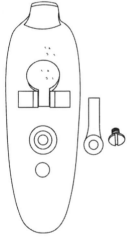

Fig. 2-9. Butt Trap Assembly.

The cap was 0.840 inch in diameter. It had a "tail" 0.480 inch long by 0.270 inch wide. The cap was 0.120 inch thick. The tail was drilled with a pin hole 0.130 inch in diameter for the cap spring pin. The top edge of the cap was rebated to allow the soldier to pry it open with a cartridge rim or knife point.

The cap was case-hardened in water, which produced mottled reds, yellows and blues.

All but the earliest caps will show fitting numbers stamped in serif type 0.09 inch high. The fitting numbers on the cap should match those stamped on the butt plate.

Butt Trap Cap Spring
A flat spring 1.290 inches long by 0.425 inch wide at its widest point and 0.245 inch wide at its narrowest point was used to close the butt trap cap. Its narrow end pressed against the tail of the cap to hold it closed or open. It was fastened to the butt plate with a screw turned into the lower, circular lug.

Butt Trap Cap Spring Screw
The cap spring screw was 0.360 inch high. Its head was 0.370 inch in diameter and was slightly domed. It had five threads and was blackened by being dipped in oil which was then burned off.

Butt Trap Cap Pin
This steel pin held the cap in the upper lug. It was 0.130 inch in diameter and 0.545 inch long. The pin was oil blackened and peened at both ends.

The American Krag Rifle and Carbine

Stock Assembly

The rifle and carbine stock and its component parts remained remarkably stable throughout the production of the Krag rifle. The most noticeable changes in the stock during its eleven-year production period were the rounding of the toe, the thickening of the wrist (or small) and the apparent diminishment of the comb, the reduction of the bolt handle cutout, and in the carbine stock, the lengthening of the forearm for the Model 1899 carbine. Less noticeable were the addition of air chambers, or lightening cuts, in the barrel channel and lightening holes in the butt to which were also added holes for the segmented ramrod and oiler. From the Model 1896 on, the ramrod channel and ramrod stop were omitted.

All Krag rifle and carbine stocks had two finger grooves, one on either side of the forend or forearm. The grooves on the rifle stock and the Model 1899 carbine stock were 6.8 inches long. They were 5.5 inches long on the Models 1892, 1896 and 1898 carbine stocks. On the Type 4C Model 1899 carbine stock used to restock serviceable Model 1896 carbines in and after 1900, they were 6.8 inches long. All were 0.625 inch wide at the widest point and the ends drew to rounded points. The finger grooves were 0.6 inch wide at the front and 0.7 inch wide at the rear on all rifles and carbines.

RIFLE STOCKS
Four types of rifle stocks were developed. The Krag cadet rifle used a slightly modified Model 1892 stock until 1900, when all were restocked with the standard Model 1896 rifle stock and reissued as standard infantry rifles.

The rifle stock was 49 inches long and the Model 1896 and 1898 carbine stocks were 30 inches long. The Model 1899 carbine stock

The American Krag Rifle and Carbine

was 31.75 inches long. All stock length measurements are from the forend or forearm to heel. The Krag rifle and carbine stock butts were both 4.480 inches high and 1.75 inches wide at the thickest point.

The stock, shown in Figure 2-10, includes: 1) butt, 2) lower lightening hole, 3) upper lightening hole which contains the cleaning rods and oiler, 4) lower sling swivel plate inletting, 5) wrist or small, 6) receiver bed, 7) bolt handle recess, 8) trigger inletting, 9) finger grooves, 10) lightening channels in the stock, 11) lower band pin hole, 12) upper band screw hole, 13) lower shoulder for the lower band, 14) upper shoulder for the upper band, 15) upper barrel band inletting, 16) hand-guard spring inletting, 17) hinge bar head cut, 18) front trigger guard screw hole, 19) receiver tang inletting, 20) rear trigger guard screw

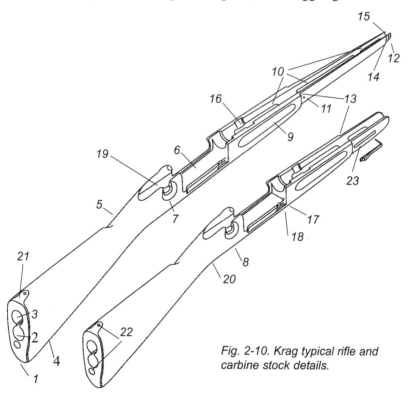

Fig. 2-10. Krag typical rifle and carbine stock details.

33

The American Krag Rifle and Carbine

hole, 21) butt plate tang inletting, 22) butt plate screw holes and 23) band spring inletting. Band springs were not used in the Krag rifle (except the Cadet model) or the Model 1892 carbine stocks to retain barrel bands. Instead, the upper band was retained by a screw which passed through the stock forend or forearm and the band. The lower band was retained by a pin driven crosswise through the stock the band's width ahead of the lower shoulder. The pin protruded just enough on the right side to hold the lower band, when tightened with the cross screw, in place against recoil.

The inletting for the stock removed a greater amount of wood in the critical receiver bed area than in any other U.S. military rifle before or since. The extensive

bedding required by the side-opening magazine was a definite weak point in the stock. It is not unusual to see hairline or larger cracks running diagonally from the bedding back toward the wrist, see Figure 2-11.

Fig. 2-11. Stock receiver inletting.

Model 1892 Rifle Stock, Type 1

Two variations of the **Type 1** stock were developed. The chief identifying characteristic of the Model 1892 stock is the channel cut for the ramrod in the underside of the forend, see Figure 2-12. The exposed part of the channel stretches from the stock nose to the lower band position. Where the ramrod channel enters the stock, the cut comes to a rounded point. At the stock nose, the channel is cut into a "tulip" head.

The ramrod channel is 17.0 inches long from the stock nose to the lower band position, 0.220 inch wide and 0.245 inch deep. Occasion-

34

The American Krag Rifle and Carbine

Table 2-2 U.S. Krag Rifle Stocks		
Model	**Characteristics**	**Attributes (cumulative)**
1892	Ramrod channel, small (1.675-inch dia.) wrist, flared bolt handle recess, vertical channel on either side of trigger pin recess for 0.455-inch pin	**Type 1A:** Flat butt, high wood in bolt handle recess
		Type 1B: Low wood in bolt handle recess
		Type 2A: Toe cut forward, low bolt recess, two lightening holes in buttstock, forend air chambers
		Type 2B: Lower band spring inletting, no inletting for lower sling plate on Cadet rifle only
1892 Modified to 1896	Ramrod channel filled, small (1.675-inch dia.) wrist, flared bolt handle recess, cleaning rod holes in buttstock, no lightening cuts (air chambers) added to forend NOTE: Springfield did not stamp a new cartouche on M1892 rifles modified to the M1896 configuration. Type 3A stocks will show original cartouches but Type 3B will not	**Type 3A:** Type 1A or 2A stock with ramrod channel filled with round dowel, toe cut forward, two lightening holes in butt with three 0.22-inch dia. cleaning rod holes in upper. (M1892 rifles refurbished in 1897)
		Type 3B: Type 1A or 2A stocks with ramrod channel filled with square cross section filler strip, toe cut forward, two lightening holes in butt with three 0.24-inch dia. cleaning rod holes in upper. (M1892 rifles refurbished after 1899)
1896	No ramrod channel, flared bolt handle recess, curved toe, four air chambers in forend, thicker wrist (1.80-inch dia.), two lightening holes in buttstock, vertical channel for 0.455-inch trigger pin eliminated	**Type 4A:** Two lightening holes in butt, no oiler channel, three cleaning rod holes 0.22 inch in dia. drilled in upper lightening hole
		Type 4B: Two lightening holes in butt with oiler channel between, three cleaning rod holes 0.22 inch in dia. drilled in upper lightening hole

The American Krag Rifle and Carbine

Table 2-2, cont.
U.S. Krag Rifle Stocks

Model	Characteristics	Attributes (cumulative)
	No cleaning rod channel, thick wrist (1.80-inch dia.), bolt handle recess cut square, no bolt handle ramp cutout	**Type 5:** Cleaning rod holes enlarged to 0.24-inch dia.
	Reduced-length M1898 stock made for 100 Board of Ordnance and Fortifications test rifles	**Type 6:** Forend reduced to 11.5 inches long ahead of lower band, two air chambers in forend
1898	Model 1898 stock shortened at Manilla Arsenal	**Type 7A:** Forend reduced to 9.75 inches long ahead of lower band, front air chamber plugged for the "U.S. Magazine Carbine, caliber .30, Model of 1899, altered for Knife Bayonet and Sling" for use by the Philippine Constabulary
	Model 1898 stock shortened at Springfield Armory and Rock Island Arsenal	**Type 7B:** Forend reduced to 9.75 inches long ahead of lower band, front air chamber plugged for the "U.S. Magazine Carbine, caliber .30, Model of 1899, altered for Knife Bayonet and Sling" for use by military schools

ally, the collector will find a Model 1892 stock with a ramrod channel that exceeds these dimensions for depth and width by more than 0.01 inch and is square in cross section. This is a Type 3A or B stock (see below) with the filler strip removed.

The wood around the Type 1 stock bolt handle recess is flared to the outside, see Figure 2-13. The recess is large enough to accommodate the sloped ramp extending from the side of the receiver. It was designed to protect the wood of the stock in case the bolt handle was slammed closed.

The American Krag Rifle and Carbine

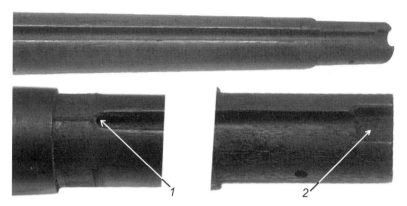

Fig. 2-12. Type 1 stock cleaning rod channel, above; below, left to right, rounded end where cut enters stock ahead of the lower band shoulder (arrow 1); tulip-head cut at the stock nose (arrow 2).

NOTE: This same flared recess was used on all Types 1, 2, 3 and 4 rifle stocks and all Type 1, Type 2 and Type 4C carbine stocks.

All Type 1 stocks to circa serial #25,000 have a vertical channel on either side of the trigger slot to accommodate the 0.455 inch Type 1 trigger pin.

Fig. 2-13. Type 1 bolt handle flared recess. Note the ramp extending from the receiver into the recess (arrow).

The **Type 1A** stock has a flat butt and no lightening holes, high wood in the bolt handle recess, small (1.675-inch diameter) wrist and no air chambers (lightening cuts) in the barrel channel.

The American Krag Rifle and Carbine

The wood in the bolt handle recess rises higher than later models. While it is difficult to measure, you can always tell as the wood directly under the bolt handle will show a deep crescent pressed into the wood by the underside of the bolt handle. Later models may show the same crescent but because the wood is lower, the mark has the appearance of a dent, refer to Figure 2-13.

The wrist or small, as it was termed by the Springfield Armory, was rather narrow at 1.675 inches in diameter when measured vertically at the narrowest point ahead of the comb.

The **Type 1B** stock has the wood in the bolt handle recess relieved or lowered after May 1894. In these stocks you will not see a crescent pressed into the wood by the bolt handle or if you do, it will take the form of a small dent. It also has the flat butt, no lightening cuts in the buttstock or barrel channel and retains the small (1.675-inch diameter) wrist.

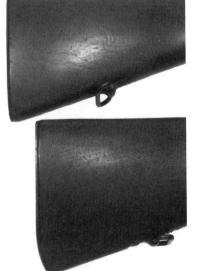

Fig. 2-14. Types 1 and 2 stocks showing change to the toe of the Model 1892, Type 2 and all later stocks.

Model 1892 Rifle Stock, Type 2

The **Type 2** stock was also used on the Model 1892 rifle. It is the same as the Type 1 but in two variations with the following alterations.

In August 1895 at circa serial #18,900, to protect the stock from splitting, the toe was cut forward (Figure 2-14) so that it did not make contact with the ground when the command to "order arms" was given. The **Type 2A** stock retained the thin wrist (1.675 inches), the ramrod channel and ramrod stop slot. The lightening cuts in the buttstock were also added at circa serial #s 19,000–21,000. These changes were approved in August 1895.

NOTE: Model 1892 rifle, serial number 19,3XX (circa September 1895), has been observed with the changes enumerated above.

The **Type 2B** stock was used on the Krag Model 1896 Cadet rifle and issued to cadets at the U.S. Military Academy at West Point, New York. Two modifications distinguish it from previous Model 1892 stocks. First, the cadet lower band (without the sling swivel) was installed and a carbine band spring was used to retain it. This required that the Type 2B Cadet stock be inletted for the band spring just forward of the lower band shoulder which, of course, means that the lower band retaining pin was not used nor a hole for it drilled.

Secondly, the buttstock was *not* inletted for the standard lower sling swivel plate as slings were not used at West Point at that time.

All remaining Cadet rifles were returned in 1900 to the Springfield Armory where they were restocked as standard infantry rifles. Apparently, at least four authentic Cadet rifles have survived. One is in the U. S. Military Academy at West Point (donated by Franklin B. Mallory) and the other three are in private collections.

Model 1892 Rifle Stock Modified to the Model 1896, Type 3
The **Type 3** stock was either the Model 1892 Type 1 or 2 rifle stock with the ramrod channel filled to eliminate the ramrod channel. Two variations of these stocks exist and are distinguished by the way the ramrod channel was filled, see Figure 2-15.

The **Type 3A** stock was used on rifles refurbished in 1897 to bring them up to the Model 1896 standard. These were new, unissued rifles

The American Krag Rifle and Carbine

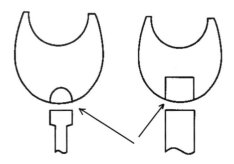

Fig. 2-15. Type 3A and 3B modified M1892 stocks showing the two different methods of filling the cleaning rod channels.

and so the ramrod channel was simply filled with a round walnut dowel 0.220 inch in diameter for all but the top 0.5 inch of its length where it was increased in diameter to 0.4 inch to fill the tulip-head-shaped cut. When the stock nose is viewed end on, the filler strip is round. In all probability, the majority of these were converted from the Type 2A stock.

The toe of the stock was also cut forward for the Type 2 butt plate.

The **Type 3B** stock was used on rifles refurbished in 1900 and later to bring them up to Model 1896 standards. As these rifles had been issued and used in the field, the edges of the ramrod channel were dented and chipped. Armory craftsmen milled a rectangular cut 0.395 inch wide the length of the ramrod channel and filled it with a rectangular strip of walnut. When the stock nose is viewed end on, the filler strip is square, refer to Figure 2-15.

The Type 3 stock retained the 1.675-inch-diameter wrist but with the lightening cuts in the buttstock added. Look closely at the bottom of the forend between the lower and upper bands and you will see the outline of the walnut strip that filled in the ramrod channel.

NOTE: The Type 3 rifle stocks did not have the air chambers, or lightening cuts, added in the forend. The Type 3B will not have a cartouche.

Model 1896 Rifle Stock, Type 4
The **Type 4** rifle stock retained the Type 1 stock bolt handle flared recess. It omitted the ramrod channel and the ramrod stop just ahead

The American Krag Rifle and Carbine

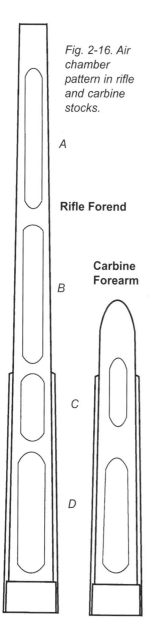

Fig. 2-16. Air chamber pattern in rifle and carbine stocks.

A

Rifle Forend

Carbine Forearm

B

C

D

of the receiver bed, which allowed "air chambers" or "lightening grooves" to be cut in the forends and forearms, see Figure 2-16. The four "air chambers" were of varying lengths to lighten the stock. Dimensions of the lightening cuts seen in Figure 2-16 were, width and length, A) 0.425 x 6.5, B) 0.45 x 6.5, C) 0.480 x 1.7 and D) 0.480 (front) by 0.635 (rear) x 5 inches long. Figure 2-17 compares the stockbeds of a Model 1892 and 1896 stock.

The Type 4 stock was used exclusively on the Model 1896 Krag rifle. It is easily identifiable by its rounded toe, flare surrounding the bolt handle recess on the right side of the stock and its thicker wrist (1.80-inch diameter), see Figure 2-18. Two variations of the Type 4 stock were used.

The **Type 4A** was similar to the Type 2 stock except that the butt was drilled for two lightening holes. The upper is 0.975 inch in diameter and 3.7 inches deep; the lower is also 0.975 inch in diameter but 7.1 inches deep. The upper hole had three smaller-diameter holes 0.22 inch in diameter drilled into it, arranged in a triangle for the three-piece rifle cleaning rod. Note that there is as yet no channel for the oiler, see Figure 2-19. The **Type 4B** stock had a shallow channel added to the bottom of the top lighten-

41

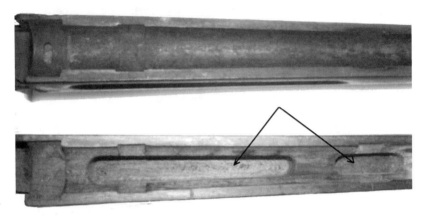

Fig. 2-17. "Air chambers" were cut into the barrel channel to decrease the weight of the stock. Compare the M1892 above to the M1896 below.

ing hole under the holes drilled for the three-piece cleaning rods to make room for the oiler at circa serial #69,000 in August 1897. At the same time, the wood separating the upper and lower lightening holes was removed for 0.25 to 0.50 inch, see Figure 2-20. And, if you look down into the lightening holes, you will often see where the cutting tool sliced through the separating wall into the lower lightening hole. Many of the earlier stocks had the oiler channel cut during repairs or refurbishment.

Fig. 2-18. Type 1 (above) and Type 4 (below) stock wrists compared.

The American Krag Rifle and Carbine

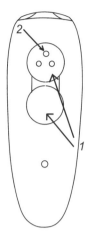

Fig. 2-19. Type 4A rifle buttstock with lightening holes (1) and cleaning rod holes (2) drilled but no oiler channel.

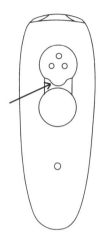

Fig. 2-20. Type 4B rifle buttstock with oiler channel.

Model 1898 Rifle Stock, Type 5

The most visible change in the **Type 5** stocks used on the Model 1898 rifle was in the bolt handle seat. The chamfer that was cut in the Model 1892 and Model 1896 stocks was omitted. Instead, the cut was reduced to a straight-sided rectangular cut, see Figure 2-21.

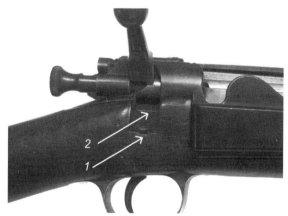

Fig. 2-21. Model 1898 stock bolt handle recess (1). Note that the ramp (2) extending from the receiver into the recess has been eliminated.

At the same time, the "ramp" on the receiver under the bolt handle, which Springfield termed the bolt handle seat, was omitted. It is this change that makes it impossible to place a Model 1892 or Model 1896 receiver in a Model 1898 stock.

43

The American Krag Rifle and Carbine

The size of the holes drilled in the buttstock for the cleaning rods was increased from 0.22 inch to 0.24 inch in diameter to make the rod segments easier to remove, circa serial #150,000 (November 21, 1898).

BOARD OF ORDNANCE AND FORTIFICATIONS RIFLE STOCK, TYPE 6

On August 25, 1900, by verbal authority of the Chief of Ordnance, a Krag rifle with a shorter barrel was submitted to the Board of Ordnance and Fortifications to test the feasibility of issuing a shorter-barreled arm for use by both cavalry and infantry. The experiment led ultimately to the Model 1903 Springfield with a 24-inch barrel.

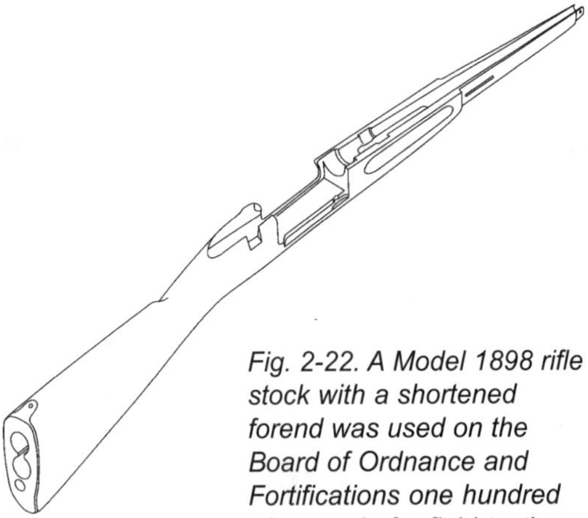

The principal change made in the BOF rifle was the reduction of the barrel length from 30 inches to 26 inches. A new stock, the **Type 6** started life as a Model 1898 stock but with a forend 6 inches shorter to fit the rifle's 26-inch barrel, see Figure 2-22. The forend wood faired smoothly into the upper barrel band as on a standard-length rifle. Only two air chambers were cut in the Type 6 stock and so no wooden filler strip was needed at the stock nose.

Fig. 2-22. A Model 1898 rifle stock with a shortened forend was used on the Board of Ordnance and Fortifications one hundred rifles made for field testing.

Only one hundred of these short rifles were produced for field trials by the 23rd Infantry Regiment before the project was dropped by the impending adoption of the "United States Magazine Rifle, Caliber .30, Model of 1903."

44

The American Krag Rifle and Carbine

Fig. 2-23. An example of a Springfield Armory–remanufactured Model 1898 stock for a "U.S. Magazine Carbine, caliber .30, Model of 1899, altered for Knife Bayonet and Sling." Note the junction of the forearm and barrel band and the barrel turned down for the knife bayonet. From the Jonathan Peck Collection, courtesy of Little John's Auction Service.

"U.S. Magazine Carbine, caliber .30, Model of 1899, altered for Knife Bayonet and Sling," Stock, Type 7

The **Type 7** was a shortened rifle stock remanufactured from Model 1898 stocks at the Manila Arsenal (**Type 7A**) and at the Springfield Armory (**Type 7B**) to provide short rifles for the Philippine Constabulary force and for high schools, academies and colleges providing military training, see Figure 2-23. The standard Model 1898 rifle stock's forend was shortened 8 inches behind the muzzle to fit Model 1898 and Model 1899 carbine barreled receivers. The resulting forearm was not tapered to fit the upper barrel band, and so the wood is larger than the diameter of the forward barrel band and proud of the metal. The milling under the barrel band is smooth and does not show cutting marks. The last 0.75-inch of the first lightening channel in the barrel bed crossed the point where the forearm was shortened. It was carefully cut square and filled in with a rectangular piece of walnut which was smoothed to shape.

The Type 7A stocks remanufactured at the Manila Arsenal had a carefully fitted upper barrel band. It is not known if a cartouche was applied to the stock or who the inspector would have been. Nor is it known what other markings might serve to identify it. The only true

The American Krag Rifle and Carbine

Constabulary rifle known to the author was in a privately owned display case that could not be opened. The stock was in such poor shape that it is doubtful that a cartouche would have been observed.

A total of 4,980 "U.S. Magazine Carbine, caliber .30, Model of 1899, altered for Knife Bayonet and Sling" were made at the Manila Arsenal using Model 1899 carbine barreled receivers as reported by the Chief Supply Officer to Headquarters, Philippine Constabulary, dated August 17, 1908. See Appendix G, Bibliography.

NOTE: Very few true Philippine Constabulary rifles are believed to have survived both the adoption of the Model 1903 rifle and the later Japanese Occupation (1942 to 1945) of the Philippines. The Constabulary carbine the author saw was brought to the United States after World War II. The owner stated that it had been used by his father against the Japanese while he was a member of a guerrilla unit on Mindanao during the war.

The Type 7B stock was remanufactured at the Springfield Armory. It can be identified by the cartouche of J.F. Coyle as "J.F.C." or Charles Valentine, "C.V.," in script or "C.V.V." in block letters inside a rectangular box with rounded corners, and by careful fitting of the upper barrel band. The milling under the upper barrel band is smooth without tool marks. A total of 4,074 "U.S. Magazine Carbine, caliber .30, Model of 1899, altered for Knife Bayonet and Sling," were made at Springfield Armory, plus 613 at the Rock Island Arsenal. They included a few Model 1896 carbines and thirty-nine Model 1898 carbines.

CARBINE STOCKS

Four types of carbine stocks were developed and used on the Krag carbine: the Model 1892, Model 1896, Model 1898 and Model 1899. The Model 1892 stock was made only in quantities sufficient for a prototype weapon. The Model 1896 and later Model 1898 and Model 1899 stocks are not interchangeable although the latter two are, see Figure 2-24.

The American Krag Rifle and Carbine

	Table 2-3	
	U.S. Krag Carbine Stocks	
Model	**Chief Characteristics**	**Attributes (Cumulative)**
1892 Type 1	Long forearm fairing smoothly into forward barrel band; inletted for carbine swivel; flared bolt handle recess	Cleaning rod channel, no lightening cut in forearm or butt; thin wrist (1.675-inch diameter); finger grooves (5.5 inches long)
1896 Type 2A	Short forearm with long nose; flared bolt handle recess; inletted for carbine swivel	30 inches long; round toe; 1.675-inch dia. wrist; two lightening holes in butt, no oiler channel; two 0.22-inch dia. holes in upper lightening hole for two-piece cleaning rod; circa serial #19,000 to 19,300
1896 Type 2B		Three holes for cleaning rod, wrist 1.80 inch in dia., circa #19,000 to 19,301-21,500 to 68,999
1896 Type 2C		Channel for oiler between upper and lower lightening holes in butt beginning at circa serial #69,000
1898 Type 3	Short forearm; square bolt handle recess; inletted for carbine swivel	Chamfer around bolt handle seat omitted; ramp for receiver bolt handle seat omitted
1899 Type 4A	Long forearm with short nose; no inletteing for carbine swivel; finger grooves are 6.8 inches long	Overall length increased to 31.75 inches. Diameter of three holes for cleaning rod segments increased to 0.24 inch
1899 Type 4B		Inletted for lower rifle sling plate on buttstock (field modification)
1899 Type 4C		Flared bolt handle recess (used to restock the Model 1896 carbine only)

The American Krag Rifle and Carbine

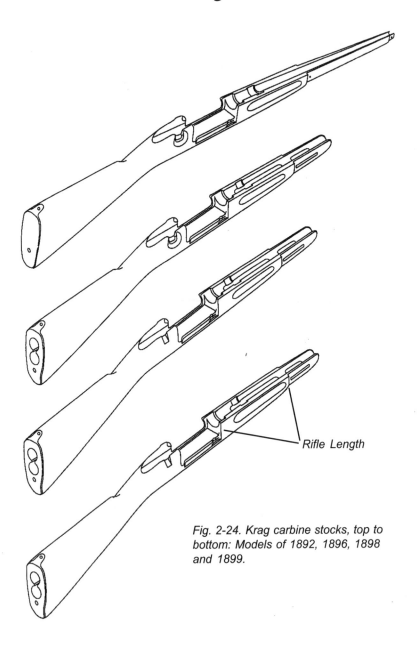

Rifle Length

Fig. 2-24. Krag carbine stocks, top to bottom: Models of 1892, 1896, 1898 and 1899.

The American Krag Rifle and Carbine

The Model 1892 carbine stock retained the flared bolt handle recess on the right side of the stock.

Besides the obvious difference in being shorter than the rifle stocks, the carbine stocks were fitted with barrel bands without sling swivels and with band springs to hold them in place. The barrel band pin was omitted. The stock was also *not* inletted for the lower sling swivel plate except on 372 Model 1899 Type 4B carbine stocks made for Engineer troops. The carbine stocks for the Models of 1892, 1896 and 1898 but not the Model 1899 were inletted on the left side for the carbine swivel. By the time the Model 1899 carbine was introduced, the carbine sling was no longer used.

Model 1892 Carbine Stock, Type 1

The Model 1892 stock has the appearance of a short Model 1892 rifle stock ending three inches from the barrel's muzzle. But unlike the later "U.S. Magazine Carbine, caliber .30, Model of 1899, altered for Knife Bayonet and Sling" used by the Philippine Constabulary and military schools which was made by cutting the forend of the rifle stock to accept a carbine barreled action, the Model 1892 carbine stock was tapered from the lower band forward to fair smoothly into the upper band. It was also inletted for the one-piece ramrod under the barrel, a carbine swivel on the left side of the narrow wrist, a clamping barrel band without a sling swivel and for a short forward barrel band, see Figure 2-25.

The Model 1892 carbine stock did not have the lightening holes in the buttstock or the lightening channels in the barrel bed. It had the thin wrist (1.675 inches in diameter) of the Model 1892 Type 1A rifle stock as well and finger grooves on either side of the forearm. It also used a lower band pin rather than a band spring like later-model carbines to retain the lower barrel band.

The American Krag Rifle and Carbine

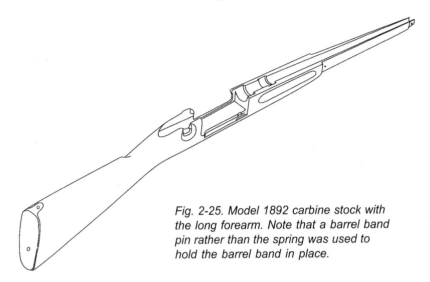

Fig. 2-25. Model 1892 carbine stock with the long forearm. Note that a barrel band pin rather than the spring was used to hold the barrel band in place.

As both specimens of the two Model 1892 carbines manufactured with the long forearm are known, one in private hands and the other in the Rock Island Arsenal Museum, it is unlikely that the collector will encounter one.

Model 1896 Carbine Stock, Type 2

As noted above, the changes made to the Model 1892 carbine and submitted by the Springfield Armory in May 1895 were all adopted, and formal production of the Model 1896 supposedly began in mid-1896 according to reports from the Ordnance Department. In actual fact, the pressure to provide carbines for mounted troops was so intense that production of the new carbine actually began in late 1895, probably in mid-November or very early December. These are the carbines with "1895" marked receivers. Those made in January and early February of 1896 were marked "1896" on the receiver, without the word "Model" in both cases.

Changes affecting the **Type 2** stock involved 1) shortening the stock to 30 inches and rounding the nose to make insertion into the carbine boot easier, 2) thickening the wrist as in the Model 1896 Type 4 rifle stock

The American Krag Rifle and Carbine

at circa serial #27,000, 3) at circa serial #18,000, the introduction of a thicker butt plate and rounding the toe of the stock, 4) the addition of the two lightening holes in the butt, circa serial #s 19,000–19,300, 5) drilling 0.22-inch holes in the upper lightening hole to hold the newly adopted two-piece cleaning rod, and the three-piece cleaning rod circa serial #21,500 and 6) the addition of two lightening channels in the forearm, see Figure 2-26.

Retained from the original Model 1892 (Type 1) design were the flared bolt handle recess, carbine swivel on the left side and the finger grooves in the forearm.

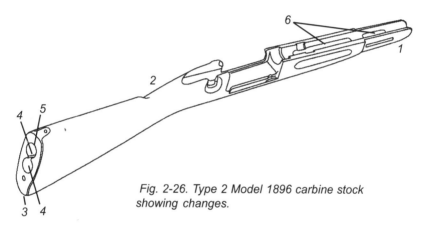

Fig. 2-26. Type 2 Model 1896 carbine stock showing changes.

The one-piece ramrod under the barrel was eliminated in favor of the two-piece cleaning rod in the buttstock (but with the three 0.22-inch-diameter holes drilled as in the rifle stock). The Type 2 carbine stock originally had only two holes for the two segments of the cleaning rod as called for in the Ordnance regulations.

The forearm from the magazine receiver well to the barrel band cut was 6.9 inches long and the nose, from the barrel band forward to the tip of the stock, was 4.0 inches.

51

The American Krag Rifle and Carbine

Finger grooves were cut into the stock's forearm. They were 5.5 inches long and 0.6 inch wide at the front and 0.7 inch wide at the rear. The dimensions of the rest of the stock including stock bed and buttstock remained the same as those of the Model 1896 rifle stock.

The Type 2 Model 1896 Carbine stock was developed in three variations. The **Type 2A** stock had the same narrow wrist 1.675 inches in diameter) as the Model 1892 Type 1 rifle. The lightening holes did not have a channel between for the oiler. In the upper lightening hole, two holes 0.22 inch in diameter, one above the other, were drilled for the two-piece cleaning rod circa serial #s 19,000–19,300, see Figure 2-27. No carbines or rifles were assembled from mid-February to early May due to a shortage of suitable steel for barrels. During this period, approval was given to drill three holes in the upper lightening hole of the carbine buttstock for the three-piece cleaning rod even though only two parts of the rod were issued with the carbine, see Figure 2-28. This step was taken as a laborsaving measure, since it used the same tooling as for the rifle.

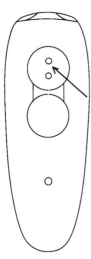

Fig. 2-27. Type 2A (Model 1896); note the two cleaning rod holes in the buttstock.

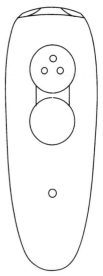

Fig. 2-28. Type 2B (Model 1896) with three cleaning rod holes in buttstock.

The **Type 2B** Model 1896 carbine stock from between circa serial #s 19,000–19,300 to 21,500 on will have three holes for the cleaning rod drilled in the shape of an equal triangle. The Type 2B stock also had the thicker (1.80 inches diameter) wrist like the Type 4 rifle stock.

The American Krag Rifle and Carbine

NOTE: A carbine with serial number #26,998 has been examined that has a 1.675-inch, small-diameter wrist. A carbine with serial #28,884 was observed that had the large 1.80-inch-diameter wrist.

The **Type 2C** stock was approved in August 1897 at circa serial #69,000. A channel for the oiler was cut along the bottom of the upper lightening hole, see Figure 2-29.

Model 1898 Carbine Stock, Type 3

The Model 1898 **Type 3** carbine stock saw the same changes made as the Model 1898 rifle stocks, see Figure 2-30. Retained from the Model 1896 carbine stock were the 1) thicker wrist, 2) inletting for the carbine swivel, the 3) short forearm and 4) long nose of the Model 1896 carbine stock and 5) the three 0.22-inch holes drilled in the upper lightening hole in the buttstock for the cleaning rods, even though only two pieces of the cleaning rod were issued with the carbine. The

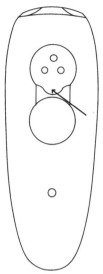

Fig. 2-29. Type 2C (Model 1896) cleaning rod holes in buttstock with oil channel (arrow) added.

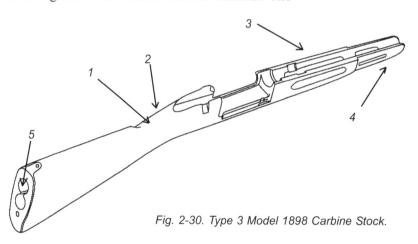

Fig. 2-30. Type 3 Model 1898 Carbine Stock.

most visible change in the Model 1898 carbine stock was in the bolt handle seat. The flared recess that was cut in the Model 1892 and 1896 stocks was omitted. Instead, the cut was reduced to a straight-sided rectangular cut, see Figure 2-31.

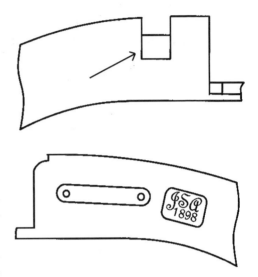

At the same time, the "ramp" on the receiver under the bolt handle, which Springfield termed the bolt handle seat, was omitted. It is this change that makes it impossible to place a Model 1896 carbine receiver in a Model 1898 carbine stock.

Fig. 2-31. Type 3 (Model 1898) carbine stock changes: top, bolt handle recess squared and bolt handle ramp eliminated and below, carbine sling plate inletting retained.

In the Type 3 Model 1898 carbine stock, the holes for the three-piece cleaning rod were 0.22 inch in diameter.

NOTE: As with the rifle, the Model 1898 carbine stock is not interchangeable with the Model 1896 carbine stock, but is interchangeable with the Model 1899 carbine stock.

Model 1899 Carbine Stock, Type 4

The Model 1899 carbine stock was approved in August 1899 and production began immediately. The Model 1899 carbine stock was longer by 1.8 inches than the Model 1896/98 carbine stock. The forearm was increased to 9.4 inches in length (from the receiver well forward to the barrel band cut) while the length of the nose beyond the barrel band cut was reduced from 4.0 inches to 3.3 inches, see Figures 2-32 and 2-33.

The American Krag Rifle and Carbine

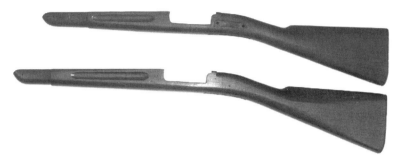

Fig. 2-32. Top, M1898 carbine stock; bottom, M1899 carbine stock.

Two reasons for the change in the carbine stock have been given. The Fiscal Year 1899 Annual Report states that the Model 1899 stock was designed to reduce production costs by using the same fixtures and jigs as for the rifle. This also allowed the Armory to use Model 1898

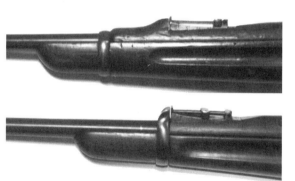

Fig. 2-33. Top, Model 1899; bottom, Model 1898 carbine stocks. Note the location of the rear sights as well as the longer forearm and shorter nose of the Model 1899.

rifle stocks with damaged forends or which had been rejected during manufacture for flaws in the forend. The second reason given is supposedly based on a number of complaints from the field that when carrying Model 1896 and 1898 Krag carbines at the "trail arms" position (carried in the shooting hand at the point of balance), the shooter could receive a burn from the Model 1896 rear sight if the barrel was very hot.

The American Krag Rifle and Carbine

While there are objections to both explanations, the reason given in the Annual Report is probably correct, even though the rifle stock would have to be converted to a carbine stock before the air chambers (lightening cuts) were milled.

As for the second explanation, the point of balance on the Krag carbine is at the position of the magazine. The most comfortable carrying position at "trail arms" is with the magazine gate tucked into the palm of the right hand with the gate wedged under the length of the thumb. Or, if instead of "trail arms" the carbine was carried diagonally across the chest, the shooting hand would have held the stock wrist and the off hand would grasp the finger grooves. In either position, neither hand would make contact with a hot barrel or rear sight.

Three variations of the Model 1899 carbine stock were developed. The **Type 4A** stock is distinguished by the fact that the three holes in the buttstock for the two-piece cleaning rod were enlarged to 0.24 inch to make their insertion easier. At the same time, the inletting for carbine swivel plate was eliminated from the left side of the wrist (Figure 2-34). This was done as the carbine scabbard or sheath had replaced the cavalry shoulder sling and boot.

Fig. 2-34. Close-up of the left wrist of Model 1898 and Model 1899 stocks. Note that the Model 1899 stock is not inletted for the carbine swivel.

The **Type 4B** was a field modification performed on 372 Model 1899 carbines at Ft. Riley, Kansas, in 1903. A lower sling swivel plate was inletted into the buttstock. A rifle lower band with the

The American Krag Rifle and Carbine

forward sling swivel replaced the carbine band. These Model 1899 carbines with stocks modified for a sling were issued to Engineer troops.

The **Type 4C** stock was used to restock serviceable Model 1896 carbines. It had the flared bolt handle recess of the Type 1 and Type 2 carbine stock but the longer forearm and finger grooves of the Model 1899 Type 4 carbine stock, see Figure 2-35

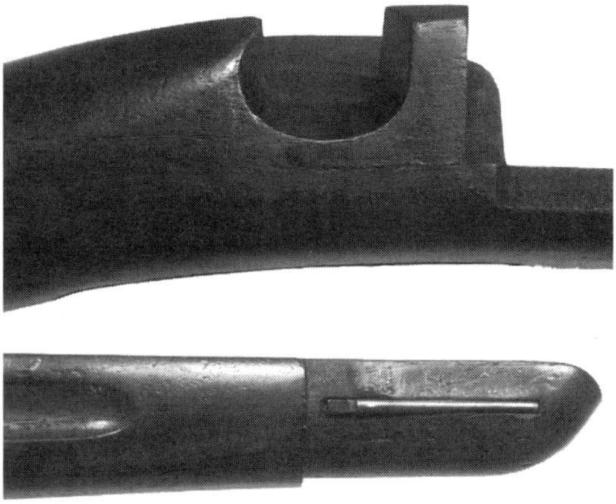

NOTE: The Director of Civilian Marksmanship (DCM) sold the Model 1898 rifle and carbine in 1922 only, at $6.00 and $10.00, respectively. In 1926–1927 and again from

Fig. 2-35. The Model 1899 Type 4C stock was used to restock serviceable Model 1896 carbines. Note the flared recess for the bolt handle, the longer forearm and short nose.

1928–1930, Krag carbines were also offered. But in fact, these carbines were made from Model 1898 rifles with the barrel reduced to carbine length (22 inches) and mounted in Model 1899 carbine stocks. When the Model 1899 carbine stocks ran out, Model 1898 rifle stocks were reduced to fit. These will have the rear sling swivel plate inletting. The Model 1905 front sight and band was installed instead of the Krag carbine front sight. In the absence of original paperwork from the DCM, it is nearly impossible to identify a cut-down rifle in a Model 1899 Krag stock as a DCM gun rather than one modified in the same manner by a surplus dealer. Apparently, the DCM did not keep records of Krag serial numbers sold or if so, they have long been discarded or lost. But records from the Benicia Arsenal suggest that 11,245 Krag

The American Krag Rifle and Carbine

rifles were converted to carbines between 1925 and 1930, according to Frank Mallory of the Springfield Research Service.

Commercial Stocks for the Krag

These were short rifle stocks that were remanufactured by various surplus dealers (W. Stokes Kirk and others) primarily in the late 1920s and 1930s to provide inexpensive hunting rifles, see Figure 2-36. They can be identified by the relatively sloppy workmanship involved in fitting the upper barrel band, relatively careless plugging of the upper air chamber where the cut was made to reduce the stock's length, the substitution of the Model 1905 front sight for the Krag sight and by the variety of cartouches, if any, found on the stocks. The milling under the barrel band often shows tooling and cutting marks.

Fig. 2-36. A Krag short rifle remanufactured from a Model 1898 standard rifle by W. Stokes Kirk in the late 1920s or early 1930s. Note the Model 1905 front sight base and blade.

Another type of commercial stock was a cut-down Model 1903 rifle stock installed on Krag barreled receivers that had their rifle barrels shortened to carbine length. The stocks were simply cut just ahead of the barrel band retaining spring and rounded into a blunt nose. The receiver well was cut into the '03 stock and the magazine well was filled in with a block of walnut cut to shape. The Model 1898 bolt handle cutout was milled into the right side. The Model 1903 stock bolt was just to the rear of the magazine gate. On the left side of the stock, behind the Krag receiver's side plate, the well for the '03 cutoff and stock bolt can be seen. These stocks were made up primarily by the Francis Bannerman Company of New York City after World War I.

58

The American Krag Rifle and Carbine

MARKINGS, STOCKS

Armory Subinspector's Cartouche

It was the practice of the Springfield Armory to stamp into the wood of the left side of the stock, just above the rear of the trigger guard, a rectangular box with beveled corners containing the initials of the Master Armorer responsible for a final quality control check to make certain that the arm met all specifications and functioned properly. The calendar year was stamped below the initials, inside the box.

Samuel W. Porter was the Master Armorer at Springfield Armory and served as Armory Subinspector at the time Krag production got underway. Mr. Porter died unexpectedly of diphtheria on June 18, 1894. He was succeeded by J.S. Adams, who did not receive the title of Master Armorer but did serve as Armory subinspector. Mr. Adams' initials appear on nearly all Krag rifles and carbines built from the middle of 1894 through the end of production. His initials are in script.

Certain nonstandard rifles and carbines such as the .22-caliber gallery practice rifles show the cartouche of J.F. Coyle (*J.F.C.*) in script or Charles Valentine (*C.V.*) in script letters. Both will also be found in block letters for the "U.S. Magazine Carbine, caliber .30, Model of 1899, altered for Knife Bayonet and Sling," rebuilt at the Springfield Armory. The Charles Valentine block letter cartouche uses three letters (C.C.V.). Table 2-4 and Figure 2-37 provide a list of stock cartouches observed.

NOTE: Samuel W. Porter's "*S.W.P./1894*" cartouche was struck on the *right* side of Model 1892 Krag stocks between circa serial #'s 1,177 and 1,932, after his death from diphtheria on June 18, 1894. The cartouche was returned to the left side when J.S. Adams assumed the responsibility for final inspections at circa serial #1,933. The author owns serial #1,178 and the ownership of #1,933 is known to the author and others.

NOTE: The two long-stock Model 1892 carbines (serial #'s 1,015 and 1,575) have survived. Number 1,015 is in the Rock Island Arsenal Museum. The other is owned by a private collector and shows an "*S.W.P./ 1894*" cartouche on the right side. (Private communication.)

The American Krag Rifle and Carbine

Refurbishment Cartouches

In 1908, the U.S. Ordnance Department began marking the stocks of arms refurbished at any government arsenal. The markings were usually the initials of the Arsenal and the inspector, often separated by a hyphen and always in block letters. The most commonly seen are "S.A." for Springfield Armory and "B.A." for Benicia Arsenal in California. Rock Island Arsenal also began to refurbish small arms in 1898. Their marking would have been "R.I.A." The location initials are followed by the initials of the inspector. See Figure 2-38 for an example of a Benicia Arsenal refurbishment cartouche.

The American Krag Rifle and Carbine

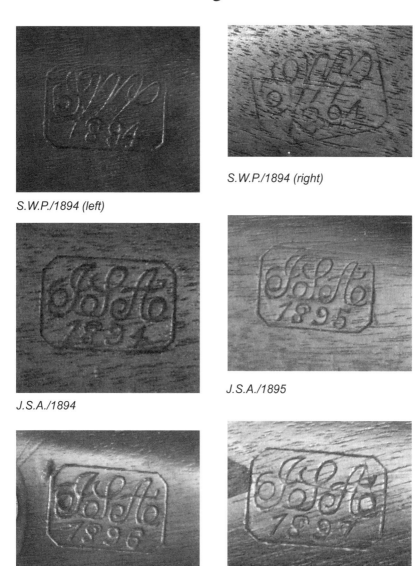

S.W.P./1894 (left)

S.W.P./1894 (right)

J.S.A./1894

J.S.A./1895

J.S.A./1896

J.S.A./1897

Fig. 2-37. U.S. Krag Inspection Cartouches.

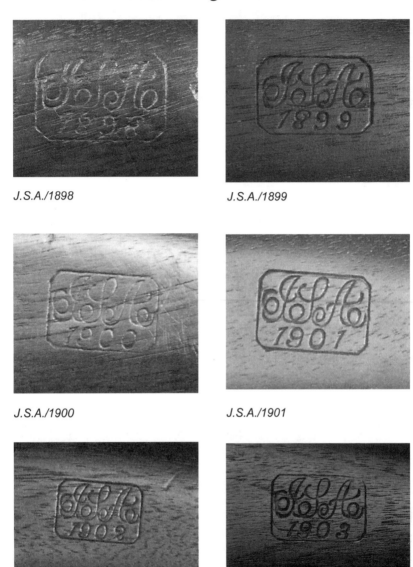

J.S.A./1898

J.S.A./1899

J.S.A./1900

J.S.A./1901

J.S.A./1902

J.S.A./1903

Fig. 2-37. U.S. Krag Inspection Cartouches, continued.

J.F.C. undated in script

J.F.C. undated in Roman

C.V. undated in script

Fig. 2-37. U.S. Krag Inspection
Cartouches, continued.

J.S.A./1897 stamped sideways

Proof Mark

Krag rifles and carbines were
proof tested before and after
assembly. Before assembly,
finished barrels were tested
with a proof cartridge that developed 100,000 lbs per square
inch (psi). After assembly, finished rifles were tested with a

Fig. 2-38. Refurbishment cartouche
found on the Krag rifle or carbine,
"B.A.–W.J."

proof cartridge that developed 70,000 psi. Barrels were stamped with
a small "P" to indicate they had passed proof. The finished rifle was

The American Krag Rifle and Carbine

Fig. 2-39. Firing proof on Krag rifles and carbines behind the trigger guard.

marked on the bottom of the stock, just behind the trigger guard plate with a *script "P"* inside a circle, see Figure 2-39. During refurbishment, it was sometimes necessary to fit a new barrel or bolt to a receiver. If so, proof testing was again required. The new proof mark was almost always a sans serif "P" inside a circle usually stamped over the original proof mark, see Figure 2-40.

Stock Inspection Markings

Stocks were carefully inspected and gauged before being fitted with the barreled receiver. If the stock met all specifications, it was stamped with a one- or two-digit number, or a single letter, immediately behind the trigger guard plate, see Figure 2-41.

If a replacement stock was later fitted at a post remote from one of the arsenals, it shows only a number or a single letter behind the trigger guard plate and will not show an inspection cartouche or a firing proof cartouche, see Figure 2-42. A letter to the side of the "P" proof is that of the "stocker" who scraped the stock during a refurbishment process.

Fig. 2-40. Refurbishment proof mark. Note the block letter "P" without serifs.

Other Stock Markings

Regular Army, Navy and Marine Corps units rarely marked their small arms with permanent unit or rack numbers. But Krag rifles and carbines were issued to National Guard units starting in 1900 and many of these did. Such markings are often found on stocks, and even on the barrels or receivers. Krag rifles and carbines were also sold through

The American Krag Rifle and Carbine

Fig. 2-41. Stock inspection marking on the Krag rifle and carbine.

the Director of Civilian Marksmanship Program in the 1920s, and through surplus dealers until after World War II. Given the treatment and abuse that many of these rifles and carbines endured, it is not surprising to see the names or initials carved into stocks by those who never have defaced an expensive hunting rifle in that way.

HANDGUARDS, RIFLE AND CARBINE

Eight different types of handguards were used on the Krag rifle and carbine, four on rifles and four on carbines. All handguards were attached to the barrel with spring steel clips, riveted to the handguard with steel rivets. The handguard used with a rifle or carbine varied within the Model 1898 rifle and carbine and the Model 1899 carbine depending on which rear sight was used, see Table 2- 5.

Handguard, Model 1892 Rifle, Type 1

This **Type 1** rifle handguard was used on the M1892 rifle. It is unique in that it did not extend far enough to the rear to cover the receiver ring. The handguard was 8.562 inches long, 1.5 inches wide at the rear (just ahead of the lip) and 0.812 inch wide at the front, see Figure 2-43.

Fig. 2-42. Initials or numbers stamped into the stock behind the trigger guard and no inspection cartouche indicate a stock that was replaced in the field.

NOTE: The Type 1 handguard was used on all M1892 rifles on which the M1892 or Model 1896 rifle sight was used except for those rebuilt in 1900 and later. On those rifles, the Type 3 Model 1896 handguard was used with the Model 1896 rear sight. These sights and handguards may have been further updated at a later date.

The American Krag Rifle and Carbine

		Table 2-5	
	Handguards Used on U.S. Krag Rifles and Carbines		
Rifle or Carbine/ Serial #s	Hand-guard Type	Handguard Model	Rear Sight Model
1892 Rifle	1	1892 Rifle	1892 Rifle and 1896 Rifle
1892 Carbine	2	1892 Carbine	1892 Carbine 1896 Carbine
1892 Rifle (late) 1896 Rifle 1896 Cadet Rifle 1898 Rifle (109,000 146,000 and 207,000 to 330,000)	3	1896 Rifle	1896 Rifle
1896 Carbine 1898 Carbine	4	1896 Carbine	1896 Carbine
1898 Rifle 1899 Carbine (242,242- 272,000 to 285,000)	5	1898 Rifle and Carbine	1898 Rifle 1902 Rifle 1898 Carbine 1902 Carbine
1899 Carbine (216,000 to 242,241)	6	1899 Carbine with Type 4 carbine stock	1896 Carbine

The American Krag Rifle and Carbine

Rifle or Carbine	Hand-guard Type	Handguard Model	Rear Sight Model
		Table 2-5, cont.	
		Handguards Used on U.S. Krag Rifles and Carbines	
1898 Rifle 1899 Carbine	7	M1901 Rifle and Carbine (without sight protector)	1901 Rifle 1901 Carbine (questionable)
"U.S. Magazine Carbine, caliber .30, Model of 1899, altered for Knife Bayonet and Sling"	8	1902 Carbine with sight protector used on those altered carbines for Philippine Constabulary and military schools M1902 Carbine with sight protector used on those short rifles commercially remanufactured	1901 Carbine 1902 Rifle

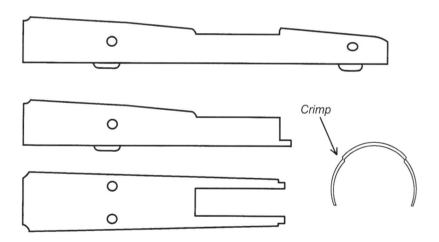

Fig. 2-43. Type 1 Handguard for the Model 1892 Rifle and Type 2 for the M1892 Carbine. Note the crimped clip.

The American Krag Rifle and Carbine

Two steel spring clips were riveted to the underside of the handguard. They are 0.620 inch wide and are crimped just past the rivets, refer to Figure 2-43.

The rivets holding the clips are 0.250 inch in diameter and are barely recessed below the wood.

The cutout for the rear sight was 2.562 inches long by 0.182 inch wide. The Type 1 handguard is distinguished not only by its smaller size but by the fact that the clips that snap around the barrel are crimped.

NOTE: The Model 1892 Type 1 and the Model 1896 Type 3 rifle handguards could be and were used interchangeably on the Model 1892 rifle. The change to the latter was always done in the field.

Handguard, Model 1892 Carbine, Type 2
The four prototype Model 1892 carbines used a Type 1 rifle handguard modified so that its forward edge fit under the rear-facing lip of the barrel band. The front lip of the handguard was removed and the right and left legs were notched to fit into notches in the lower band. Only one clip was used to hold the handguard to the barrel, refer to Figure 2-43.

Handguard, Model 1896 Rifle, Type 3
The **Type 3** handguard was somewhat of a transition piece in that it was used on both the Model 1892 rifles manufactured circa serial #s 24,000–26,000 (January–February 1896) and on the Model 1896 rifle on which the Model 1896 rifle sight was mounted. It was made longer to cover the receiver ring to prevent burns when a hot rifle was grabbed by a soldier to carry at "trail arms," see Figure 2-44.

The handguard was 9.375 inches long and rebated on the underside 0.8 inch to cover the receiver ring. It was 1.5 inches wide at the rear and 0.95 inch wide at the front.

The American Krag Rifle and Carbine

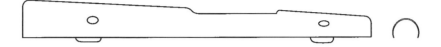

Fig. 2-44. Type 3 Handguard for the Model 1896 Rifle. Note that the clip is not crimped.

Like the Type 1 for the Model 1892 rifle, it had two spring steel clips to secure it to the barrel. The clips were not crimped like those on the Model 1892 handguard.

Because heat from the barrel could be transferred through the spring clips to their rivets and cause pinpoint burns to the shooter's hand if he grabbed the rifle or carbine across the handguard, the rivets were recessed evenly from 0.020 to 0.030 inch below the wood.

At the back of the cutout for the rear sight, a sloping flat ramp was milled to make it easier to see the sight. The ramp was 1.5 inches long. It was also rebated slightly at the front in a semicircle.

Handguard, Model 1896 Carbine, Type 4
The **Type 4** handguard (Figure 2-45) was used on both the Model 1896 and Model 1898 carbines on which the Model 1896 carbine sight was mounted. It was shorter (6.2 inches) than the Type 3 handguard for the

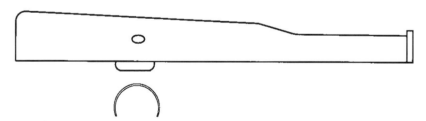

Fig. 2-45. Type 4 Handguard for the Model 1896 Carbine. Note that the clip is not crimped.

The American Krag Rifle and Carbine

rifle as it ended at the front just past the cutout for the rear sight. A short lip slipped under the barrel band to hold it in place at the front, and the rear was held by a single spring steel clip. The clip was not crimped and the rivets were recessed evenly from 0.020 to 0.030 inch below the wood.

Handguard, Model 1898 Rifle and Carbine, Type 5

The **Type 5** handguard was used on all rifles and those Model 1899 carbines on which the Model 1898 or Model 1902 rear sight was used, see Figure 2-46.

Fig. 2-46. Type 5 Handguard for the Model 1898 Rifle and 1899 Carbine with either the Model 1898 or Model 1902 rear sight. Note that clip is not crimped.

NOTE: It was also used on those Model 1896 carbines restocked with the Type 4 Model 1899 carbine long forearm stock when the Model 1898 or Model 1902 carbine rear sight was used.

The handguard was 9.375 inches long and rebated on the underside 0.8 inch to cover the receiver ring. It was 1.5 inches wide at the rear and 0.95 inch wide at the front.

The Type 5 handguard can be easily distinguished by the deeper cut and flared sides at the back of the recess for the larger sight bar.

Two spring steel clips hold the handguard to the barrel, as with the Model 1896.

The clips are not crimped. The rivets are recessed evenly from 0.020 to 0.030 inch below the wood.

70

The American Krag Rifle and Carbine

Handguard, Model 1899 Carbine, Type 6

The **Type 6** carbine handguard was designed to be used on the Model 1899 carbines equipped with the Type 4 (long forearm) stock and the Model 1896 carbine rear sight. It was as long (9.375 inches) as the rifle handguard. The extra length reduced the excessive breakage that had occurred with the short Type 3 handguard and provided additional protection for the soldier's hand from a hot barrel, see Figure 2-47.

Fig. 2-47. Type 6 Handguard for the Model 1899 Carbine equipped with the Model 1896 rear sight. Note the sight protector hump.

The Type 6 handguard had a notched hump directly in front of the rear sight cutout. The hump protected the rear sight when the carbine was shoved into or drawn out of the cavalry scabbard. The hump was 0.905 inch high. The U-shaped notch in its center served as a sighting groove and was 0.515 inch wide and 0.135 inch deep.

The Type 6 carbine handguard was also used on those Model 1896 carbines that were refurbished and reissued with the Type 4C carbine stocks.

The rivets are recessed evenly from 0.020 to 0.030 inch below the wood.

Handguard, Model 1901 Rifle and Carbine, Type 7

The **Type 7** handguard was used on the Model 1898 rifles and Model 1899 carbines fitted with the Model 1901 rear sight. The Type 7 handguard is considered original equipment on those Model 1898 rifles made after August 1901 (circa serial #330,000), see Figure 2-48.

71

The American Krag Rifle and Carbine

Fig. 2-48. Type 7 Handguard used on the Model 1899 Carbine and the Model 1898 Rifle, both equipped with the Model 1901 rear sight.

The Type 7 handguard's dimensions are the same as the Model 1896 and Model 1898 rifle handguards. The opening for the Model 1901 rear sight is 3.3 inches long by 0.7 inch wide and is 2.2 inches behind the front of the handguard. It does not have a sight protector hump and was used only a short time on the Model 1899 carbine.

The rivets were evenly recessed 0.020 to 0.030 inch below the wood.

Handguard, Model 1902, Carbine, Type 8

The Model 1901 rear sight used on Model 1899 carbines fitted with the Type 7 handguard was prone to damage when pushed into the carbine scabbard with the sight leaf down. The leaf often hooked over the lip of the scabbard and either snapped the leaf back or prevented the carbine from being inserted completely. In response to complaints from the field, the **Type 8** Model 1902 handguard was designed. Like the Type 6 handguard for the Model 1899 carbine, it had a sight protector hump. But the hump on the Type 8 was moved forward so the binding lever had room to move. The area behind the hump was relieved on the right side as well, see Figure 2-49 (arrow).

The Type 8 handguard was installed on Model 1899 carbines manufactured after February 1902 and on earlier-model carbines that had Model

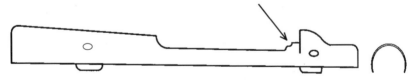

Fig. 2-49. Type 8 Handguard for Model 1899 Carbine equipped with the Model 1901 rear sight. Compare to the Type 6 Handguard in Figure 2-47.

The American Krag Rifle and Carbine

1896 or 1898 rear sights replaced with Model 1901 rear sights. Research authorities Mallory and Olson suggest that both rifles and carbines with Model 1901 rear sights were issued to the regular Army and those with Model 1902 rear sights to the Militia (National Guard).

NOTE: There are reproductions of Krag carbine and rifle handguards available. They can readily be distinguished by the rivets used to hold the clips to the wood. The original rivets used at Springfield Armory had a flat head and will show a tiny dimple on the outside center. The reproduction handguard rivets will also show a dimple on the outside but it is quite pronounced. Circular grinding marks are almost always visible as well. On the inside of the reproductions, there is an inverted dimple where the rivet comes through the clip of at least one half the diameter of the rivet head. The reproduction rivets are also rarely recessed properly flush with the wood (Model 1892), or below the wood (all other models).

HANDGUARD MARKINGS

Krag rifle and carbine handguards, with the exception of the Type 1 Model 1892, are marked only with a letter or number that identified the stock fitter. The number is a single digit or letter 0.1 inch high located on the inside, just ahead of the relief for the receiver ring, see Figure 2-50.

Fig. 2-50. Handguards are marked on the underside with a stock fitter's mark, a small letter or number. Numbers 6 and 66 are quite common.

While the number of original Model 1892 handguards examined is quite small, none observed were so marked.

Reproduction handguards are not marked in any way.

The American Krag Rifle and Carbine

BARREL BANDS

The barrel bands helped secure the barrel to the stock. Two types were used. The upper barrel band was used on all rifles and the Model 1892 carbine to secure the barrel at the muzzle end. It also served as a bayonet mount on the rifle using a Mauser-style lug and it had a lug, or ears, for the stacking swivel.

The lower barrel band was placed at mid-barrel. All rifle lower barrel bands, with the exception of the Cadet rifle, had a lug for the sling swivel.

All rifle lower barrel bands, with the exception of the Cadet rifle, were held in place by a cross screw through the barrel band lugs and by a steel pin inserted crosswise through the stock forend ahead of the barrel band position. The Model 1896 Cadet rifle used a carbine band spring.

Carbines, with the exception of the Model 1892, had only one barrel band placed approximately at mid-barrel. With the exception of the "Engineer Carbine," with its rifle lower band, carbine barrel bands did not have either a sling or stacking swivel lug. The carbine barrel band was held in place against recoil with a barrel band spring installed in the stock. In the carbine, the barrel band retaining pin was not used.

Rifle Upper Band

The upper band was 1.955 inches long by 1.070 inches wide at the rear, tapering to 1.067 at the front. It was 1.305 inches high overall, not including the bayonet mount or sling swivel lug.

One inch behind the front end, a hole was drilled through both side walls. A boss was forged on the side of the band with the top milled flat and drilled through to seat the upper band screw. The screw hole in the right side was threaded. The stacking swivel lug was positioned 0.10

inch ahead of the rear end of the band. It was 0.630 inch wide and divided into two ears, each 0.130 inch wide. The stacking swivel depended 0.340 inch below the bottom of the band.

In all but the Types 1A and B barrel bands, the top center section of the upper band was removed to lighten the piece. The cutout was 0.780 inch wide by 1.215 inches long.

NOTE: The upper band cannot be removed from the rifle barrel without first removing the front sight blade. The upper band can be moved forward on the barrel to allow it to be dismounted by first removing the upper band screw and sliding the band toward the muzzle and off the forend. If the band will not move, tap lightly on the stacking swivel lug with a plastic or brass hammer.

The various rifle barrel bands are described in Table 2-6 and the following paragraphs.

Model 1892 Upper Band, Type 1

The Type 1 barrel band was solid for its entire length without the lightening cutout. A verti-
cal projection at the bottom front of the lug was drilled through to allow the ramrod to pass (arrow 1). This barrel band was used as original equipment from the start of the production to circa serial #2,100, see Figure 2-51.

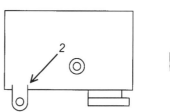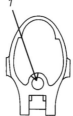

Fig. 2-51. The Types 1A and B solid upper barrel bands were used on the Krag Model 1892 Rifle. Shown is the Type 1A.

The Type 1 barrel band has two variations: the **Type 1A** barrel band was rounded on either side of the bayonet mount and the stacking swivel lugs formed a 90-degree angle (arrow 2) with the body of the barrel band.

Table 2-6 U.S. Krag Rifle Barrel Bands		
Upper Band		
1A	Model 1892	Solid band with lug for stacking swivel at 90-degree angle, bayonet mount, ramrod lug. In use to circa serial #200
1B	Model 1892	Flats ground on either side of bayonet mount, fillets added to stacking swivel lug, circa serial #201
2	Model 1892	Top center cut away to lighten band, circa #2,100
3	Model 1896 and 1898	Ramrod lug eliminated
4	Model 1898 retrofitted to prior production	1.0-inch-long slot cut in bottom, circa serial #250,000
5	Board of Ordnance and Fortifications Rifle	Type 4 upper band enlarged on mandrel
Lower Band		
1	Infantry models	Lug for swivel
2	M1896 Cadet Rifle	No lug for swivel

At circa serial #201, the **Type 1B** upper band had raised flats ground on either side of the bayonet mount to make it easier to attach and remove the bayonet. Stacking swivel lugs were faired into the body of the upper band with fillets to strengthen them, see Figure 2-52.

Model 1892 Upper Band, Type 2
On April 2, 1894, the **Type 2** barrel band was approved to replace the Type 1. The top was cut away in a rectangle 0.780 inch wide by 1.215 inches long to lighten the band. It retained the lug for the ramrod. This

change was made at circa serial #2,100, see Figure 2-53. This upper band was also used on the 404 Model 1896 Cadet rifles made for use at the U.S. Military Academy at West Point.

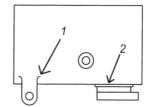

Fig. 2-52. Detail showing the fillets (arrow 1) and raised flats around the bayonet mount (arrow 2) on the Type 1B upper band and successive upper bands.

Model 1896 Upper Band, Type 3

When the one-piece ramrod was replaced by the three-piece cleaning rod for the rifle, the lug for the ramrod was also eliminated. In all other respects, the **Type 3** upper band resembles the Type 2. It was used on all subsequent rifle models to July 1899, see Figure 2-54.

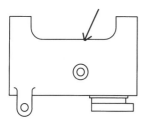

Fig. 2-53. Type 2 upper barrel band with the top portion (arrow) removed was used on the Model 1892 service rifle and the Model 1896 Cadet rifle.

Model 1898 Upper Band, Type 4

Reports from the field indicated that after extensive bayonet practice, the upper band tended to loosen and

wobble. To eliminate the problem, a slot 1.0 inch long was cut from the rear of the band forward between the stacking swivel ears. This allowed the band to be tightened securely around the rebated forend. The **Type 4** upper

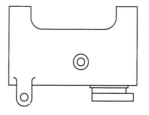

Fig. 2-54. Type 3 upper barrel band without the lug for the cleaning rod.

The American Krag Rifle and Carbine

band was identical to the Type 3 in all other respects except for this slot. This change became effective at circa serial #250,000, see Figure 2-55. The Type 4 band was also installed on rifles turned in for repairs or refurbishment.

Fig. 2-55. Type 4 upper barrel band with the slot (arrow) cut to allow it to be tightened securely about the forend rebate.

Board of Ordnance and Fortifications Rifle Upper Band, Type 5

The **Type 5** upper band used on this rifle was the Type 4 band which was forced onto a mandrel to enlarge it to fit the larger diameter of the 26-inch barrel, see Figure 2-56. It measured 1.955 inches long by 1.072 inches wide by 1.564 inches high overall, not including the bayonet mount or swivel lug. The Type 5 upper band had the 1.0-inch-long slot cut between the stacking swivel ears so that it could be tightened securely.

Fig. 2-56. The Board of Ordnance and Fortifications rifle upper band was enlarged slightly to fit the larger-diameter 26-inch barrel. Compare to Figure 2-23.

Upper Band Markings and Finish

All upper barrel bands were milled from steel stock and blued. None show inspector's or other official markings.

Upper Band Screw

The upper band screw held the upper band in place on the forend. It was 1.280 inches long with a slotted, fillister head 0.270 inch in diam-

The American Krag Rifle and Carbine

eter. It had four threads just below the head and the shaft had a rounded end. The upper band screw was niter blued, see Figure 2-57.

Fig. 2-57. Upper barrel band screw.

Bayonet Lug

The bayonet lug used on the Krag rifle was a Mauser-style lug. It was 0.425 inch wide by 0.660 inch long. It projected 0.240 inch below the bottom of the upper band. The front of the mount was rounded to make it easier to slide the bayonet on. At circa serial #201, the flats on either side of the bayonet stud were added to make it easier to attach and remove the bayonet, see Figures 2-58 and 2-52.

Fig. 2-58. Bayonet mount (arrow) on the rifle upper band.

Stacking Swivel

The stacking swivel permitted three rifles to be fastened together into a self-supporting tripod by hooking the stacking swivels together.

The stacking swivel was an open oval 0.630 inch wide and 1.656 inches long made from iron wire 0.170 inch in diameter. The bottom of the oval was open for 0.205 inch.

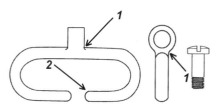

Fig. 2-59. Krag rifle stacking swivel and screw.

Three Types were used. The **Type 1** stacking swivel had square cut ends to circa serial #100. The

The American Krag Rifle and Carbine

Type 2 had round beveled edges, and fillets (arrow 1) were added to the sides of the stacking swivel lug to strengthen them at circa serial #201. The **Type 3** had round edges (arrow 2) to the end of production, see Figure 2-59.

The stacking swivel was held to the stacking swivel lug on the upper band with a screw 0.755 inch long. The screw had a slotted fillister head 0.270 inch in diameter that was 0.095 inch thick at the rim. The screw was threaded on the lower 0.20 inch of its length. The stacking swivel screw was niter blued.

NOTE: For a short period at circa serial #80,000, the end of the stacking swivel screw was upset to prevent it from backing out.

Rifle Lower Band, Model 1892

Only two types of the Model 1892 rifle lower band were used on the Krag rifle. It was milled from a steel forging into an oblong ring that encircled the barrel and forend, see Figure 2-60.

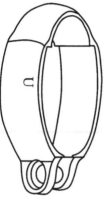

Fig. 2-60. Model 1892 Krag lower rifle band.

The band was split at the bottom and had an ear or lug on either side of the split which allowed the band to be tightened with a screw. The lower band pin, a straight pin of steel, rounded at both ends, was placed crosswise through the forend to hold the band in place against recoil.

The lower band was 1.37 inches wide by 2.140 inches high (including the sling swivel lug) and 0.510 inch wide. The lugs for the sling swivel were 0.365 inch high and 0.220 inch thick. They were drilled through for the lower band swivel screw. The screw hole in the right lug was rebated and recessed to 0.265 inch and 0.05 inch deep for the lower band swivel screw head.

The American Krag Rifle and Carbine

The Model 1892, **Type 1** rifle lower band was used on all infantry rifles from production start to finish.

The **Type 2** lower band was similar to the Type 1 with the exception that it lacked the lugs for the sling swivel and was not split at the bottom. It was used on the Model 1896 Krag Cadet rifle and the Model 1899 carbine, only. The Type 2 lower band on the Cadet rifle was retained by a band spring, similar to that used on the carbine models, and so did not require the use of the lower band pin, see Figure 2-61.

The Type 2 lower band measured 1.285 inches high by 1.932 inches across and 0.5 inch wide.

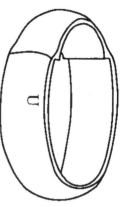

Fig. 2-61. Krag Cadet lower rifle band. Note the absence of the sling swivel lug.

Fig. 2-62. The lower rifle band was marked "U" to indicate that it should be placed with the open end toward the muzzle.

Lower Band Markings and Finish

The lower band was stamped "U" on the right side. The open end of the "U" points to the muzzle. Barrel bands were blued, see Figure 2-62.

Rifle Swivel, Lower Band

The swivel to hold the upper bight of the sling was formed from iron wire 0.170 inch in diameter bent into an oval. A lug was welded to the top of the swivel and drilled through for the lower band sling swivel screw, see Figure 2-63.

The American Krag Rifle and Carbine

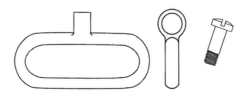

Fig. 2-63. Krag rifle lower band sling swivel and screw.

The swivel was 1.710 inches long and 0.670 inch high. The lug was 0.425 inch high and 0.210 inch thick. The hole for the lower band sling swivel screw head was 0.282 inch in diameter on the right lug and 0.184 on the left lug for the screw shank.

The same swivel was used throughout the production of the Krag rifle.

Lower Band Swivel Screw

This screw was 0.710 inch long by 0.184 inch in diameter. It was threaded for one half its length. The slotted fillister head was 0.268 inch in diameter and 0.085 inch thick at the edge. The same screw was used throughout Krag production, refer to Figure 2-63.

Lower Band Pin

The lower band pin was a steel pin 0.10 inch in diameter and 1.056 inches long, with rounded ends. The band pin was placed crosswise in the stock, 0.5 inch ahead of the rebate for the lower band. Its ends projected sufficiently to hold the tightened barrel band in place against recoil, see Figure 2-64.

The band pin was blued and unmarked.

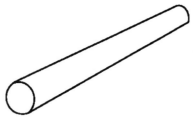

Fig. 2-64. Krag lower band pin.

NOTE: To remove the lower band, it is sometimes necessary to remove the lower band pin if it protrudes farther than the lower band can be opened after the lower band swivel screw is removed. First try tapping the pin farther into the stock.

The American Krag Rifle and Carbine

If that does not work, use a flat-face punch with a 0.10-inch-diameter face and a light hammer. Gently (!) tap the pin out from left to right, being careful not to allow the punch to slip and enlarge the band pin hole. If signs of splintering appear, drive the pin back to its original position and treat both ends with lemon oil for several days to dissolve the natural varnishes adhering the pin to the wood. Reinsert after the lower band has been replaced and gently tap in from right to left.

Carbine Barrel Bands

The carbine barrel band (see Table 2-7) differed from the infantry rifle lower barrel band in that it lacked the lugs for the sling swivel and was not split. Except for the Model 1892 carbine, only one band was used on the Krag carbine to hold the barrel to the stock. It was retained by a barrel band spring and not by the lower band pin.

Table 2-7 U.S. Krag Carbine Barrel Bands		
Upper Band		
Type 1	Model 1892 Carbine, 1st Type	0.75 inch wide, screw hole in side, no stacking swivel or bayonet lug
Forearm Band		
Type 1A	Model 1892, 1st Type Carbine	0.5 inch wide, no sling swivel lug, lug for clamping screw, sight protector hump with shallow sighting groove
Type 1B	Model 1892, 2nd Type Carbine	Sight protector hump with deep sighting groove
Type 2	Model 1896 and 1898 Carbines	No lug for clamping screw, sight protector hump with deep sighting groove
Type 3	Model 1899 Carbine and retrofitted to prior production carbines fitted with Type 5 (1898); Type 6 (1899); Type 7 (1901) and Type 8 (1902) handguards	Same as the Type 2 M1896 Cadet Rifle lower band, no sight protector hump, no lug for clamping screw

The American Krag Rifle and Carbine

Carbine Upper Band, Model 1892, Type 1

The **Type 1** upper band for the Model 1892 carbine was similar to that used on the rifle but was only 0.75 inch long and lacked the lug for the bayonet mount. It was held in place by a shortened upper band screw. As only two prototypes using this particular upper band were built for the long-forearm Model 1892 carbine, the likely production of the Model 1892 upper band was rather limited.

Carbine Lower Band, Model 1892, Type 1

Two variations of the lower band were used on the four prototype Model 1892 carbines (two long forearm and two short-forearm stocks). The Type 1 carbine barrel band had a projection at the top that served to protect the rear sight when the carbine was shoved into a carbine boot. The band was also split at the bottom and had two ears or lugs drilled for a lower band screw to clamp the band tightly about the barrel. The rear of the band was recessed to hold the Type 1 handguard in place. It was made in two variations and both were held in position against recoil with the lower band pin.

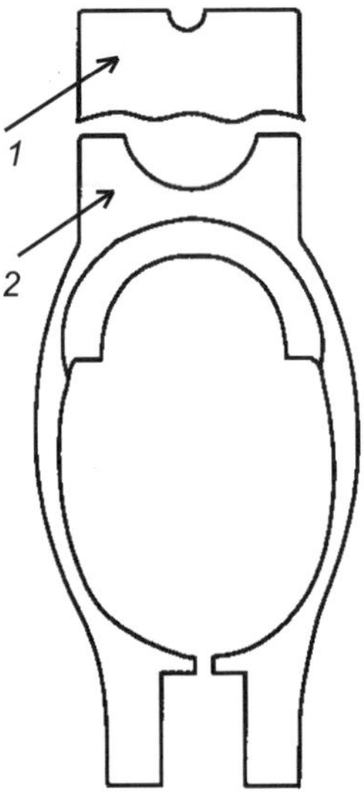

The **Type 1A** carbine band had a shallow "U" sighting groove milled in the top of the sight protector, see Figure 2-65 (arrow 1).

The **Type 1B** carbine band had a deeper "U"-shaped sighting groove. It was 0.540 inch wide; at its deepest, 0.220 inch deep (arrow 2).

Fig. 2-65. Model 1892 Type 1A (above) and 1B (below) carbine barrel bands.

Carbine Lower Band, Model 1896, Type 2

The **Type 2** lower band developed for the Model 1896 carbine was essentially the Type 1, 2nd Variation carbine band without the split

The American Krag Rifle and Carbine

and lugs for the lower band clamping screw. It retained the raised sight protector with the deep "U"-shaped sighting groove, see Figure 2-66.

The Type 2 band measured 2.230 inches high by 0.495 inch thick. The sight protector projection was 0.917 inch wide and the "U"-shaped sight clearance cut was 0.540 inch wide and 0.220 inch deep. The sight clearance cut opened out to the front.

The Type 2 carbine barrel band was used on all Model 1896 and Model 1898 carbines equipped with the Model 1896 rear sight.

Fig. 2-66. Model 1896/1898 carbine barrel band.

Carbine Lower Band, Model 1899 Carbine, Type 3

The **Type 3** carbine band was essentially the same band used on the Krag Cadet rifle. It was the Model 1896 Cadet rifle lower band without the lugs for the sling swivel, see Figure 2-67.

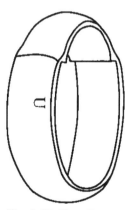

The Type 3 lower band measured 1.285 inches high by 1.932 inches across and 0.5 inch wide. It was used on all Model 1899 carbines equipped with the Model 1896, Model 1898, Model 1901 and Model 1902 rear sights.

Carbine Barrel Band Markings and Finish

The Type 3 carbine band only was stamped "U" on the right side. The open end of the "U" points to the muzzle. Types 1 and 2 barrel bands were unmarked as they could only be installed in the correct direction. Barrel bands were blued, refer to Figure 2-62.

Fig. 2-67. Type 3 carbine barrel band.

The American Krag Rifle and Carbine

Barrel Band Spring

The barrel band spring was first developed for the Model 1812, Third Pattern, Caliber .69 Musket in 1816 and was in continual use for 129 years through the Model 1903 rifle and the M1 Carbine (end of production in 1945). It was made from spring steel in the shape of an "L" with the short or bottom stroke inserted crosswise through the stock. The long, or upright stroke lies flat in a groove milled in the right side of the stock. The top of the upright stroke is rebated so that a portion slides under the barrel band and the front on the rebated portion holds the barrel band secure against recoil, see Figure 2-68.

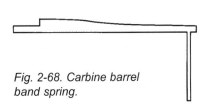

Fig. 2-68. Carbine barrel band spring.

The barrel band spring was used on the Krag Cadet Rifle and all models of the Krag carbine except the Model 1892 Carbine which used the lower band pin. It was blued as a result of the heat treatment process.

Butt Swivel Assembly

The butt swivel assembly consisted of the 1) butt swivel plate, 2) swivel, 3) butt swivel pin and 4) butt swivel plate screws. The butt swivel plate was fastened to the buttstock with two butt swivel plate screws (similar to the upper butt plate screw and rear carbine swivel screw). The swivel was inserted into a hole drilled in the boss of the swivel plate and secured with the butt swivel pin screw, see Figure 2-69.

The butt swivel plate was 0.545 inch wide and 1.725 inches long. It had two 0.216-inch-diameter holes drilled through the top, each countersunk to 0.290 inch for the screw heads. The boss was 0.390 inch high and drilled through the center for the swivel. A 0.10-inch-diameter hole was drilled through the bottom center for the butt swivel pin which retained the swivel. The swivel was made from iron wire 0.160 inch in diameter formed into a "C." The open ends were inserted into

86

The American Krag Rifle and Carbine

the hole drilled in the butt swivel plate boss and were retained by the butt swivel pin. The swivel was 0.684 inch high and 1.743 inches long. The butt swivel pin was 0.10 inch in diam-

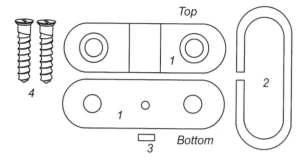

Fig. 2-69. Butt Swivel Assembly.

eter and 0.20 inch long. It was cut from iron wire. Two butt swivel plate screws secured the butt swivel plate to the stock. Both were 0.885 inch long overall with slightly domed heads, 0.3 inch in diameter. The shanks had seven threads. The butt swivel assembly was unchanged throughout U.S. Krag production.

CARBINE SWIVEL

Fig. 2-69a. Carbine Swivel

The carbine swivel was mounted on the left side of the Models 1892, 1896 and 1898 Krag carbines, see Figure 2-69a. It consisted of a flat plate 0.505 inch wide by 2.715 inches long by 0.110 inch thick, a round bar bent into a staple 1.705 inches long by 0.225 inch in diameter riveted to the plate and a ring 1.00 inch in diameter made from iron wire 0.175 inch in diameter. Two wood screws similar to the upper butt plate screw attached the plate. The rear screw (0.885 inch long) was the same as the upper butt plate screw while the front screw was shorter at 0.60 inch long. The use of the Model 1885 carbine sling as well as the Models 1885 and 1887 carbine boot was discontinued with the introduction of the Model 1899 carbine. The **Type 1** carbine swivel was quenched in oil, which produced a deep black color; the **Type 2** was blued.

The American Krag Rifle and Carbine

Barrels

The Krag service barrel was made in three lengths: rifle, 30 inches; Board of Ordnance and Fortifications rifle, 26 inches; and carbine, 22 inches, see Figure 2-70. Only two service calibers were produced, .30-40 Krag and .22-caliber rimfire. Only a few minor changes were made to the barrel during the production life of the Krag.

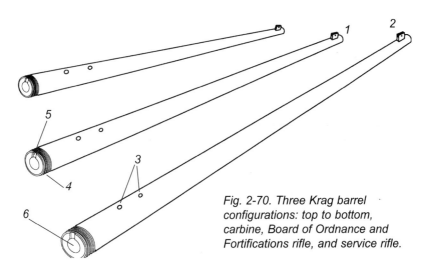

Fig. 2-70. Three Krag barrel configurations: top to bottom, carbine, Board of Ordnance and Fortifications rifle, and service rifle.

The Krag barrel had a bore diameter of 0.300 inch and a groove diameter of 0.308 inch. The rifling had four grooves and lands with one turn in ten inches (1:10).

Three types of special barrels were produced, all in rifle length and only in very small, experimental quantities. One type was chambered for an experimental .30-40 Krag rimless cartridge and the other two for the experimental .20- and .22-caliber service cartridges.

The Krag barrel had six major parts: 1) muzzle, 2) front sight stud, 3) rear sight screw holes, 4) barrel threads, 5) extractor groove and 6) bore.

The American Krag Rifle and Carbine

The bore was drilled in a steel rod, reamed to final size and rifled and chambered. The barrel was proofed with a 70,000 psi cartridge, then marked on the bottom, ahead of the chamber, with a small "P" 0.10 inch high. The front sight base was brazed on and two holes for the rear sight screws were drilled and tapped. The barrel was polished and de-oiled in a caustic soda solution, then browned (blued) in a solution of mercuric chloride, spirits of niter and alcohol, then placed in a steam cabinet for a period of time before being carded (polished) to remove the fine rust that developed. The process was repeated until the desired depth of color was obtained. Table 2-8 provides identifying dimensions for all barrels:

Table 2-8 U.S. Krag Rifle and Carbine Barrel Dimensions (inches)				
Type/ Caliber	Barrel Length	Muzzle Diameter	Lower Barrel Band Position	Receiver
Rifle .30	30	0.620	0.766	0.985
Rifle .22	30	0.620	0.766	0.985
Rifle .30*	26	0.630	0.766	0.985
Carbine M1896/-98	22	0.635	0.766	0.985
Carbine M1899	22	0.635	0.765	0.985
* Board of Ordnance and Fortifications Rifle				

SERVICE RIFLE BARRELS

Four types of service rifle barrels were developed and used in the Krag rifle. The changes from one type to another are very minor and are readily visible in only one or two cases. Rear sight screw holes were located in exactly the same place on the rifle barrel as on the carbine barrel, 4 1/16 inches ahead of the right side of the bolt well or race opening for the rear screw and 6 1/2 inches for the forward screw.

The American Krag Rifle and Carbine

NOTE: Changes are cumulative unless otherwise noted.

Service Rifle Barrel, Type 1

The **Type 1** barrel was used on Model 1892 rifles manufactured to circa serial #12,500 at the end of April 1895. It had a flat muzzle and the rear of the barrel, visible through the open receiver, was also flat, see Figure 2-71.

Fig. 2-71. Krag Type 1 barrels had a flat, uncrowned muzzle. North Cape Publications collection.

The cut for the extractor was 0.20 inch wide. An index mark was scribed on the right side of the barrel and receiver to assure that the barrel was properly set. Both index marks should be in exact alignment, see Figure 2-72.

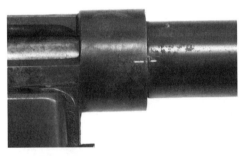

Fig. 2-72. The barrel and receiver had matching index marks to line up the barrel properly.

Service Rifle Barrel, Type 2

The **Type 2** barrel was used from circa serial #s 12,500 to 216,000. It had a rounded or crowned muzzle, see Figure 2-73. The chamber was 2.30 inches long with the length, base to shoulder, 1.65 inches long. Shoulder diameter was 0.424 inch and neck diameter was 0.340 inch. The rear of the barrel, visible through the open receiver, remained flat. The cut for the extractor was 0.20 inch wide.

The American Krag Rifle and Carbine

Service Rifle Barrel, Type 3

From circa serial #213,000 to the end of production in 1904, the chamber of the **Type 3** barrel was reduced slightly in size. The chamber

was shortened to 2.27 inches long and the distance from base to shoulder became 1.62 inches long. Shoulder diameter was reduced to 0.419 inch and neck diameter to 0.338 inch. At the same time, the rear of the barrel, visible through the open receiver, was rounded slightly. The extractor cut was also enlarged slightly to 0.210 inch wide.

Fig. 2-73. The Types 2,3 and 4 Krag barrels had a crowned muzzle.

Board of Ordnance and Fortifications Barrel, Type 4

The **Type 4** barrel is the service barrel shortened to 26 inches for testing as a suitable arm for both infantry and cavalry. The muzzle diameter was 0.01 inch greater in diameter.

GALLERY PRACTICE RIFLE BARRELS
Gallery Practice Rifle Barrel, Type 1

The **Type 1** gallery rifle barrel was developed in an effort to reduce the cost and space required for marksmanship training. They were not manufactured by Springfield Armory but by the Stevens Arms Company at the request of the Chief of Ordnance of the Pennsylvania National Guard in 1905. The .22-caliber barrel extraction system was designed by Harry M. Pope. Most were marked "STEVENS–POPE/ J. STEVENS ARMS & TOOL CO. CHICOPEE FALLS, MASS. U.S.A." Both rifle and carbine barrels were manufactured. The legend was centered between the receiver ring and front sight on both kinds of barrels, see Figure 2-73a.

The American Krag Rifle and Carbine

Fig. 2-73a. The "Stevens-Pope" barrel legend was centered between the receiver ring and front sight on both .22-caliber rifle (top) and carbine (bottom) barrels. William R. Mook collection.

The bore was drilled at a slight upward offset from muzzle to breech with the breech end of the bore at the top of the barrel so that the .30-caliber service extractor could be used. These .22-caliber gallery rifles were used by the National Guards of Pennsylvania, New Jersey and Washington State before the Chief of Ordnance of the U.S. Army declared them an unauthorized rifle and stopped their use.

Gallery Practice Rifle Barrel, Type 2

The **Type 2** barrel was made in .22 rimfire caliber to replace the Stevens-Pope system. Two variations of this barrel were made at the Springfield Armory. The .22-caliber barrel had 8 grooves and a rifling rate of 1:18 inches. The Springfield .22-caliber barrel bore was offset from muzzle to breech so that the end of the bore was at

Fig. 2-74. Type 2B .22-caliber barrel manufactured by the Springfield Armory. From the Jonathan Peck Collection, courtesy of Little John's Auction Service.

the bottom of the barrel, see Figure 2-74.

92

The American Krag Rifle and Carbine

The **Type 2A** barrel had a groove diameter of 0.226 inch. This was 0.003 inch larger than the diameter of the .22-caliber long bullet and was based on the diameter of a .22-caliber Extra Long bullet which had been tested earlier. The Type 2A barrel was therefore quite inaccurate.

Springfield subsequently produced a new barrel (**Type 2B**) with a bore diameter of 0.223 inch which provided acceptable accuracy. The rifles with the Type 2A barrels were recalled and they were replaced with the Type 2B barrels. Barrels were chambered for both the .22-caliber short and long cartridge.

The Krag .22-caliber Gallery Rifles were produced starting in 1905 and issued starting in 1906 but were withdrawn starting in mid-1907 in favor of the Hoffer-Thompson-equipped Model 1903 Springfield. They numbered 717 complete rifles and 124 barreled receivers, or a total of 841. Most, but not all, were in the circa serial #476,500+ range and were made from receivers taken from inventory. They were not service rifles and so royalties were not paid to the Norwegian government for their manufacture.

MATCH RIFLE BARREL

A special .30-caliber target barrel chambered for the Model 1898 .30-caliber cartridge was manufactured by the Stevens Arms Company and designed by Harry M. Pope. They were not manufactured under contract for the military but were made for match target shooting. The barrels outwardly resembled the standard 30-inch infantry barrel but had 8 grooves and a rifling rate of 1:8 inches. The rifling was cut with a right-hand twist to overcome the

Fig. 2-75. The Krag carbine barrel was 22 inches long.

bullet's tendency to drift left with the right-hand service rifling. The American team used the Krag rifle equipped with Stevens-Pope barrels at Bisley, England, on July 11, 1903, to win the Palma Trophy. Eight American shooters fired 15 rounds each at distances of 800, 900 and 1,000 yards for a cumulative score of 1,570, 15 points higher than the British team which placed second. A few match barrels were also made by the Winchester Repeating Arms Company.

CARBINE BARRELS

The Krag carbine barrel was 22 inches long, see Figure 2-75. Table 2-8 provides identifying dimensions. In all other respects besides length, the carbine barrel was identical to the rifle barrel. Chamber dimensions were the same and changed at the same time as in the rifle barrel. Rear sight screw holes were located in exactly the same place on the carbine barrel as on the rifle barrel, 4 1/16 inches ahead of the right side of the bolt well or race opening for the rear screw and 6 1/2 inches for the forward screw. The carbine barrel had the same taper breech to muzzle as the rifle barrel. It was simply cut off at 22 inches long which provided it with the same muzzle diameter as the rifle barrel (0.635 inch) if it was also cut at 22 inches. All carbine barrels were manufactured for the .30 U.S. Government cartridge (.30-40) only.

Carbine Barrel, Type 1

The **Type 1** carbine barrel was used on the at least two of the four Model 1892 carbines (serial #s 1,015 at the Rock Island Arsenal Museum and 1,575 in a private collection), on the Model 1896 carbine (circa serial #s 21,500 to 87,500) and on the Model 1898 carbine (circa serial #s 123,100 through 131,000). The carbine barrel had a rounded muzzle (except for the Model 1892, which had a flat muzzle). The chamber was 2.30 inches long with the length, base to shoulder, of 1.65 inches. Shoulder diameter was 0.424 inch and neck diameter was 0.340 inch. The rear of the barrel, visible through the open receiver, remained flat. The cut for the extractor was 0.20 inch wide. A barrel index mark is found on the right side of the barrel. It should match exactly a similar index mark on the right side of the receiver face.

The American Krag Rifle and Carbine

Carbine Barrel, Type 2

From circa serial #226,100 (Model 1899 carbine) to the end of production in 1904, the chamber of the **Type 2** barrel was shortened to 2.27 inches long and the distance base to shoulder to 1.62 inches long. Shoulder diameter was reduced to 0.419 inch and neck diameter to 0.338 inch. At the same time, the rear of the barrel, visible through the open receiver, was rounded slightly. The extractor cut was also enlarged slightly to 0.210 inch wide.

NOTE: The collector will occasionally encounter Krag carbines with barrels that show the initials "S A" over the Ordnance Department logotype, the Flaming Bomb, over the "month/year-date." These barrels are Model 1903 Springfield Rifle barrels fitted to Krag carbines by a surplus military dealer for commercial sale.

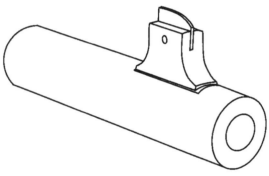

Fig. 2-76. Front sight stud and blade.

Krag Front Sight Stud

The Krag front sight stud was brazed onto a flat milled onto the top of the barrel, see Figure 2-76. The front sight stud was 0.252 inch wide by 0.920 inch long at the base, 0.453 inch at the top and had a slot 0.055 inch wide for the front sight blade. The base was 0.420 inch high. A hole was drilled crosswise through the center of the stud and a rivet passed through holes in the stud and sight blade and its ends were peened and polished smooth. The **Type 1** stud slot was 0.055 inch wide for the Type 1 blade on all Model 1892 rifles and carbines. The **Type 2** stud slot was 0.50 inch wide on all production beginning with the Model 1896.

The American Krag Rifle and Carbine

Rear Sight Screw Holes

The rear sight on all Krag models was attached by two slotted flat head screws. Two holes were drilled into the center top of the barrel and threaded. Screw holes for both the rifle and carbine were located at the same distance ahead of the right-side opening of the bolt well or race: 4 1/16 inches for the rear screw hole and 6 1/2 inches for the front.

KRAG BARREL MARKINGS AND FINISH

Krag barrels will usually show only three marks, 1) a small alphanumeric code stamped on the breech end indicating the steel supplier, 2) a small "P" 0.1 inch high indicating that the bar- rel had been tested with a

Fig. 2-77. Barrel proof mark.

proof cartridge (Figure 2-77) and 3) the barrel index mark on the right side at the breech. Steel suppliers can be identified by consulting the "Reports of the Chief of Ordnance to the Secretary of War" for the year the barrel was manufactured.

Every Krag barrel was tested with a 70,000 pound per square inch proof cartridge. Ten barrels were selected from each lot of barrel steel for further testing with a 100,000 psi proof cartridge.

Barrels were browned (blued), including muzzles. The breech end of the barrel showing through the receiver will be "in the white" if original. If blued, the barrel may have been refinished. Do not mistake age and discoloration for bluing. No Krag barrel was ever Parkerized at the Springfield Armory as Parkerizing was not begun there until November 1918, fourteen years after the end of Krag production.

The American Krag Rifle and Carbine

Receivers

The Krag had one of the most complicated receivers ever machined at the Springfield National Armory. It was forged to rough shape and machined to final specifications, Figure 2-78.

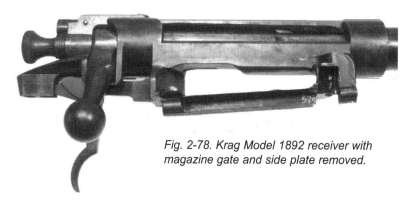

Fig. 2-78. Krag Model 1892 receiver with magazine gate and side plate removed.

The receiver with its side-mounted magazine was a marvel of precision machining at a time in the Armory's history when an unreliable steam-powered electrical plant was replacing the century-old water plant that drove the extensive web of belt-driven machinery. A total of 121 separate machining operations were required by the summer of 1900 to complete one receiver. It should be noted that the electrical plant continued to drive the belt-driven machinery for many more years. If you have ever wondered what happened to the majority of the millions of buffalo skins from the wholesale destruction of the great buffalo herds between 1865 and 1880, you have only to look at the miles and miles of industrial belting that drove the machinery of the mid-industrial age. The power belts were manufactured from buffalo leather because of its thickness, resilience and strength.

Whether used on a rifle or a carbine, the receiver was the same. As lists of serial numbers that distinguished between rifles and

The American Krag Rifle and Carbine

carbines were not kept at the Springfield Armory, the collector's task in determining authenticity is complicated by the fact that the receiver could be used for either rifle or carbine before circa serial #226,000. After circa serial #226,000, receivers intended for use on carbines were stamped "MODEL 1899."

Toward the end of the Krag's production life in 1904, a few rifles were converted to carbines by the simple expedient of changing barrels, rear sights and stocks. These can be identified by the fact that the "8" in "MODEL 1898" was overstamped "9." Collectors should note that the "9" was stamped with a die of the same type font and size as the "8" it replaced.

While the majority of changes to the Krag rifle and carbine occurred in the receiver itself, most were minor and resulted from field service observations or else had to do with increased efficiency during production.

Finally, while a Krag Model 1892 or Model 1896 receiver will not fit into a Model 1898 stock, a Model 1898 receiver will fit into any Krag stock made at the Springfield Armory.

Receiver Description

The Krag receiver was 1.92 inches wide at its widest point, 8.2 inches long and 1.841 inches high at its highest point. The magazine well provided a mounting point for the magazine gate along the bottom right side. A single locking lug was milled in the floor just below the breech to accept the single locking lug on the bolt. The right side of the split bridge formed a safety locking shoulder against which the safety lug on the bolt body would impinge if the locking lug failed.

The receiver consisted of a machined forging to which was attached the barrel, magazine assembly, cutoff, side plate, ejector sear spring and trigger/sear assembly. The parts of the receiver are shown in Figure 2-79. They include the: 1) bolt channel, 2) magazine well, 3) channel to the magazine, 4) bullet ramp, 5) left wall, 6) locking shoulder, 7) cocking shoulder, 8) cutoff switch recess, 9) cutoff hole, 10) bolt handle

The American Krag Rifle and Carbine

seat, 11) locking lug recess, 12) ejector seat, 13) cocking groove, 14) sear nose slot, 15) side plate tenon mortise, 16) guide lip, 17) guide lip rivet, 18) extractor spring lip, 19) hinge bar holes, 20) magazine spring channel, 21) carrier arbor hole, 22) sear seat hole*, 23) side plate screw hole*, 24) ejector pin hole*, 25) extractor pin notch, 26) trigger heel bearing, 27) hinge bar spring seat*, 28) trigger guard screw holes* and 29) extractor hook slot, 30) barrel ring. Items with an asterisk are not visible in the drawing.

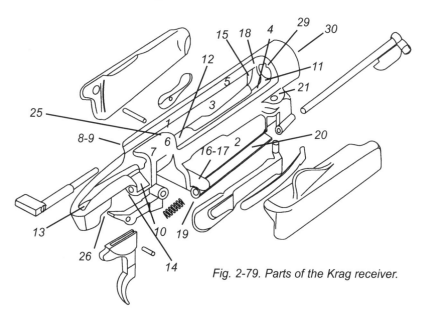

Fig. 2-79. Parts of the Krag receiver.

The parts of the Krag receiver which changed in form or dimension are summarized in Table 2-9. Only one aspect of the receiver was changed that was significant enough to allow the Krag receivers to be divided into two types. That change was at circa serial #109,000 when the extension on the bolt handle seat was eliminated. That change made it impossible for Model 1892 and 1896 receivers to fit into Model 1898 stocks, see Figure 2-80.

Table 2-9 U.S. Krag Receiver Changes		
Part*	**Serial Number Range**	**Date or Model When Change Was Approved**
Magazine well groove for guide lip tenon omitted, guide lip made thinner and riveted to magazine well floor	circa 2,000-2,500**	September 8, 1894 M1892
Slot for ejector pin head omitted on left rear wall below the magazine side plate screw hole	circa 7,400***	January 28, 1895 M1892
Notch for cutoff spring-loaded spindle deepened and extended upward by 0.1 inch	circa 12,000***	October 15, 1895 M1892
Extractor pin notch added to rear wall of the receiver	circa 24,000**	December 1895 M1896
Trigger heel walls removed	circa 25,000***	Approved May 27, 1895, appears at circa 25,000
Index mark on side of barrel tenon omitted but retained on front	circa 26,000**	January 1896 M1896
Cutoff hole reduced 0.5 inch and moved downward slightly	circa 109,000 ****	July 1898 M1898
Lip or tenon for mortise for side plate increased by 0.02 inch	circa 109,000***	July 1898 M1898
Bolt handle seat or ramp eliminated	circa 109,000**	July 1898 M1898
Bearing surface for carrier in carrier arbor lowered 0.02 inch	circa 109,000****	July 1898 M1898
Magazine spring channel wall reduced	circa 109,000****	July 1898 M1898

The American Krag Rifle and Carbine

Table 2-9, cont.
U.S. Krag Receiver Changes

Part*	Serial Number Range	Date or Model When Change Was Approved
Top of arbor for carrier lowered 0.08 inch	circa 109,000**	July 1898 M1898
Bottom of the channel for the magazine spring raised slightly	circa 109,000***	July 1898 M1898
Fillet added to the barrel seat in receiver	circa 240,000***	Approved June 1899 M1899
"8" in "MODEL 1898" overstamped "9" to turn Model 1898 rifles into Model 1899 carbines	circa 371,000**	January 1902 M1899
Larger dies used to stamp Model 1898 serial numbers	circa 477,000**	November 1903 M1898

* Changes are carried through Krag production. Changes were sometimes introduced before written authorization was issued, and sometimes they were introduced after. The actual start date for a change in manufacturing procedure also depended on stock inventory as well as production methods.
** Easily visible
*** Visible
**** Not readily visible

Therefore, **Type 1** receivers were manufactured before circa serial #109,000 and used only on the Model 1892 and Model 1896 rifles and carbines. The **Type 2** receiver was manufactured after circa serial #109,000 and used on all Model 1898 rifles, Model 1898 carbines and Model 1899 carbines.

Ejector

The ejector's function is to knock the empty cartridge case from the grip of the extractor as the bolt is drawn to the rear. The ejector has

The American Krag Rifle and Carbine

Fig. 2-80. The bolt handle extension (arrow) was eliminated in the Models 1898 and 1899 receivers.

four significant aspects: 1) heel, 2) point, 3) pin hole and 4) bearing surface, see Figure 2-81. The ejector was pinned into a slot in the floor of the receiver. The pin hole was located behind the ejector's center of gravity so that the point always pivoted up. When the bolt was pushed forward or pulled back, the ejector rode in a slot in the bottom. The bolt slot does not reach all the way to the front and as a consequence, as the head of the bolt passed over the ejector, it tipped upward, knocking the cartridge case from the extractor and out of the open breech.

Type 1 ejectors had a bearing surface 0.001 inch high around the

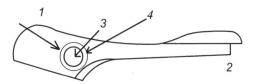

Fig. 2-81. Ejector.

ejector pin hole (arrow 4) and were numbered to the receiver between circa serial #s 31–300. The Type 2 ejectors lacked the bearing surface and were not numbered or marked in any way (arrow 4).

Ejector Pin

The ejector pin held the ejector in place in the receiver and allowed it to pivot up and down. The Type 1 ejector pin was "L" shaped and 0.820 inch long and 0.095 inch in diameter. The head was the short end of the "L" and was 0.222 inch long by 0.098 inch wide. The ejector pin hole in the receiver was immediately below the side screw

The American Krag Rifle and Carbine

hole. A slot was cut on a bias from the center of the hole to the five o'clock position to hold the head in place. The inside of the head was cut on a bias so that a tool could be inserted to pry it out, see Figure 2-82.

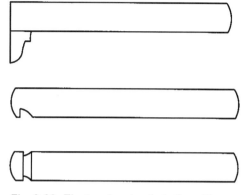

Fig. 2-82. Ejector pins, top to bottom, Type 1, Type 2 and Type 3.

The **Type 2** ejector pin was modified at circa serial # 7,400 by removing the "L"-shaped head and substituting a hook-shaped cut in the outside end. The pin was lengthened to 0.272 inch.

The **Type 3** ejector pin was introduced at circa serial #23,000, just prior to the start of Model 1896 receiver manufacturing. The undercut notch was changed to a circular groove.

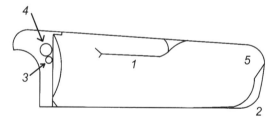

Fig. 2-83. Side Plate.

Side Plate

The side plate is a separate part of the receiver that forms the left wall. The front of the side plate attaches to the receiver by a tenon which fits into a mortise machined in the front, left side of the magazine. The rear is held to the receiver by a screw. The side plate (Figure 2-83) is 1.165 inches high at the rear, 0.935 inch at the front (ahead of the curve) and 7.75 inches long (including the tail). The features are: 1) rib, 2) tenon, 3) ejector pin hole recess, 4) side plate screw hole and 5) the ramp.

The American Krag Rifle and Carbine

Four major types of side plate were used. The **Type 1** side plate was slightly curved on the inside and did not have a rib or a hole for the ejector pin. The **Type 1A** side plate was numbered by the assembler to the receiver with a Roman numeral in the first thirty produced. The

Type 1B side plate was used from circa serial #s 31 to 7,399 but with the receiver serial number stamped in Arabic numbers on the rear flat as shown below in Figure 2-84. The **Type 1C** side plate was used from circa serial #s 7,400 to 10,999. It had a blind hole drilled for the longer Type 2

Fig. 2-84. (L-r) Types 1A and 1B side plates. Note the Roman numeral "XXV" chiseled on the Type 1A and the stamped Arabic "100" on the Type 1B. William R. Mook collection. Type 1C (inset) has the ejector hole.

ejector pin, refer to Figure 2-84, arrow. The practice of stamping the receiver serial number on the inside of the side plate was intermittent and discontinued with the **Type 1D** side plate after circa serial #11,000.

In the **Type 2** side plate the thickness of the upper half was increased from 0.06 to 0.07 inch and the cartridge rib was elongated from 1.360 inches to 2.26 inches to improve feeding, starting with the Model 1896 at circa serial #24,000. The Type 2 side plate was not serial numbered to the receiver.

The tenon of the Type **3A** side plate was increased from 0.230 inch to 0.250 inch in the Model 1898 at circa serial #109,101 to hold it more securely at the front.

The American Krag Rifle and Carbine

Starting with the **Type 3B** side plate at circa serial #145,000, the high polish to the inside of the side plate was no longer applied. At circa serial #195,000, the upper, rear corner of the **Type 4** side plate was given a more pronounced curve to the outside.

Side Plate Screw

The side plate screw had a fillister head and was originally 0.465 inch long overall. The diameter of the slotted head was 0.265 inch. The **Type 1** screw was 0.465 inch long overall; the **Type 2** was shortened one thread to 0.462 inch overall, see Figure 2-85.

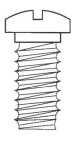

Fig. 2-85. Side Plate Screw.

Trigger Heel Bearing

The trigger heel bearing is the flat part on the underside of the receiver tang immediately ahead of the rear guard screw hole. The heel of the trigger contacts the bearing surface on the underside of the tang when the finger piece is pulled back, which causes the sear (which is pinned to the trigger) to be pushed downward, releasing the cocking piece and allowing the firing pin to be driven forward by the mainspring, see Figure 2-86.

Originally, the bearing surface was a slot cut in the bottom of the tang, and the walls of

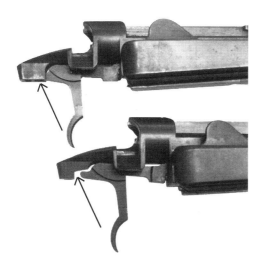

Fig. 2-86. Trigger bearing surfaces: above, M1892; below, M1896 and later receivers.

the slot served as a guard for the trigger heel. It was determined that the walls served no practical purpose and that it was more efficient to mill a flat bearing surface from the tang material than to cut the slot. From circa serial #25,000 to the end of production, the bearing surface was a flat on the bottom of the tang immediately ahead of the rear guard screw hole.

Sear Seat Hole

The sear seat hole was a rounded cut milled in the left side rear of the receiver, along the midline and behind the magazine box. The hinge of the sear was inserted into the hole. The sear rotated up and down on this bearing surface.

Guard Screw Holes

Two guard screw holes were drilled and tapped in the bottom of the receiver. The guard screws pass through the trigger guard and stock, and thread into the screw holes in the receiver. The rearmost screw hole is drilled into the tang. The forward guard screw hole is drilled into the bottom of the magazine box just forward of the sear seat hole. The guard acts as a clamp to hold the receiver and stock together.

TRIGGER ASSEMBLY

The trigger assembly consists of seven parts, four of which are shown in Figure 2-87: 1) trigger, 2) trigger pin, 3) sear and 4) sear spring. Other parts associated with the trigger assembly are the trigger guard and two trigger guard screws. The trigger is attached to the sear by the trigger pin behind the sear's point of balance. The hinge on the front of the sear slides into the sear seat hole in the receiver just behind the magazine box. The sear spring fits into a hole in the front end of the sear, below the hinge, and bears against the wall of the receiver. When the trigger is pulled to the rear, its heel rises and bears against the trigger heel bearing point on the bottom of the receiver tang. This forces the back end of the sear down, which pulls the sear nose out of engagement with the cocking piece on the bolt. The sear spring in the

The American Krag Rifle and Carbine

front of the sear forces the sear nose back up, ready to be engaged by the cocking piece the next time the bolt is operated.

Trigger

The trigger has five features: A) finger piece, B) sear recess, C) bearing, D) heel and E) trigger pin hole (refer to Figure 2-87). The sear recess is milled into an open box in the top center for the rear of the sear.

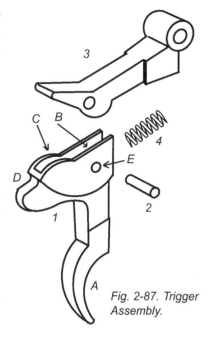

Fig. 2-87. Trigger Assembly.

Three types of triggers (see Figure 2-88) were used during Krag production. In the **Type 1** trigger the sear recess was 0.24 inch wide. The trigger was originally case-hardened in oil to produce a deep blue-black color to circa serial #400.

The **Type 2** trigger was case-hardened in water to produce a distinctive mottled, green, yellow and blue coloration. The colors produced by this process often fade on exposure to ultraviolet light and air to a mottled gray. Color case-hardening of the trigger was in use from circa serial #'s 401 to 148,000.

Fig. 2-88. This cut from a 1900 edition of the American Machinist Magazine *shows the method for face milling five Krag triggers at a time.*

107

The American Krag Rifle and Carbine

The **Type 3** trigger was again case-hardened in oil starting at circa serial #148,001 to the end of production. The sear recess was widened by 0.01 inch to 0.25 inch.

Trigger Pin

The trigger pin was made of hardened steel and was 0.10 inch in diameter. The pin tapered slightly along its length. The pin's narrow end was inserted from the right and was upset with a hammer on the left side to hold it in place, see Figure 2-89.

Fig. 2-89. Trigger Pin.

Two types of pins were used: The **Type 1** pin was 0.455 inch long. The **Type 2** was reduced to 0.395 inch in length at circa serial #25,000.

Sear

The function of the sear is to hold the cocking piece in the retracted position so that the mainspring is compressed and the firing pin is drawn back and held until the trigger is pulled to the rear to release it.

The sear, see Figure 2-90, was 0.345 inch wide at the hinge, 0.234 inch wide at the sear nose and 2.05 inches long. The front of the sear immediately below the hinge had a hole 0.240 inch in diameter and 0.387 inch deep for the sear spring.

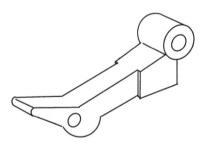

Fig. 2-90. Sear.

Four types of sears were used during Krag production. The **Type 1** sear was made of high-carbon steel from the start of production to circa serial #20,000. The **Type 2** sear was made from low-carbon steel and case-hardened in oil at circa serial #22,500. The nose of both types was 0.585 inch long. The **Type 3** sear nose was shortened by 0.005 inch to 0.580 inch at circa serial #24,000 to the end of production. This was not an official change. The

Type 4 sear was manufactured under subcontract. It was similar to the Type 3 but was stamped "A" on its side. Its exact period of use is unknown.

Sear Spring

This was a coil spring tapered at the end that drove the sear nose to return to the "up" position after the rifle or carbine was fired. The spring was made from steel wire in 7 coils. The outside diameter of the spring was 0.234 inch, see Figure 2-91.

Fig. 2-91. Sear Spring.

Two types of springs were used. The **Type 1** spring was made from steel wire 0.041 inch in diameter. The **Type 1A** spring was left black from the hardening and tempering process to circa serial #9,000. After, the **Type 1B** spring was polished.

At circa serial #146,000, a larger-diameter (0.047 inch) steel wire was used to make the **Type 2** spring. It was polished as well.

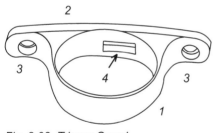

Fig. 2-92. Trigger Guard.

Trigger Guard

The trigger guard serves two functions: the first, to surround the trigger and protect it from being accidently pulled, and the second to secure the receiver to the stock. It consisted of 1) the trigger guard and 2) the trigger guard plate, see Figure 2-92.

The trigger guard plate was 0.6 inch wide by 3.725 inches long. 3) Two counterbored holes 0.250 inch in diameter were drilled for the guard screws and 4) a rectangular slot 0.230 inch wide and 0.590 inch long was cut for the trigger.

The American Krag Rifle and Carbine

The trigger guard was bow shaped 0.650 inch wide with an oval-shaped opening 1.765 inches in diameter at its widest.

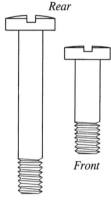

Rear

Front

Fig. 2-93. Type 1 Guard Screws.

The trigger guard was unchanged throughout production. It was unmarked and blued.

Guard Screws

Two guard screws were used to attach the trigger guard and stock to the receiver, see Figure 2-93. The front guard screw was 1.20 inches long with a slotted fillister head 0.345 inch in diameter. It was threaded on the lower 0.440 inch of its length. The rear guard screw was 1.515 inches long with a slotted fillister head 0.345 inch in diameter. It was threaded on the lower 0.550 inch of its length.

Two types of guard screws were used. The **Type 1** guard screw had a flat end to circa serial #40,000. After, the tip of the **Type 2** screw was beveled slightly. Both were threaded 0.25 inch in diameter with 25 threads per inch.

MAGAZINE ASSEMBLY

The Krag rifle had a side-loading box magazine that held five cartridges. To load, the gate on the right side was lowered and five cartridges were laid across the palm and fingers of the right hand and "rolled" into the magazine. When the gate was snapped closed, a follower pushed the first cartridge up into position to be captured by the bolt as it was moved forward. If the rifle or carbine was to be fired in the "single shot" mode, the cutoff lever, or thumbpiece, was activated to block the cartridges in the magazine from rising, and allowing a cartridge to be inserted into the open breech.

The need for a magazine cutoff was thought necessary to prevent the soldier from firing excessively and overburdening the logistics system. Keep in mind that prior to the widespread use of automobiles

The American Krag Rifle and Carbine

and trucks, ammunition was distributed by train to way points where it was picked up by horse-drawn wagons and carried to forts and camps, or during combat, to the front lines. One thousand .30-40 cartridges in their wooden shipping crate from Frankford Arsenal weighed 75 lbs and supplied twenty-five soldiers with a standard garrison issue of forty rounds per day. A company of 120 men in garrison therefore required 360 lbs of ammunition per day. A combat issue was one hundred rounds and a 75 lb crate supplied only ten men. A 120-man company required 900 lbs of ammunition per day in combat.

While loading the Krag rifle sounds easy and quick, in fact it was not, especially under combat conditions. The act of removing single cartridges from the cartridge belt, balancing the five cartridges on the hand and then orienting them to roll into the magazine was not easily accomplished, especially when the soldier was under fire and his hands were shaking. It was far too easy to drop one or more cartridges or insert them the wrong way and jam the load.

A clip-loading device was developed and patented by Edward G. Parkhurst and Lyman E. Warren. The Parkhurst device used a Mauser-style metal clip holding five cartridges. The clip was inserted into a special holder at the rear of the Krag magazine with the gate open. Pushing down with the thumb loaded the cartridges into the magazine. The gate was snapped shut and the rifle's bolt cocked to load the first round. The Parkhurst device functioned well enough but was still slower than the Mauser system, which allowed the cartridges to be pushed straight down into a vertical magazine.

In any event, soon after the Parkhurst device was developed and tested, the Krag was replaced in service with the Model 1903 rifle which used the Mauser-style clip-loading system. As a consequence, only two hundred receivers, plus at least one known prototype, were equipped with the Parkhurst-Warren clip-loading device.

NOTE: In the Model 1892 series, certain magazine parts were stamped with the receiver's entire serial number as, presumably, these parts were handfitted. The practice was completely discontinued at about

The American Krag Rifle and Carbine

circa serial #11,000. The entire number was always stamped on the gate. Some parts were numbered longer than others, i.e., numbering of the follower ended at circa serial #670 while the carrier was numbered to circa serial #11,000.

The parts of the magazine include 1) the gate, 2) hinge bar, 3) magazine spring, 4) carrier, 5) follower, 6) follower pin, 7) side plate and 8) side plate screw, see Figure 2-94.

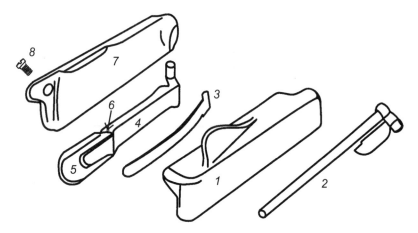

Fig. 2-94. Magazine Assembly.

Magazine

The magazine is the open space below the bolt race (well) and just inside the gate. The magazine connects the bolt race or well by the magazine channel which allows the cartridges to be forced up one at a time into the path of the bolt face.

Gate

The gate is the cover or door to the magazine. It is hinged at the bottom and uses a flat spring, curved along its length to apply pressure to hold it in the open or closed position. The gate has a thumbpiece on its

The American Krag Rifle and Carbine

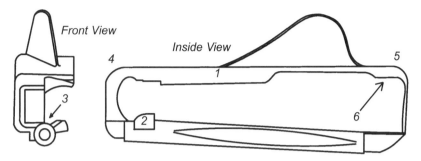

Fig. 2-95. Magazine Gate.

upper outer surface, see Figure 2-95.

Two types of gates were used. The **Type 1** gate used on the Model 1892 and Model 1896 Krags is characterized by a wide bevel on its upper outer surface (1).

Six variations of the Type 1 gate were used. Gates on the first thirty rifles form the **Type 1A**. Most are believed to have had the receiver serial number chiseled into the metal as a Roman numeral by the assembler. The **Type 1B** gates had the receiver serial numbers in Arabic numbers stamped into the front vertical edge from serial number 31 to circa 11,000. The relief for the lug, or protrusion, milled into the receiver at the top rear of the magazine well and the matching relief cut on the magazine gate (arrow 6) was discontinued at circa serial #24,000 in the **Type 1C** gate. In the **Type 1D** gate at circa serial #10,000, the length of the lug (2) that carries the cam that directs the carrier from the recess in the gate into the magazine was changed from 0.267 inch to 0.270 inch (0.003 inch). Serial numbering of all magazine parts to the receiver was discontinued at circa serial #11,000.

NOTE: The entire serial number was stamped on gate and side plate between circa serial #s 31–10,000.

The American Krag Rifle and Carbine

The **Type 1E** had a small fillet (3) added where the lug and hinge hole meet. The curve where the front and side of the gate meet was decreased (4).

The **Type 2** gate retained the changes made to the Type 1 gate and in addition, the wide bevel (1) on its upper surface was eliminated starting with the Model 1898 at circa serial #109,000. The rear of the gate was also changed, giving it a more squared appearance (5).

Hinge Bar Head and Pin

The hinge bar was made in two parts, the head and the pin, see Figure 2-96. The pin passes through two lugs with holes drilled through them (hinge bar holes) on the front edge of the magazine well in the receiver and through the hinge hole in the gate. The hinge hole is a long tunnel drilled through a round protrusion on the inside bottom edge of the gate. The pin is a steel rod 0.150 inch in diameter and 4.290 inches long. The end of the pin is rounded. Three types of pins were used.

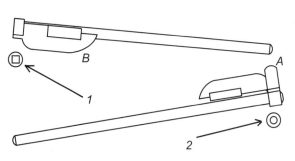

Fig. 2-96. Hinge Bar.

The head end of the **Type 1** pin is squared for 0.210 inch and press-fitted into the head and filed flat from the start of production to circa serial #6,000, refer to Arrow 1 in Figure 2-96. The pin was spring tempered and black in color.

The head end of the **Type 2** pin is round for 0.210 inch and press-fitted into the head from circa serial #6,001 to the end of production. The head of the pin was peened, leaving a rounded end protruding slightly from the head (refer to Arrow 2 in Figure 2-96). The pin was spring tempered and black in color.

After circa serial #16,000, the **Type 3** pin was no longer spring tempered and was blued.

NOTE: One hinge pin has been observed that was threaded.

The head was an intricately machined piece that was press-fitted to the pin. It was spring-loaded to retain the pin in place. The head was composed of A) the lug by which the hinge bar head and pin could be turned and withdrawn and B) a spring with a lug on its inside surface which snapped into place against the forward hinge bar hole on the receiver. The spring flexed and held the lug in place so that it would not rotate or work its way out under recoil or hard use. Five types of hinge bar heads were used. The **Type 1** had a square mortise for the square head of the pin to circa serial #6,000, refer to Arrow 1 in Figure 2-96.

In the **Type 2** head, the mortise was made round after circa serial #6,000 to the end of production. It was easier to drill a round hole than cut a square mortise and so increased production efficiency, refer to Arrow 2 in Figure 2-96.

The right, inside edge of the spring on the head was rounded slightly to make it easier to turn up and withdraw. The change was made to the **Type 3** head at circa serial #10,500.

The **Type 4** head, at circa serial #13,600, had a small fillet ground at the point where the spring joined the lug to increase its strength.

At circa serial #22,400, the lug on the **Type 5** head was reduced from 0.205 inch to 0.197 inch. Specifications published in the *Description and Rules for the Management of the U.S. Magazine Rifle and Carbine, Calibre .30*, dated 1898, stated that the lug was reduced 0.03

The American Krag Rifle and Carbine

inch. Measurements of fourteen examples show that the average reduction was closer to 0.01, with a variance of 0.005 inch, suggesting that this piece was ground partly by hand in a fixture.

Magazine Spring

The magazine spring was 0.210 inch wide and 3.04 inches long. The breech end of the spring was round while the muzzle end had a lip which bore against the heel of the carrier. The springs were hardened and tempered and show a characteristic black color, see Figure 2-97. Two types of springs were used throughout the production of the Krag.

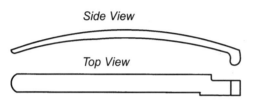

Fig. 2-97. Magazine Spring.

The **Type 1** spring was polished on its reverse side to circa serial #400. After, the **Type 2** spring was polished only in the middle third of its reverse side.

Carrier

The carrier and follower were two separate pieces connected by the follower pin. They were assembled at the factory and not intended to be separated. If one segment needed to be replaced, they were usually replaced together. The carrier and follower were numbered together from circa serial #s 31–670, see Figure 2-98.

The carrier had the following parts: 1) face, 2) arbor, 3) heel, 4) cam, 5) point and 6) follower pin hole. The point was milled into a convex curve to guide the cartridge into the magazine channel. The carrier was 3.75 inches long and 0.475 inch wide at the axle end. The opposite end was machined into the arbor and heel.

A number of major type changes were made to the carrier during its production with some variations as well. The **Type 1A** carrier may

116

The American Krag Rifle and Carbine

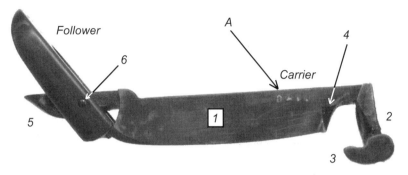

Fig. 2-98. Carrier and Follower Assembly showing partial serial number on early carrier (arrow A).

have had a Roman numeral fitting number chiseled on it to serial #30 by an assembler. The Type **1B** carrier carried the serial number of the receiver in Arabic numbers stamped onto bottom surface adjacent to the heel circa serial #s 31 to 11,000. The numbers were 0.08 inch high and had serifs.

Prior to circa serial #1,200, the convex surface of the carrier was polished to a glossy finish before bluing; after, it was not polished to the same high degree. If you can see vertical polishing marks in the curved surface, the carrier was made after circa serial #1,200.

NOTE: Other authorities give the changeover point at circa serial #1,000. Direct observation of serial number 1,148 shows a highly polished convex surface.

The lug against which the magazine spring bore was shortened from 0.4 inch to 0.365 in the **Type 2** carrier at circa serial #9,200.

The arbor on the **Type 3** carrier was shortened from 1.049 to 1.0 inch at circa serial #s 108,000–109,000. The metal was removed from the bottom of the arbor. This was the final form of the carrier.

The American Krag Rifle and Carbine

Follower

The follower acts on the last cartridge in the magazine. The carrier's point pushes the last cartridge onto the follower, which forces it high enough in the magazine channel to be caught by the bolt face. Followers were only numbered from circa serial #s 31–670.

The **Type 1**'s curved face was 0.454 inch wide at its widest point. Only one modification was made to the follower during production.

The curved face of the **Type 2** follower was reduced in width by 0.1 inch to 0.354 inch, forcing the first cartridge in the magazine to rise higher. The change was made at circa serial #233,000.

Follower Pin

The follower pin connected the carrier and follower. It was 0.08 inch in diameter and 0.55 inch high. The pin was hardened and the ends were polished flush with the surface of the follower.

MAGAZINE CUTOFF ASSEMBLY

The cutoff switch for the magazine shut off cartridge flow from the magazine to allow the shooter to load single cartridges through the open breech. The cutoff was mounted in a socket on the left side of the receiver, see Figure 2-99.

Fig. 2-99. The cutoff switch is located on the left side of the receiver behind the top of the side plate. North Cape Publications collection.

The cutoff consisted of three parts: 1) thumbpiece, 2) spring and 3) spring spindle. The earliest cutoff used a flat spring with a detent or tab perpendicular to the

118

spindle shaft to hold the cutoff in the open or closed position. The detent traveled in a recess cut into the receiver wall. The later cutoff exchanged the flat spring for a spring-driven spindle. The spring drove the spindle into the cutoff groove where it dropped into one of two detents drilled in the cutoff recess to hold the cutoff in "ON" (down) allowing the cartridge to be fed from the magazine or "OFF" (up) position. This raised the carrier just enough to prevent cartridges from feeding from the maga-zine until circa serial #s 107,000 to 108,000 when its action was re-versed, see Figure 2-100.

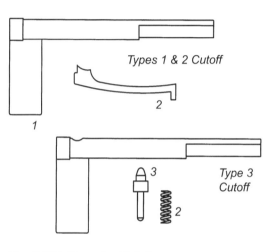

Types 1 & 2 Cutoff

Fig. 2-100. Magazine Cutoff

Type 3 Cutoff

The **Type 1** cutoff was 2.497 inches long over-all. The spindle was 0.218 inch in diameter and 2.144 inches long. The thumbpiece was 0.361 inch long and 0.575 inch high. It was 0.240 inch thick at the thickest point and the edge was scored with eight grooves. The **Type 1A** was numbered to the receiver to circa serial #150 (see Figure 2-106A) and its spindle was rebated half its diameter for 0.865 inch. The rebate ended in a 90-degree cut. The **Type 1B** was not numbered and its rebate ended in an angled cut circa serial #s 151–500, see Figure 2-101.

The **Type 2** cutoff was identical to the Type 1 except that number of grooves cut along the edge of the thumbpiece to make it easier to grasp was changed from eight to four. Also, the end of the rebate was an angled cut or upward slope to the full diameter of the spindle. The Type 2 cutoff was used from circa serial #s 501–11,900.

119

The American Krag Rifle and Carbine

Fig. 2-101. (Top to bottom) Types 4, 3 and 1 cutoffs compared.

At circa serial #11,900, the flat spring with a lug-bearing surface was replaced by the spring-loaded spindle in the **Type 3** cocking piece, refer to Figure 2-101. The thickness of the thumbpiece below the grooved edge was also increased from 0.185 to 0.225 inch at the narrowest point.

Two variations were used. The **Type 3A** was darkened by immersing in molten potassium nitrate to circa serial #16,350. After, the **Type 3B** cutoff was chemically blued. It is very difficult to tell the difference on most after a century of use.

The action of the **Type 4** cutoff was reversed in the very late Model 1896 rifles and carbines so that after circa serial #'s 107,000-108,000, when the thumbpiece was up, cartridges fed from the magazine and when the cutoff was down could be single loaded Additionally, the rear edge of the thumbpiece was beveled to prevent it from cutting the scabbard when the carbine was shoved in. A fillet of leather was also added to the scabbard at the junction of the thumbpiece and spindle.

In the **Type 5** cutoff, the length of the spring spindle was increased by 0.013 inch. The spindle shaft of the cutoff was also decreased from 1.495 inches to 0.995 inch at circa serial #109,000 (Model 1898).

In the **Type 6** cutoff, the Armory stopped bluing the thumbpiece to make it more visible on the firing line. The bluing ceased at circa serial #152,000. When new, the cutoff had a "straw yellow" color from the tempering process that quickly wore off.

The American Krag Rifle and Carbine

With the **Type 7** cutoff, the Armory resumed bluing the thumbpiece but polished the underside to make it visible at the end of the firing line, starting at circa serial #242,000 to the end of production.

The final action concerning the cutoff was to install the Type 4 cutoff with its reversed action in all Models 1892 and 1896 arms still in service as of May 1900.

PARKHURST CLIP-LOADING DEVICE

The Parkhurst-Warren clip-loading device was a rectangular steel unit 0.876 inch wide by 0.630 inch long by 1.410 inches high that was mounted on the right rear wall of the receiver behind the magazine on a dovetail (Parkhurst's original prototype device on the Model 1892 rifle was bolted to the receiver). A sheet metal guide 1.8 inches long was slotted into the bottom of the magazine to guide the cartridges in the magazine, see Figure 2-102. A modified cartridge guide bolted to the bottom rear of the magazine box guided the cartridges into the magazine. The outside edge of the cartridge guide was extended and tilted upward to roll the cartridges smoothly into place, see Figure 2-103. Because the device was mounted to the rear of the magazine opening, no changes had to be made to the gate or other parts of the magazine.

Fig. 2-102. Parkhurst-Warren clip-loading device. Craig Riesch collection.

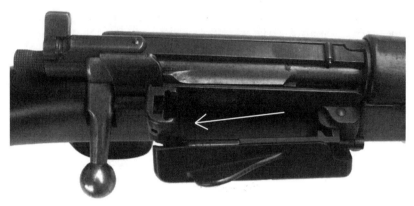

Fig. 2-103. Modified cartridge guide at bottom rear of the magazine box used with the Parkhurst-Warren clip-loading device. Craig Riesch collection.

The cartridge clip was made of steel in one piece. The edges of the clip were folded over to grasp the cartridge rims. "T"-shaped springs were cut from the clip body. Their ends rested in slots cut in the left and right edges of the body and were folded inward to hold the cartridges in place, see Figure 2-104.

SERIAL NUMBERS AND OTHER MARKINGS

The receiver, from start to end of production, was marked on the left side above the side plate with the legend "U.S./ SPRINGFIELD ARMORY" and the serial number, see Fig-

Fig. 2-104. Krag Parkhurst clip and cartridges. Craig Riesch collection.

ure 2-105. Table 2-10 below presents the various styles of markings and serial numbers used throughout Krag production.

The American Krag Rifle and Carbine

Fig. 2-105a. Model 1892. ("1894." No "MODEL.") North Cape Publications collection.

Fig. 2-105b. "1895." (No "MODEL.") William R. Mook collection.

Figs. 2-105a-h: U.S. Krag Rifle and Carbine Receiver Markings.

Fig. 2-105c. "1896." (No "MODEL.") William R. Mook collection.

Fig. 2-105d. Model 1896, North Cape Publications collection.

Figs. 2-105a-h: U.S. Krag Rifle and Carbine Receiver Markings, cont.

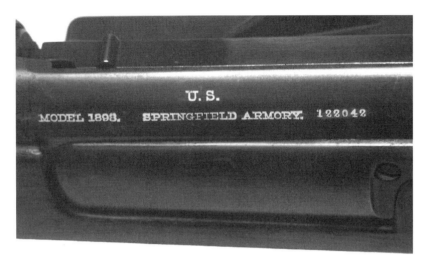

Fig. 2-105e. Model 1898, Craig Riesch collection.

Fig. 2-105f. Model 1899 (Carbine only), John Jordan collection.

Figs. 2-105a-h: U.S. Krag Rifle and Carbine Receiver Markings, cont.

Fig. 2-105g. Model 1898 .22 Caliber Rifle. Jonathan Peck collection, courtesy of John Gangel Auction Service.

Fig. 2-105h. Model 1899 carbine receiver with overstamped "8." William R. Mook collection.

Figs. 2-105a-h: U.S. Krag Rifle and Carbine Receiver Markings, cont.

The American Krag Rifle and Carbine

	Table 2-10 U.S. Krag Receiver Assembly Markings		
Receiver Part	**Year or Model & Year**	**Manufacturer's Legend**	**Serial Number**
Receiver	Serif letters 0.10 inch high to 1903; after, letters were 0.12 inch high **1894.** All Model 1892 rifles to circa 24,120 **1895.** To circa 30,701 **Model 1896.** On rifles, carbines, and Cadet rifles to circa serial #109,200 **Model 1898.** Rifles and carbines to circa 476,045+ **Model 1899.** Carbines to circa 223,300-420,810	**U.S./SPRINGFIELD ARMORY.** Letters with serifs, 0.10 inch high to 1903; after, 0.12 inch high The **U.S.** was 0.150 inch high throughout production	**No.** preceded serial number on #s 1 through 14, with numbers handstamped. #s 15 to circa 477,000 had numbers 0.10 inch high; after, they were 0.12 inch high. All were stamped with machine dies
Side Plate	None	None	Circa 1-30, Roman numerals chiseled in by hand. Circa 31-11,000, stamped numerals with serifs, 0.08 inch high
Gate	None	None	Circa 1-30, Roman numerals chiseled in by hand. Circa 31-11,000, stamped numerals with serifs, 0.08 inch high
Carrier	None	None	Circa 1-30, Roman numerals chiseled in by hand. Circa 31-11,000, stamped numerals with serifs, 0.08 inch high

The American Krag Rifle and Carbine

All Krag rifle and carbine receivers, after circa serial #37,100, bear the word "MODEL" before the model year.

NOTE: The first fourteen Krag rifle receivers produced were marked "No." before the "serial number." Was this because they were essentially pre-production "tool room" rifles?

Before 1896, the intent was to stamp the year the receiver was manufactured on the left side of the Krag receiver in the Scandinavian manner. In practice, all Model 1892 service receivers were stamped "1894." Very early Model 1896 receivers (primarily used on carbines) were stamped "1895" when they were made in the last month of that year (circa serial #30,700), "1896" between January of that year and sometime in February (circa serial #37,045) when the word "MODEL" was inserted before the year in all subsequent manufacture. Both letters and numbers had serifs. In February 1896, General D.W. Flagler, Chief of Ordnance, formalized the practice of stamping the model year on the receiver and continued the practice of stamping the year of acceptance in the inspector's cartouche on the stock. See Appendix D for an alternate theory on the dating of Model 1892 Krag receivers.

Markings on rifle and carbine receivers are shown in Figures 2-105a-h and include: "1894." "1895." "1896." "MODEL 1896." and "MODEL 1898." "MODEL 1899." was also stamped on carbines only and reportedly, on a very few rifles made for experimental purposes. A few late Model 1899 carbines were made at Springfield Armory using Model 1898 receivers. The last "8" in "MODEL 1898" was overstamped "9" using a die of the same size and font (refer to Figure 2-105h). The experimental Model 1892 carbine receivers were marked "1894."

After the Model Year, "U.S./SPRINGFIELD ARMORY." was stamped. The "U.S." was 0.150 inch high and the "SPRINGFIELD ARMORY." was 0.10 inch high. The letters had serifs and a period after the "Y," refer to Figures 2-105a-h.

The American Krag Rifle and Carbine

The serial number followed and was stamped in numbers with serifs 0.10 inch high until the last few rifles made in 1903 starting at circa serial #477,000. These were stamped with dies that were 0.12 inch high, refer to Figures 2-105a-h.

NOTE: Some markings on the left side of the Krag receiver appear to be larger than the dimensions given above. The apparent size will depend on how hard the die was struck and how far it penetrated the metal.

Gallery practice rifle receivers were marked "CAL/ .22" following the serial number, in sans serif letters and numbers 0.150 inch high, refer to Figure 2-105g.

Fig. 2-106. Model 1892 serial numbers (arrows) on side plate and carrier (inset).

A variety of inspector's initials and numbers were stamped on the face of the receiver. The majority of these markings are single letters and/ or numbers 0.08 inch high and indicate Springfield employees and inspectors. They can be identified by consulting the "Official Register of the United States, Officers and Employees, Vol. I, Legislative, Executive and Judicial." See Appendix G.

From the start of production to circa serial #30, the side plate, gate and carrier were marked with a fitting number chiseled in Roman

The American Krag Rifle and Carbine

numerals onto the part by the assembler. After, the entire serial number was stamped on the part using die stamps with serifs, 0.08 inch high, see Figure 2-106. The practice was discontinued in early 1895 at circa serial #11,000.

Ejectors were numbered from serial #s 31–300 and cutoffs were numbered from circa serial #s 31–150.

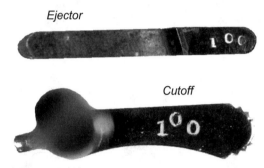

Ejector

Cutoff

A Model 1892 rifle, serial No. 14, has the Arabic number 14 stamped on the carrier and cocking piece.

The side plate serial number was stamped vertically on the inside rear edge; the

Fig. 2-106A. Type 1A cutoff and Type 1 ejector showing the serial number of rifle receiver #100. William R. Mook collection. Photos by Nick Ferris.

gate serial number was stamped vertically on the front inside edge; the carrier serial number was stamped on the reverse side but not on the follower. Followers were marked only with Arabic numbers between circa serial #s 31–670. These observations are taken from more than thirty-five Model 1892 rifles ranging from #s 9 through 19,3XX.

Note: The observation that early receiver/magazine (and) bolt parts under serial number 25 were marked with assembler's number in Roman numerals is based on the existence of a barreled receiver, serial number 25, that has the gate, side plate and carrier, marked XXV. In addition, observation by William R. Mook has found a bolt sleeve and cocking piece with a later firing pin marked XIV. It is not known if this was an official practice or because these very early rifles may have been "tool room" or pre-production models.

Bolt Assembly

While the Krag-Jørgensen was the first bolt action to enter military service with regular troops of the United States, it was not the first bolt-action, cartridge rifle employed by the regular U.S. military. The Model 1871 Ward-Burton (.50-70), Model 1879 Winchester-Hotchkiss (.45-70), Model 1882 Remington-Lee (.45-70) and Model 1882 Chaffee-Reese (.45-70) had all been tested under field conditions by the Army. And the U.S. Navy and Marine Corps had tested and adopted both the Model 1882 Remington-Lee (.45-70) and the Model 1895 Winchester-Lee Straight Pull rifle in 6 mm.

The bolt assembly is composed of 1) the bolt body, 2) cocking piece, 3) sleeve, 4) firing pin, 5) mainspring, 6) striker and 7) the extractor. The Model 1892 bolt also had the 8) extractor screw which later was changed to a rivet, see Figure 2-107.

BOLT BODY
The bolt body is a cylinder with a handle on the rear right side. The parts of the bolt body are: 1) locking lug, 2) guide rib, 3) locking shoulder, 4) bolt handle, 5) handle collar, 6) ejector groove, 7) cock-

Fig. 2-107. Krag-Jørgensen Bolt Assembly.

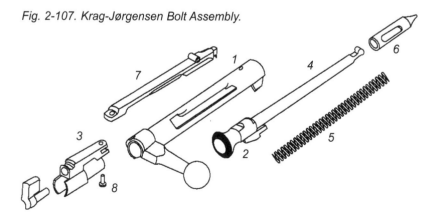

131

ing cam, 8) safety lock spindle notch, 9) cocking nose notch, 10) striker hole, 11) gas escape vent, 12) bolt face and 13) the slot for the securing stud on the barrel of the cocking piece, omitted from the Type 3 and later bolt bodies, see Figure 2-108.

The Early Model 1892 bolt will also have a slot (13) for the securing stud on the cocking piece. It was eliminated after circa serial #15,500.

The bolt body is 0.626 inch in diameter and 5.7 inches long. The locking lug (1) on the front is 0.390 inch wide, 4.30 inches long and

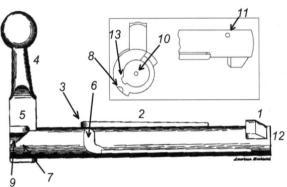

0.18 inch high. The guide rib (2) is 0.388 inch wide and 2.74 inches long. The bolt handle (4) is 2.420 inches long. It is surmounted with a ball for grasping that is 0.890 inch in diameter. The handle is mounted on a collar (5) that encircles the left side of the bolt

Fig. 2-108. Bolt body. Illustration from American Machinist Magazine, *April 5, 1900, inset added.*

from the 12 to 5 o'clock positions (bolt closed). The collar is 0.10 inch high and 0.576 inch wide. The safety notch and cocking nose notch (9) are located on the rear of the collar at the 12 and 8:30 o'clock positions (bolt closed).

The guide rib served two purposes. The first was to allow the bolt to move back and forth in the bolt well without binding and is responsible for the Krag's exceptionally smooth bolt throw. The second purpose was to serve as a safety device in case the locking lug on the front of the bolt should fail, in which case the rear of the guide rib would form the locking shoulder (3) and bear against the cam on the right front of the receiver bridge, refer to Figure 2-79 (6).

The safety notch (8) was the recess into which the safety lock spindle would rest when the safety lever was thrown to the right. It locked the cocking piece, which held the firing pin and striker in place, and did not allow it to move forward.

The cocking nose notch (9) was a V-shaped indentation at the 8:30 o'clock position when the bolt was closed. The nose of the sear on the cocking piece rested in this notch when the bolt was cocked. When the cocked bolt was withdrawn from the receiver, the sear nose in the notch prevented the cocking piece from turning under pressure from the mainspring.

The ejector groove (6) lay along the bottom of the bolt body when the bolt handle was raised. It allowed the ejector nose to pass when the bolt was drawn back.

The gas escape vent (11) was a hole in the top of the bolt body (bolt closed). If a cartridge ruptured, the excess gas flowed back into the bolt body. The greater portion of the gas vented through the gas escape vent and the rest out the rear of the bolt, where it was deflected from the shooter's face by the flared head (called the comb by Ordnance Department).

The bolt face (12) was 0.625 inch in diameter and recessed. A full-diameter collar 0.035 inch thick surrounded the entire rim of the flanged cartridge. The hole for the striker was 0.075 inch in diameter.

Five types of bolt bodies were used during the production of the Krag rifle.

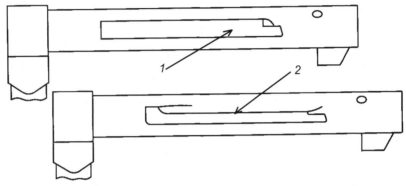

Fig. 2-109. Type 1 and Type 2 bolt bodies compared to show the differences in the guide rib.

The **Type 1** bolt body had a full-width guide rib (0.388 inch) for its entire length, see Figure 2-109 (arrow 1). The gas vent hole was 0.110 inch in diameter and located 0.590 inch behind the bolt face. The bolt face was case-hardened using potassium cyanide. The flat beneath the bolt handle was 0.840 inch long. A square securing stud was riveted to the right side of the barrel on the bolt sleeve that entered a matching slot in the back of the bolt body.

The Type 1 was marked with the receiver serial number stamped on the bottom flat of the bolt handle with Arabic numbers 0.08 inch high from circa serial #s 31 to 400, see Figure 2-109A. Starting at circa serial #400, the bolt face was hardened with potassium cyanide to eliminate erosion from hot gases if the primer was punctured.

Fig. 2-109A. Type 1 bolt handle numbered to receiver. William R. Mook collection. Photo by Nick Ferris.

The American Krag Rifle and Carbine

A modification was made to the guide rib in the **Type 2** bolt at circa serial #14,600. The left side of the guide rib was cut away to a width of 0.218 inch wide. The change was made to lighten the bolt body, refer to Figure 2-109 (arrow 2).

In the **Type 3** bolt body, the slot for the securing stud on the sleeve barrel was eliminated at circa serial #15,500, see Figure 2-110. The steel lot number was often stamped on the bolt body starting with the Type 3. The lot number, usually consisting of one or two letters and a number, was often stamped on the rear flat of the bolt handle.

The gas escape vent was moved to 0.825 inch behind the bolt face in the **Type 4** bolt body at circa serial #36,000.

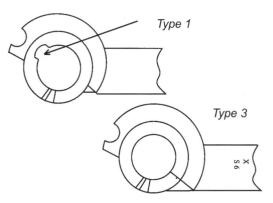

In the **Type 5** bolt body, the length of the flat beneath the bolt handle was increased to 0.950 inch at circa serial #109,000 (Model 1898). This change was intended to prevent the underside of the bolt handle from striking the stock.

Fig. 2-110. The slot (arrow) used for holding the securing stud was eliminated in the Type 3 bolt body.

Bolt Body Finish and Markings

The bolt body was case-hardened in oil and then polished bright. The **Type 1** bolt body was numbered to the receiver from circa #'s 31 to 400 with Arabic numerals 0.08 inch high.

The American Krag Rifle and Carbine

Starting with the Type 3 bolt body at circa serial #15,500, the steel lot number code was sometimes stamped on the rear flat of the bolt handle in the form of one or two letters and a number. The markings usually had serifs and were 0.08 inch high, refer to Figure 2-110.

No other markings or inspector's marks were stamped on the bolt body.

NOTE: Stamping the full or partial serial number on the bolt body, and all other bolt parts, ended at serial #400.

Cocking Piece/Firing Pin Assembly

The cocking piece held the firing pin/striker against the tension of the mainspring after the bolt was cocked. The sear notch on the bottom of the cocking piece engaged the sear nose and held it until the trigger was pulled back, tipping up the front of the sear and disengaging the sear nose. The cocking piece and firing pin left the factory as one piece. If either part was damaged, they were replaced as a unit. The cocking piece/firing pin assembly, see Figure 2-111, consisted of the 1) cocking piece, 2) firing pin, 3) comb, 4) lug, 5) cocking cam, 6) nose, 7) sear notch, 8) safety lock notch, 9) locking notch (Models 1896–98 and 99), 10) striker lug or point. A total of four types of cocking piece/firing pin assemblies were used.

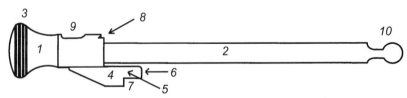

Fig. 2-111. Cocking piece and striker assembly.

The **Type 1** cocking piece/firing pin was used on the Model 1892. It had a square lug, no locking notch (9), and a flared comb or head, see Figure 2-112. The firing pin screwed into the cocking piece and was

The American Krag Rifle and Carbine

riveted in place by peening the head of the firing pin. The width of the safety lock notch on the top of the cocking piece was only 0.025 inch. The comb was knurled to make it easier to grasp. It had four grooves cut around the circumference of the "comb" to provide five rows of knurling. The cocking piece was made of carbon steel. The Type 1 cocking knob had two variations.

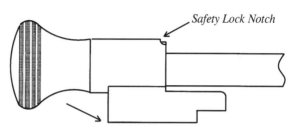

Safety Lock Notch

Fig. 2-112. Type 1 cocking piece with the square lug.

The **Type 1A** cocking piece (Figure 2-112A) was serial numbered to the receiver with Arabic numerals 0.08 inch high from circa serial #s 31 to 400 on the bottom of the lug. The **Type 1B** was not serial numbered.

The **Type 2** cocking piece/firing pin assembly was also used on the Model 1892. It was identical to the Type 1 but was made of high carbon steel starting at circa serial #16,000.

Fig. 2-112A. Type 1A cocking piece with numbered lug. Jonathan Peck collection. Photo by Nick Ferris.

The **Type 3** cocking piece/firing pin (long considered a characteristic of the Model 1896) was used starting as early as circa serial #s 30,000–35,000 (approved June 30, 1895). A locking notch (9) was added, the bottom of the lug (4) was beveled and the safety notch (8) width was increased to 0.08 inch.

137

The American Krag Rifle and Carbine

The **Type 4** cocking piece/firing pin eliminated the flared comb, or head, see Figure 2-113. There was a slight reduction in the diameter toward the center of the head to allow it to be grasped by the fingers if manual cocking was required (and you had the finger strength of a gorilla). The Type 4 was introduced at serial #202,000 just prior to the start of the Model 1899 carbine. The Type 4 was installed on both Model 1898 rifles and Model 1899 carbines to circa serial #285,000. The change was made to reduce the cost of manufacture, but it proved to be slightly more expensive. The headless cocking piece was discontinued and from circa serial #285,001 on, the Type 3 cocking piece was used.

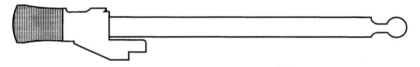

Fig. 2-113. Type 4 "Headless" cocking piece.

NOTE: The firing pin remained unchanged during Krag production.

Cocking Piece/Firing Pin Assembly Finish and Markings
The cocking piece was case-hardened in oil and then polished and blued. The firing pin was also polished bright but not case-hardened.

Only the **Type 1A** cocking piece was numbered to the receiver from circa serial #s 31–400 with the receiver serial number in Arabic numerals 0.08 inch high. Other types were not marked in any way.

Bolt Sleeve
The bolt sleeve held the extractor, safety lock and cocking piece/firing pin assembly in place. It was an intricately machined piece that underwent two major and ten minor changes during Krag production.

The American Krag Rifle and Carbine

The bolt sleeve had the following parts: 1) extractor arm, 2) extractor slot, 3) extractor screw or rivet hole, 4) safety lock seat, 5) safety lock spindle hole, 6) safety lock pin hole (Model 1892 only), 7) safety lock spindle spring groove, 8) barrel, 9) securing stud (Model 1892 only), 10) cocking piece lug slot, 11) firing pin hole, 12) dust space, 13) exterior shoulder, 14) interior shoulder and 15) grasping grooves (Model 1892 only), see Figures 2-114 (next page) and 2-115 (below).

The **Type 1** bolt sleeve, refer to Figure 2-115, had the following attributes: (1) The extractor was fastened to the sleeve with a screw through the extractor arm (2). It did not have the safety lock spindle groove (7) but did have the safety lock pin hole (6). The barrel (8) was 1.40 inches long and had a securing stud (9) 0.2 inch long by 0.185 inch wide on the front right side which engaged a slot in the bolt body well (see lower inset, Figure 2-114). The extractor arm thickness was 0.260 inch. Seven grasping grooves were machined on the rear of the bolt sleeve to make it easier to hold during assembly only on the Type 1 and Type 2 (15).

The Type 1 had the receiver serial number stamped on the bolt sleeve in Arabic numerals 0.08 inch high only from circa serial #s 31–400. The **Type 1A** safety lock pin hole (6) was 0.140 inch below the shoulder of the extractor arm. In the **Type 1B** bolt sleeve, the pin hole was raised to 0.11 inch below the shoulder of the extractor arm after circa serial #3,500.

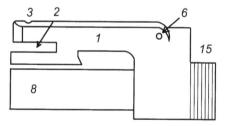

Fig. 2-115. Type 1 bolt sleeve for the M1892 Rifle.

NOTE: Stamping the full or partial serial number on the bolt sleeve ended at circa serial #400.

The American Krag Rifle and Carbine

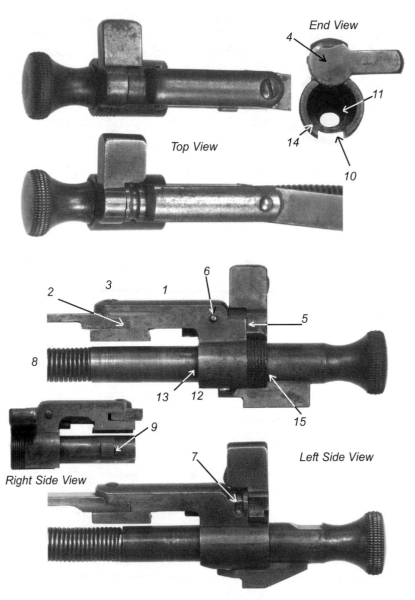

Fig. 2-114. Type 1 (above) and Type 4 (below) bolt sleeves for the Krag Rifle and Carbine. North Cape Publications collection.

The American Krag Rifle and Carbine

In the **Type 2A** bolt sleeve, the knurling or grasping grooves on the rear of the early Types 1 and 2 bolt sleeves were eliminated at circa serial #15,000. In the **Type 2B** bolt sleeve, the securing stud (9) on the barrel (8) was eliminated at circa serial #15,500.

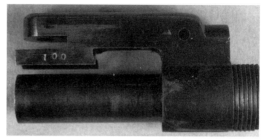

Fig, 2-115a. Type 1A bolt sleeve, numbered to the receiver. William R. Mook collection. Photo by Nick Ferris.

The **Type 3** bolt sleeve was introduced just prior to the Model 1896 carbine at circa serial #24,000. A different arrangement for the safety lock was the most important change. The Type 1 safety lock had depended on friction to secure it in the open or closed position. The new Type 2 safety lock used an internal spring-loaded plunger to secure it in place.

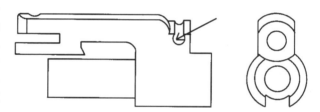

Fig. 2-116. Type 4 bolt sleeve for the Models 1896, 1898 and 1899 Rifle and Carbine.

Changes made to the bolt sleeve included the elimination of the safety lock pin hole (6) and pin and the substitution of a channel called the safety lock spindle spring groove (arrow) in the top rear portion under the overhang of the safety lock thumbpiece. Two round detents were drilled at either end of the channel for the spring-loaded spindle, see Figure 2-116.

The American Krag Rifle and Carbine

In addition, the barrel (8) was shortened from 1.40 inches to 1.055 inches to allow the extractor rivet to be installed and the extractor arm (2) thickness was reduced from 0.260 inch to 0.215 inch.

The screw securing the extractor to the extractor arm on the bolt sleeve was eliminated in favor of rivet. Tapping and threading the lower portion of the extractor arm was discontinued. The counterbored hole on the top of the extractor arm was reduced. The hole for the rivet through both sides of the extractor arm was 0.150 inch in diameter. The underside of the hole in the bottom arm was countersunk to 0.170 inch in diameter. When the rivet was inserted, the bottom was ground to conform to the contour of the underside of the arm. The top of the rivet was also upset slightly and polished into a smooth cap.

The **Type 4** bolt sleeve was the Type 1 bolt sleeve converted to the Type 3 bolt sleeve pattern starting in January 1897. These were used on Model 1892 rifles converted to the Model 1896 pattern.

Bolt Sleeve Finish and Markings
The bolt sleeve was case-hardened in oil, which gave it a slightly mottled blackish appearance when new.

From circa serial #s 31 to 400, the serial number was stamped on the bolt sleeve in Arabic numerals 0.08 inch high.

Extractor Screw
The extractor screw fastened the extractor to the bolt sleeve at the extractor arm in the Types 1 and 2 bolt sleeves to circa serial #24,000 only. The screw had a slotted fillister head. It was 0.159 inch in diameter and 0.420 inch long overall. The head diameter was 0.25 inch and it was 0.10 inch thick at the head rim. The extractor screw was used only with the Types 1 and 2, see Figure 2-117.

The American Krag Rifle and Carbine

Extractor Rivet

The extractor rivet replaced the extractor screw after circa serial #24,000 on the Types 3 and 4 bolt sleeves. The rivet head was 0.170 inch in diameter. Its length was 0.390 inch after the top or narrowest end was upset, refer to Figure 2-117.

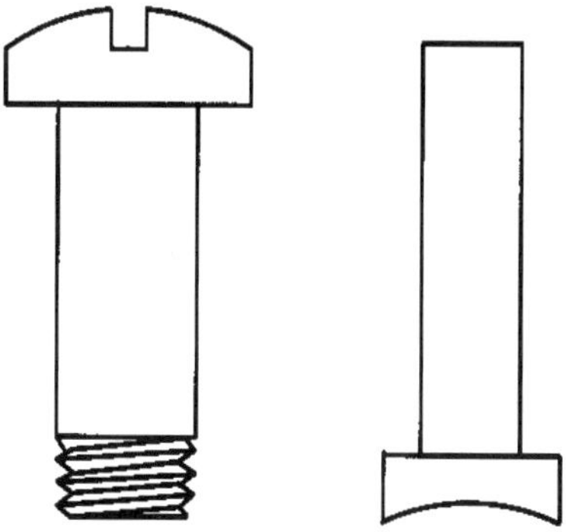

Striker

The striker was attached to the end of the firing pin by a sleeve and interlocking lug. It was 2.185 inches long and its diameter was 0.40 inch but could vary by ± 0.002 inch, see Figure 2-118.

Fig. 2-117. (Left) Extractor Screw for the Types 1 and 2 bolt sleeves. (Right) Extractor Rivet for the Types 3 and 4 bolt sleeves.

Three types of strikers were used. The **Type 1** striker had a squarish point to circa serial #21,000. The **Type 2** striker had a rounded point after circa serial #21,000. Two variations of the Type 2 striker were used. The **Type 2A**'s cutout for the firing pin lug had a square cut at the rear (broken line) to circa serial #24,000 (Model 1896). The **Type 2B** striker's cutout had a rounded or filleted cut (arrow) at the rear after circa serial #24,000 to the end of production.

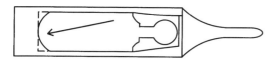

Fig. 2-118. Striker – Types 2A and 2B.

Mainspring

The mainspring drove the firing pin/striker against the cartridge primer when the sear was released by the trigger. It was a coil spring 0.385

inch in diameter, see Figure 2-119. Three types of mainspring were used.

Fig. 2-119. Mainspring.

The **Type 1** mainspring was 30.5 coils in length and had a compression weight of 18 to 22 lbs. During the hardening and tempering process, the spring was coated with black oxide which was polished off before assembly. This mainspring was in use to circa serial #7,300.

The **Type 2** mainspring was lengthened to 33.5 coils and the compression weight was reduced to 16 to 18 lbs. This was made necessary by the change to the Type 3 bolt sleeve with the shorter barrel. The Type 2 mainspring was used on all Model 1892 rifles modified to the Model 1896 pattern; also on all Model 1896 rifles with 1896-dated receivers and early Model 1898 carbines and rifles.

The **Type 3** mainspring was used from circa serial #140,000 to the end of production. It was lengthened to 38.5 coils but retained the compression weight of 16 to 18 lbs.

Extractor

The extractor, see Figure 2-120, was a long spring-tempered bar fastened to the bolt sleeve. It was 0.40 inch wide and 5.5 inches long. It was machined from a single bar of steel. A hook was shaped at the front end to grip the cartridge rim. A separate extractor spring was attached by a stud to the extractor body. The extractor had the following parts: 1) body, 2) cartridge rim hook, 3) screw or rivet hole, 4) extractor spring slot, 5) extractor spring (not shown, see Figure 2-121) and 6) cutaway to allow the extractor to move forward as the bolt locked closed, 7) heel, 8) extractor pin hole, 9) inset extractor pin hole.

The American Krag Rifle and Carbine

Four types of extractor were used. The **Type 1** extractor was flat along its full length without the hump for the hold-open pin used in the Type 4 extractor, refer to Figure 2-120. The junction of the body and heel was square. The extractor was case-hardened in oil and showed a smooth black finish. It was in use from the start of production to circa serial #19,000.

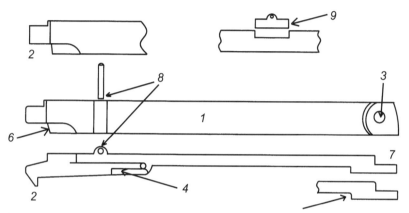

Fig. 2-120. Extractor: Top, Type 1, Middle, Type 2 and Bottom, Type 3.

Two variations of the Type 1 extractor were used. The **Type 1A** extractor spring hole was increased by 0.028 inch. The extractor spring would have to be removed to make this measurement as it is a blind hole. It was case-hardened in oil and was in use from circa serial #s 19,001 to 22,000. At circa serial #22,001, the finish on the extractor (**Type 1B**) was changed from case-hardening in oil to tempering in oil after being given a high polish. This gave them a deep, glossy blue color when new.

On the **Type 2** extractor, a change was made to prevent the bolt from sliding forward after it was opened. The right side of the receiver bridge was notched and at the same time, the extractor pin hole was added to the top of the extractor and the extractor pin was inserted, refer to Figure 2-120. The extractor pin snapped into the notch on the receiver bridge and held the bolt open. The change was made at circa serial #24,000 with the Model 1896.

On the **Type 3** extractor, a fillet was added to the junction of the body and heel to provide added strength, refer to Figure 2-120 (arrow). The change was made at circa serial #25,000. In the **Type 3A** extractor the fillet was very small, while in the **Type 3B** extractor the fillet was 0.05 inch in diameter.

The **Type 4** extractor was a replacement made from Type 1 extractors by milling a slot for a separate inset with the pin hole housing (9).

Extractor Spring

The extractor spring fits into the left, front side of the extractor. As the bolt is closed, the extractor spring is forced down by the extractor spring lip on the left receiver wall to create a positive hold on the cartridge rim. Only one type of extractor spring was used during the Krag production run, see Figure 2-121.

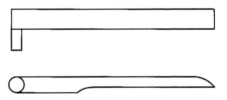

Fig. 2-121. Extractor Spring.

Extractor Finish and Markings

The Types 1A and 1B extractors were case-hardened in oil to circa serial #22,001 which gave them a mottled blackish appearance. After, the Types 1B, 2 and 3 extractors were spring tempered in oil after being highly polished. This left the extractor with a deep, glossy blue color when new. Extractors were not marked in any way.

Safety Lock Assembly

The safety lock was a lever that could be moved left (Fire) or right (Safe) to lock the firing pin in place and prevent it from flying forward

The American Krag Rifle and Carbine

under the pressure of the mainspring if the sear was accidently dislodged, see Figure 2-122.

The safety lock parts: 1) thumbpiece, 2) body, 3) cocking piece groove, 4) spindle, 5) bolt collar notch, 6) safety lock pin groove, 7) cam, 8) safety lock pin, see Figure 2-122. The following Type 2 parts were added to the safety lock: 9) spring spindle, 10) spindle spring, 11) spindle hole.

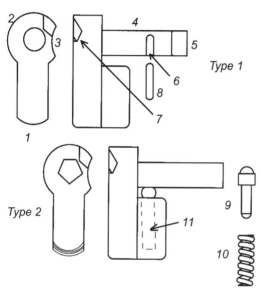

Four types of safety lock were used. The **Type 1** safety lock did not have the spring spindle hole (11), spring spindle (9) or spindle spring (10). Also, the cam (7) was a barely noticeable cut. The

Fig. 2-122. Safety Lock, Spindle and Spring.

thumbpiece and spindle were either machined from one piece of steel or were made in two parts, depending on type. The spindle had a notch at midpoint (6) for the safety lock pin. Friction retained the safety lock in either the "Fire" or "Safe" positions.

Two variations of the Type 1 safety lock were used. The **Type 1A** was made in one piece and had a deep groove (0.005 inch) in the spindle for the safety lock pin to circa serial #3,500. Its thumbpiece was 0.940 inch high by 0.225 inch thick. The **Type 1B** had a separate thumbpiece and spindle that were press-fitted. The groove depth on the spindle was reduced to 0.003 inch and the size remained the same. It was used between circa serial #s 3,501–24,000.

The **Type 2** safety lock was made in two pieces, thumbpiece and spindle. The safety lock pin was omitted. Also, a hole was drilled on the inside of the thumbpiece for the spring-loaded spindle and its spring. The dimensions of the thumbpiece were increased to 0.955 inch high and 0.250 inch thick. The cam cut (7) was also made more pronounced. The change to the Type 2 took place at circa serial #24,001 in the late stages of the Model 1892 production or the very beginning of the start of Model 1896 production.

The dimensions of the **Type 3** safety lock thumbpiece were increased to 0.965 inch high and 0.280 inch thick at circa serial #27,000.

The **Type 4** safety lock also had a separate thumbpiece and spindle press-fitted together. It had a deep (0.005-inch) groove and the thumbpiece was 0.965 inch high and 0.280 inch thick. While it is not known for certain, this thumbpiece was probably used as a replacement on the converted Model 1892 rifles.

Safety Lock Pin
The safety lock pin was 0.094 inch in diameter and 0.740 inch in length. Contrary to standard Springfield Armory practice, it was inserted from the right and removed from the left. The right end was slightly upset to prevent it from being pushed into the bolt sleeve too far. The pin was oil blackened and was used with the Type 1 safety lock only, refer to Figure 2-122.

Safety Lock Spindle and Spring
The safety lock spindle and spring were added at circa serial #24,001 for a more positive action and to prevent the safety from accidently being brushed on or off. The spindle was 0.310 inch long with a collar near the top to retain the six-coil spindle spring, refer to Figure 2-122.

The American Krag Rifle and Carbine

No changes were made to either part to the end of production. The spindle was oil blackened and the spring was hardened and tempered. The safety lock spindle and spring first appeared on very late Model 1892 rifles and those carbines dated "1895" but without the word, "MODEL."

Safety Lock Assembly Finish and Markings

The safety lock was case-hardened in water, which produced mottled reds, greens and blues when new. The safety lock spindle was spring tempered, which blackened it. The spindle spring was hardened and tempered and grayish in color from the process.

Contrary to what would be considered good practice at a later date, the safety lock thumbpiece was not marked "SAFE" or "FIRE," "ON" or "OFF," possibly again following Scandinavian practice. Nor was it stamped with any kind of inspection markings.

Sights

REAR SIGHTS

The period from 1890 to 1906 was a challenge for Ordnance officers charged with the design and manufacture of a suitable service rifle for the U.S. Army. Firearms technology led to the ability of chemical companies to produce a suitable smokeless powder (at least in the United States). The chemical and mechanical effects of combusting gases on the relatively simple steel alloys of the time were inadequately understood. And the tools for measuring trajectories of fired projectiles were fairly primitive. Complicating the situation were factions within the Army who felt that improving marksmanship scores would carry over into combat. They wanted a fully adjustable rear sight for both elevation and windage and which would compensate for bullet drift instead of a simple combat rear sight adjustable for elevation only.

As a consequence, the Krag rear sight underwent four major and several minor changes before a satisfactory one was developed and it was replaced by a fifth design that was in turn re-replaced by the satisfactory fourth design! Tables 2-11 and 2-12 provide summaries of rifle/rear sight and carbine/rear sight combinations. Details are provided in the paragraphs following.

Because the combinations of rifle and carbine model, rear sight models and handguards are so confusing, the Handguard table is repeated following Tables 2-11 and 2-12.

RIFLE REAR SIGHTS
Rear Sight, Rifle, Model 1892

The Model 1892 rear sight was a direct descendent of the Model 1873 series of rear sights for the .45-70 rifle and carbine, see Figure 2-123.

The American Krag Rifle and Carbine

Table 2-11
Rear Sights Used on U.S. Krag Rifles

Rear Sight Model	Used on Rifle Model (Serial Numbers Are Estimates)	Base Graduations (Yards)	Leaf Graduations (Yards)	Windage Graduations (Inches)	Drift Correction
1892 Type 1 Type 2 (1)	M1892 (Changes introduced before issue) M1892 and M1898 (146,000-176,000)	300-600	700-1,900	No	No
1896 Type 1 Type 2 Type 3 Type 4	M1896 Service and Cadet M1898 (109,000-146,000); all M1892 Rifles in service in June 1896; all M1892 Rifles rebuilt at any time M1898 (207,000-330,000) M1898 Rifle originally fitted with the M1898 Rear Sight	300-600	700-1,800	No	No
1898 (2) Type 1 only	M1898 Rifles mfg'd August 1899-March 1900 (217,400-253,000)	None	200-2,000	Yes	Yes
1901 (2) Type 1 Type 2 Type 3 Type 4	M1898 post-330,000. All rifles in regular service from 1904 on. All rifles in service after 1905	100-400	100-2,000	Yes	Yes
1902 (2) Type 1 Type 2 Type 3 Type 4	110,000 M1898 Rifles with M1896 rear sights converted to M1902 (1903-04). All Model 1898 Rifles mfg'd and in service after April 1903	None	200-2,000	Yes	Yes
Mixed Parts Type 5	Mix of previous model parts used after 1905. Identifiable by large binding screw	None or 300-600	700-1,800/200-2,000	Yes	Yes
BOF Type 1	Model 1901 recalibrated for 26-inch barrel Board of Ordnance and Fortifications Rifle	100-400	100-2,000	Yes	No

1) Used on M1898 rifles when the supply of Model 1896 sights ran out.
2) The Model 1898 Rifle is correct with the M1896, M1901, and M1902 rear sight as well as the M1892 and serial number ranges shown above.

Table 2-12
Rear Sights Used on U.S. Krag Carbines

Rear Sight Model		Used on Carbine Model (Serial Numbers Are Estimates)	Base Graduations (Yards)	Leaf Graduations (Yards)	Windage Graduations (Inches)	Drift Correction
1896	Type 1 Type 2	M1896 (all) M1898 (all) M1899 (216,000-242,241)	300-600	700-2000	No	No
1898	Type 1 only	M1899 (242,242 to 272,000-285,000)	None	200-2,000	Yes	No
1901	Type 1	M1899 (345,000+) "U.S. Magazine Carbine, cal. .30, Model of 1899 altered for Knife Bayonet and Sling" for Philippine Constabulary.	100-500	100-2,300	Yes	No
	Type 2	All M1898 carbines still in Regular Army Service in 1903; all carbines for Regular and National Guard post 1905				
1902	Type 1 Type 2 Type 3 Type 4	M1899 carbines with M1896 and M1898 rear sights. Original equipment on National Guard carbines post April 1903 and "U.S. Magazine Carbine, cal. .30, Model of 1899 altered for Knife Bayonet and Sling" mfg'd at Springfield Armory for schools	None	200-2,000	Yes	Rifle, yes Carbine, no

The American Krag Rifle and Carbine

Rifle or Carbine/ Serial #s	Hand-guard Type	Handguard Model	Rear Sight Model
Table 2-13 **Handguards Used on U.S. Krag Rifles and Carbines**			
1892 Rifle	1	1892 Rifle	1892 Rifle and 1896 Rifle
1892 Carbine	2	1892 Carbine	1892 Carbine 1896 Carbine
1892 Rifle (late) 1896 Rifle 1896 Cadet Rifle 1898 Rifle (109,000 146,000 and 207,000 to 330,000)	3	1896 Rifle	1896 Rifle
1896 Carbine 1898 Carbine	4	1896 Carbine	1896 Carbine
1898 Rifle 1899 Carbine (242,242-272,000 to 285,000)	5	1898 Rifle and Carbine	1898 Rifle 1902 Rifle 1898 Carbine 1902 Carbine
1899 Carbine (216,000 to 242,241)	6	1899 Carbine with Type 4 carbine stock	1896 Carbine

The American Krag Rifle and Carbine

Rifle or Carbine	Hand-guard Type	Handguard Model	Rear Sight Model
Table 2-13, cont.			
Handguards Used on U.S. Krag Rifles and Carbines			
1898 Rifle 1899 Carbine	7	M1901 Rifle and Carbine (without sight protector)	1901 Rifle 1901 Carbine (questionable)
"U.S. Magazine Carbine, caliber .30, Model of 1899, altered for Knife Bayonet and Sling"	8	1902 Carbine with sight protector used on those altered carbines for Philippine Constabulary and military schools M1902 Carbine with sight protector used on those short rifles commercially remanufactured	1901 Carbine 1902 Rifle

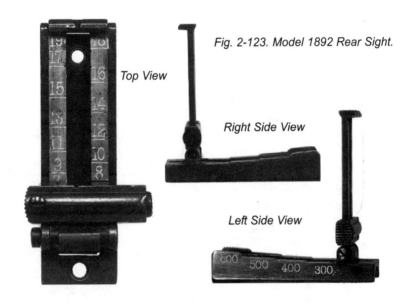

Top View

Fig. 2-123. Model 1892 Rear Sight.

Right Side View

Left Side View

The American Krag Rifle and Carbine

It used a stepped base on which the elevator bar for the leaf rested to set the range from 300 to 600 yards (stamped on the left side in 100-yard increments). Further elevation settings were obtained by raising the leaf, which was pivoted at the rear of the base, and moving the slide up or down to the desired range. Range graduations from 700 to 1,900 yards were stamped on the leaf in 100-yard increments. The right rail of the leaf was notched on the inside at the position corresponding to the range graduations. The slide contained a spring-loaded plunger that drove the slide catch into the selected notch.

The Model 1892 rear sight could not be adjusted for windage or bullet drift. Two sighting "U" notches were used, both 0.05 inch wide and deep. The sighting notch on the slide was at the top and was used at ranges between 100 and 600 yards. The trajectory of the 220-grain Krag .30-40 cartridge was (it was thought) sufficiently flat enough to strike a man standing at any distance up to 600 yards. For ranges beyond 600 yards, the leaf was raised and the slide adjusted to the estimated or known distance, and the sighting "U" notch on the now vertical side of the slide used. While both notches were slightly offset to the left to compensate for bullet drift, the compensation was not proportional to the elevation and so did not correct for the effects of bullet drift at long ranges. The plunger was knurled on its surface as was the opposite end of the slide to make it easier to operate.

The sight was graduated based on firing studies conducted during the winter of 1893–1894, which turned out to be one of the coldest on record to that time. In addition to slowing the testing because of cold and storms, the frigid temperatures resulted in denser air, which caused lower ballistic trajectories than would otherwise have been achieved. Accordingly, complaints poured into Springfield Armory about the Krag's tendency to shoot high, especially during the hot summer months. Adjustments were made to the graduations on the sight leaf that are too small to be observed without precision measuring equipment.

The American Krag Rifle and Carbine

The Model 1892 rear sight was installed as original equipment on all the Model 1892 rifles (and on the prototype carbines). It was also installed temporarily on Model 1898 rifles from circa serial #s 146,000 through 176,000 when the Model 1896 rear sights were not available. These Model 1892 sights were quickly replaced.

The Model 1892 rifle sight had problems other than lack of drift compensation and the rifle's supposed tendency to shoot high. A significant number of complaints concerned the slide catch jumping out of the notch under recoil. A stronger plunger spring was substituted but the complaints persisted.

Rear Sight, Rifle, Model 1896

The Model 1896 rear sight was basically an improved Model 1892. A binding screw was substituted for the catch to provide a more positive lock between the elevation slide and the leaf. As a result, the clamping notches on the inside of the leaf's right leg used on the Model 1892 rear sight leaf were eliminated. The four steps on the base gave way to ramped sides like those of the Model 1879 rear sight series but without the knurling on the top edges. The sighting notches on the slide and at the top of the leaf were enlarged to 0.065 inch wide and deep. Graduations remained the same on the left side of the base, 300 to 600, but were reduced by 100 yards on the leaf to 700 through 1,800 yards in one-hundred-yard increments. The graduations were also recalibrated for the 220-grain bullet with the thicker cartridge case (see Appendix C, Figure C-13) that was adopted in August 1895. Because a simple binding screw was used to clamp the slide to the leaf, the slide could be made quite a bit thinner (0.280 inch vs. 0.348 inch), and lighter.

The Model 1896 rear sight was used on the Model 1896 rifle and on the Model 1896 Cadet Rifle. Because of production problems with the Model 1898 rear sight, it was also installed as original equipment on the first run of Model 1898 rifles circa serial #s 109,000–146,000 and again at circa serial #s 207,000–330,000.

The American Krag Rifle and Carbine

In mid-1896, it was decided to upgrade all Model 1892 rifles still in service to the Model 1896 standard. Among the changes made was the substitution of the Model 1892 rear sight for the Model 1896, the main reason why so many Model 1892 rifles are found without their original rear sight.

When problems developed with the Model 1898 rear sight, all Model 1898 rifles on which they were installed as original equipment were recalled in 1900 and fitted with the Model 1896 rear sight. The rationale was sound; the Model 1898 rear sight had been calibrated for the new 2,200 fps Model 1898 cartridge. But that cartridge was removed from service in March 1900, as it had been cited as the reason why the rifle's locking lug was cracking at unexpectedly high rates. The older Model 1898 cartridge (2,000 fps) was reissued and thus the sights had to be changed back to the Model 1896 which had been calibrated for the old cartridge.

In June 1898, the range graduations on the Model 1896 rear sight were recalibrated to conform to the results of extensive test firings. Other changes were also made to the Model 1896 rear sight that led to four major variations in the rifle rear sight, see Figure 2-124.

The **Type 1** is distinguished by "high" leaf calibrations (A) and a distinctive hump over the joint screw hole (B) and a small-diameter Rear Sight Slide Screw of 0.360 inch (C). The base was 0.582 inch high at the front of the ramp.

The **Type 2** retains the "high" leaf calibrations but lacks the hump. It also uses the 0.582-inch-high ramp base.

The **Type 3** leaf was recalibrated and the range graduations are "lower," (D). The base's curve was lowered so that the front of the ramp was reduced by 0.009 inch to 0.573 inch high.

The American Krag Rifle and Carbine

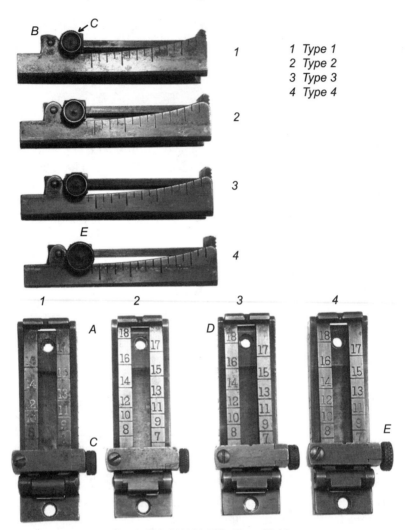

Fig. 2-124. M1896 Rifle Rear Sights

The **Type 4** rear sight retained the new "lower" range calibrations and "lower" ramp base. It also used a larger-diameter (0.425 inch) Rear Sight Slide Binding Screw (E).

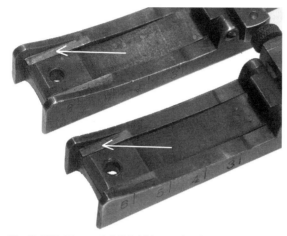

The difference in the two base heights can be most readily seen in Figure 2-125. Notice the grind marks on the inner side of the ramp. The grind marks on the 0.582-inch-high base are longer than those on the 0.573-inch-high base.

Fig. 2-125. Types 1-2 "high" base (top) and Types 3-4 "low" base Model 1896 Rear Sight bases. Note the length of grind marks (arrows).

Rear Sight, Carbine, Model 1896

The Model 1896 carbine sight (Figure 2-126) differed from the rifle sight in three particulars: the leaf is marked from 700 to 2,000 yards in one-hundred-yard increments. The top of the leaf and front edges of the slide were rounded to avoid cutting the inside of the scabbard, and the base was reduced to 0.520 inch at the front to conform to the ballistics of the 22-inch barrel. The base was marked "C" for carbine on the rear right side and the leaf on the upper right side. The aperture for the slide was also cut dif-

Fig. 2-126. Model 1896 Carbine Rear Sight, Type 1.

The American Krag Rifle and Carbine

ferently. On either side of the "U" aperture, the metal of the slide was cut lower for 0.25 inch, refer to Figure 2-126 (arrow).

Even though range calibrations on the rifle leaf had been changed because of extensive testing, they do not appear to have been altered on the Model 1896 carbine sight.

Two types of Model 1896 Carbine Rear Sights were used. The **Type 1** is distinguished by its small (0.345-inch-diameter) Rear Sight Slide Binding Screw. The **Type 2** uses the larger 0.425-inch-diameter Rear Sight Slide Binding Screw.

The Model 1896 carbine sight was used on all Models 1896 and 1898 carbines and those Model 1899 carbines to circa serial #s 216,000-242,241.

NOTE: Two different reproductions of the Model 1896 carbine sight have appeared recently. The workmanship is rather poor and they are easily identified. The sight leaf on the original Model 1896 rear sight is 0.105 to 0.108 inch thick. The reproduction leaves generally run undersize at between 0.075 to 0.085 inch. Consequently, the slide is quite loose whereas the originals are tight and move smoothly. In the second reproduction, new ladders were ground to nearly the final thickness. They were then stamped with the range numbers and graduation lines after being polished. The raised ridges around the numbers and range graduations are quite apparent. Run your finger over the leaf to feel for the displaced metal caused by the stamping process or look for lighter areas of color around the numbers and graduations with a magnifying glass.

Rear Sight, Rifle, Model 1898
The Model 1898 rear sight was a completely different design than previous rear sights, see Figure 2-127. It was based on the rear sight developed by the Danes and used on their Krag rifles. The American

The American Krag Rifle and Carbine

Fig. 2-127. Model 1898 Rear Sight.

version was designed by Lt. T.C. Dickson and it became somewhat of a political football. A large group of Dickson's supporters wanted the sight adopted because it allowed more accurate aiming. But the Chief of Ordnance at the time, Colonel Alfred Mordecai, opposed the sight as being too complicated for the soldier to use in combat. And he was probably correct. But the complaints from the field about the Model 1896 sight couldn't be ignored much longer.

The Model 1898 rear sight was composed of a base, leaf and slide and was graduated for the new 2,200 fps Model 1898 cartridge. The base had a convex curve without range markings. The leaf was hinged at the front and the slide rode along the curve as it was moved to the desired range, raising the sight aperture on the leaf to the proper height. The leaf was graduated from 200 to 2,000 yards and had no serrations on either side.

The sight bar had three "U" notch apertures. The second "U" notch was the primary sighting notch and it was cut 0.0145 inch to the right of center to compensate for the bullet's tendency to drift left. It was to be used for ranges from 100 to 1,000 yards, see Figure 2-128. The left and right notches were 0.3 inch distant from the center notch and were used in crosswinds from either side of the shooter up to twenty miles per hour. The center notch was designated by a vertical white line to help the soldier select the proper notch.

161

The American Krag Rifle and Carbine

To set the elevation, the rifle was held with the off hand under the sight. The leaf was raised with thumb of the off hand and the binding screw on the right side of the eyepiece loosened and the slide moved forward or backward on the leaf to the desired distance with the fingers of the shooting hand. The shooter then turned the binding knob down snugly to prevent the eyepiece from jumping under recoil. The distance between the elevation graduation marks was such that setting the front edge of the knob halfway between the 500 and 600 yard marks raised the elevation to 550 yards.

Fig. 2-128. Model 1898 Rear Sight Eyepiece. Note the three apertures.

The Model 1898 sight eyepiece could be moved laterally to adjust for windage. There were eight graduation marks on either side of the center index mark, 0.025 inch apart. Adjusting the eyepiece one graduation to left or right moved the point of aim 3.4 inches at 100 yards, 17.2 inches at 500 yards and 34.4 inches at 1,000 yards. The eyepiece had a range of movement totaling 0.2 inch in either direction.

There were three major complaints about the sight. 1) Under pressure, it was easy to use the wrong sighting notch. 2) The sighting notches were so shallow that they were difficult to see in low-light conditions. Trying to line up the correct notch, front sight and the target on cloudy days, in deep shade or at dawn or dusk was always difficult to do. 3) The sight would not stay set under recoil as there was no positive locking system. All of this gave renewed credence to Colonel Mordecai's objection to the Model 1898 sight that it was better suited to the target range than to combat where under intense stress, a soldier would have great difficulty manipulating the sight correctly.

The Model 1898 rear sight was used on all Model 1898 rifles assembled circa serial #s 217,400–253,000.

The question of whether or not the Model 1898 rear sight might have remained in service despite the complaints from the field was moot. It was discovered that the high rate of cracking found in the bolt locking lug was due to the excessive pressures caused by the Model 1898 (2,200 fps) ammunition. In March 1900, the ammunition was removed from service in favor of the old Model 1898 cartridge (2,000 fps) and the Model 1898 rear sights were replaced by the Model 1896 rear sight calibrated for that cartridge. The Model 1896 rear sights were in turn replaced with the Model 1902 rear sight in 1903–1904.

A final note in the ill-fated saga of the Model 1898 rifle sight: an estimated 110,000 were later converted to the Model 1902 rear sight by grinding down the eyepiece to remove the two extra sighting notches. The swing-up peep sight introduced with the Model 1902 rear sight was added to most of the converted Model 1898 rear sights.

Rear Sight, Carbine, Model 1898
The Model 1898 carbine rear sight was quite similar to the Model 1898 rifle sight. The differences were in the base, which was 0.485 inch high, the curve of the tangent on which the slide rested, the spacing of the range increments on both base and leaf which were recalibrated to match the ballistics of the carbine barrel, and the size of the numbers, which were 0.001 inch larger. The base was marked "C" on the right side and also the eyepiece.

The Model 1898 rear sight was only installed as original equipment on the Model 1899 carbine assembled circa serial #s 242,242 to 272,000-285,000. These were later converted to the Model 1902 carbine rear sight.

The American Krag Rifle and Carbine

Rear Sight, Rifle, Model 1901

When General A. R. Buffington became acting Chief of Ordnance on March 29, 1899, one of his first orders was to approve the development of a new rear sight, even though the problems associated with the Model 1898 rear sight had not yet become obvious.

The new sight was based on his Model 1884 rear sight (a.k.a. Buffington rear sight). It used a leaf hinged at the rear with a sliding eyepiece or sight bar that was moved up or down the leaf to the desired range. The base was sloped in a straight line and graduated 1 to 4 in one-hundred-yard increments on the left side. It was also marked "B" for the "battle range" setting at 375 yards. At that range, the bullet would strike a man-sized target at any distance from 100 to 550 yards without having to raise the leaf, see Figure 2-129.

Fig. 2-129. Model 1901 Rear Sight, Type 3.

The American Krag Rifle and Carbine

The leaf was marked in increments of from 100 to 2,000 yards at one-hundred-yard increments with intermediate marks for 25, 50 and 75 yards between each. The top of the leaf had a "U" notch for the 2,000-yard range. The legs of the rifle leaf were machined to provide drift correction for the Krag's tendency to shoot to the left. The Model 1901 carbine sight did not include this correction for bullet drift.

The slide was again similar to that used on the Model 1884 rear sight. The slide traveled up and down the leaf to set the elevation and was secured at the desired elevation by tightening the binding screw on the right side of the slide. When the leaf was flat on the base, the slide could be moved forward until its front edge was even with the "400" yard marking on the left side of the base.

The Model 1901 rear sight (Figure 2-130) had four sighting apertures: 1) The "U" notch on top of the slide was set at the "B" "battle range" setting of 375 yards when the sight leaf was down and the slide was moved forward to the "B" marking on the left side of the upper base; it could also be used to set the range from 100 to 400 yards by moving the slide to the desired range marked on the left side of the upper base. 2) The "U" notch on the top of the slide (leaf vertical) provided elevation adjustments from 450 to 1,900 yards. 3) The 0.046-inch-diameter hole (later changed to 0.070-inch-diameter) in the drift slide (the flat piece of metal pinned to the slide) permitted fine sighting at ranges from 100 to 1,775 yards when the leaf was raised. Horizontal lines

Fig. 2-130. Sighting apertures on the Model 1901 rear sight.

165

The American Krag Rifle and Carbine

were scribed to the left and right of the sighting hole to register with the elevations stamped on the leaf. 4) The "U" notch on the top of the leaf provided a 2,000-yard range and was reserved for volley fire.

The Model 1901 sight was adjustable for windage. This was accomplished by the use of a double base. The leaf was mounted on the upper part of the base which swiveled horizontally on the lower. A binding lever and screw at the front secured the top part of the base at the setting desired. Windage marks were scribed on the back of the upper base. The windage graduations, or windage points as they were referred to by the Ordnance Department, were 0.04 inch apart starting from the center index line and ending in "O." Similar "O"s were scribed on the lower base exactly opposite those on the upper base to permit easy alignment in either direction.

According to a calculation included in the "Description and Rules for the Management of the U.S. Magazine Rifle and Carbine, The Rear Sight, Model 1901," the correction for each point of windage for the rifle at 100 yards was 5.86 inches; 11.74 inches at 200 yards, 17.60 inches at 300 yards and out to 58.8 inches at 1,000 yards.

For you shooters, the equation is: deviation (0.04) x distance between front and rear sights divided by range equals windage correction. To calculate the amount of deviation provided by one point of windage at 400 yards for the carbine, multiply one point of deviation, (0.04) by the number of inches in the distance to the target (14,400) and divide by the distance between front and rear sights (17 inches) to obtain 33.9 inches which is the amount of windage per point at 400 yards for the carbine. For the rifle it would be 0.04 x 14,400 divided by 24.54 (the distance between front and rear sights on the rifle) to obtain 23.47 inches per point of windage. All you need to know now is how strongly the wind is blowing and at what angle to figure how many points of windage you would need at that distance. Try doping that on the range, let alone in combat, and without a pocket calculator!

The leaf was held in the vertical or horizontal position by a leaf spring set into the upper base.

166

The American Krag Rifle and Carbine

Four types of Model 1901 rear sights were used. The **Type 1** Model 1901 rifle rear sight had "V"-shaped sight notches. The slot for the binding lever screw was 0.177 inch wide and the diameter of the slide aperture was 0.046 inch.

The **Type 2** rifle rear sight had a boss added to the binding lever screw hole to protect the screw, and the slot for the binding screw in the upper base was widened to 0.221 inch to accommodate the boss. Refer to Figure 2-129 (arrow).

The **Type 3** rifle rear sight notches were changed from a "V" to a "U" and the aperture in the slide was increased to 0.070 inch diameter, refer to Figure 2-130.

In the **Type 4** Model 1901 rifle rear sight, a leaf spring was added to the underside of the upper base to eliminate any play between the two parts of the base during windage adjustment.

The Model 1901 rifle rear sight was assembled to the Model 1898 service rifle after serial #330,000, to all Krag .22-caliber gallery rifles, to all Krag service rifles issued to the regular Army after 1903, all Model 1896 rifles still in service, and all Model 1898 rifles originally assembled with the Model 1896 rear sight. It was retrofitted to all Krag rifles still in service, both regular Army and National Guard, after 1905.

NOTE: Model 1901 rear sights were extensively rebuilt and are often found with mixed parts.

Rear Sight, Carbine, Model 1901
The Model 1901 carbine rear sight was similar to the Model 1901, Type 2 rifle rear sight with these exceptions. The base was graduated from 100 to 500 yards in 100-yard increments. The upper part of the moveable base was marked "C" for carbine on the front left side, the sight bar on the upper left surface and the leaf on the upper left side, see Figure 2-131.

The American Krag Rifle and Carbine

The leaf was graduated from 100 to 2,300 yards in 100-yard increments. The leaf rails were not machined on a diagonal to provide bullet drift correction as the bullet fired from the carbine did not drift to the left.

The slide was marked "C" on its lower left front side to denote that it was to be used only for the carbine leaf.

Windage adjustment was 8.47 inches per point at 100 yards.

The Model 1901 carbine rear sight was originally assembled to all Model 1899 carbines after circa serial #345,000 and to all "U.S.

Fig. 2-131. Model 1901 Carbine Rear Sight, Type 2.

Magazine Carbine, caliber .30, Model of 1899, altered for Knife Bayonet and Sling" made for the Philippine Constabulary. It was installed on all Model 1898 and Model 1899 carbines with earlier rear sights. After 1903, it was standard equipment on all carbines issued in the regular Army mounted branches and after 1905, to all carbines still in service in both the regular Army and the National Guard.

Two types of Model 1901 carbine rear sights were used.

The **Type 1** Model 1901 carbine rear sight had a U-shaped sighting notch. A boss was added to the binding lever screw hole to protect the screw at circa serial #390,000, and the slot for the binding screw in the upper base was widened to 0.221 inch to accommodate the boss.

168

The American Krag Rifle and Carbine

In the **Type 2** Model 1901 carbine rear sight, the slide aperture was widened to 0.070 inch in diameter. A leaf spring was installed between the upper and lower bases in order to eliminate play during windage adjustment.

NOTE: Many Model 1901 rear sights appear to have a mix of various Model 1901 part types, i.e., large-diameter slide apertures with "V" notch apertures, with or without the spring between the upper and lower bases. This situation probably developed because of repairs made in the field. The Krag saw hard service in the Philippines until it was replaced with the Model 1903 Springfield starting in 1907.

Rear Sight, Rifle, Model 1902

In November 1901, General William Crozier succeeded General Buffington as Chief, Ordnance Department. The proponents of the

Fig. 2-132. Model 1902 Rear Sight.

tangent rear sight had won over the Ordnance Department with claims that the Model 1898 rear sight, for all its faults, was a sound design that improved marksmanship. To support their position, they claimed that the Model 1901 rear sight was being damaged by mounted troopers who forgot to fold the leaf before shoving the carbine into the scabbard or who caught the leaf on the edge of the scabbard mouth. They also claimed that the Model 1898 rifle handguard could be used on the Model 1899 carbine with

The American Krag Rifle and Carbine

the new Model 1902 sight, thus eliminating the cost of making the special humped handguard. Convinced, General Crozier ordered the Model 1902 rear sight to be developed and used, see Figure 2-132.

The Model 1902 rear sight was the Model 1898 rear sight redesigned to eliminate its many objections. Four types were developed. Like the Model 1898 rear sight, the Model 1902 used a base with curved (tangent) rails on which the slide rested as it was moved up or down the leaf to the desired range. The rifle rear sight base was 0.66 inch high. The left side of the leaf was serrated with a groove through the middle to allow the slide to be locked in place with a plunger and binding screw mechanism. The corners of the eyepiece were rounded so the scabbard would not be damaged

The leaf was graduated from 200 to 2,000 yards in 100-yard increments. Twenty-five-yard increments were added in April 1904 after production of the rifle and carbine had ended but the sights were still being made. Windage was accomplished by turning the eyepiece screw which moved the eyepiece from side to side. Eight graduations were stamped on either side of the center index line which extended down to the bottom of the eyepiece and was enameled white. The windage graduations were 0.04 inch apart and the equation discussed in the Model 1901 rear sight section above can be used to calculate the physical distance provided by each increment at a specific range.

The Model 1902 Rifle Rear Sight had a spring-loaded plunger which engaged a serrated leaf to hold the eyepiece in place. The triple sighting notches on the eyepiece had been eliminated in favor of a single notch. The leaf was calibrated for the 2,000 fps Model 1898 cartridge.

The **Type 1** Model 1902 rifle rear sight can readily be identified by the fact that the back of the eyepiece is plain (Figure 2-133A), the edge of the leaf is finely knurled, the graduation lines run straight across the leaf and there are no 25-yard increments. The binding screw knob on the eyepiece is unslotted.

In the **Type 2** Model 1902 rifle rear sight, the knurling on the side of the leaf was changed to vertical slots to hold the eyepiece more

The American Krag Rifle and Carbine

securely in place, see Figure 2-133B. Twenty-five-yard graduation lines were added. The 100-yard lines now ran part way across the leaf but stopped short of the range number. The rear of the eyepiece was

Fig. 2-133A. (L-r) Type 1 smooth and Type 2 knurled eyepiece. William R. Mook collection. Photo by Nick Ferris.

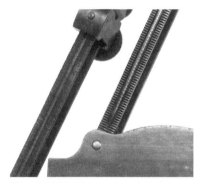

Fig. 2-133B. Types 1 and 2 sight leaves showing the different serrations.

knurled or checkered. The eyepiece binding screw knob was slotted so that a cartridge or coin could be used to tighten it.

The **Type 3** Model 1902 rifle rear sight was approved in January 1904. It was identical to the Type 2 but with the addition of a swing-up peep sight plate attached to the rear of the eyepiece. It was designed to aid long-range marksmen and target shooters by providing a finer sight. It was also touted as helping the infantryman. It did not. While the idea was good, the sight plate was so large that it unduly narrowed the soldier's focus and prevented him from seeing what was happening beyond or beside the target. Again, that was a desirable feature on the target range but not in a combat situation, see Figure 2-134.

The **Type 4** Model 1902 rifle rear sight was actually a large num-

Fig. 2-134. Model 1902 Rear Sight swing-up aperture.

ber of obsolete Model 1898 rear sights converted to the Model 1902 configuration by the grinding down the sides of the eyepiece to remove the two extra sighting notches, thus leaving the center sighting notch, see Figure 2-135A. The left side of the leaf was also serrated by rolling it with a rather fine, diagonal knurling (see Figure 2-135B) or cutting vertical slots, depending on when it was modified. The leaf slide binding screw was slotted for tightening with a coin or cartridge rim. The base curves were reground to bring the range graduations in line with the Model 1898 2,000 fps cartridge.

Many of the binding screw knobs on the Type 4 were taken from surplus Model 1903 (.30-03 caliber) rear sights. These binding screw knobs can be identified by the large coin slot with dished areas on either side, see Figure 2-136.

Two variations of the converted Type 4 Model 1898 rear sights were used. The **Type 4A** did not have the swing-up peep sight attached to the eyepiece while the **Type 4B** did.

The **Type 5** will be a mixture of 1898, 1902 and 1903 rear sight parts assembled or used for

Fig. 2-135A. M1898 Rear Sight modified to Model 1902 configuration. Note that the flanking apertures have been ground away (arrows).

Fig. 2-135B. Fine knurling on the Type 4 leaf.

repairs after 1905. They are easily identified by the 1903 binding screw, refer to Figure 2-136.

The Model 1902 Rifle Rear Sight was retrofitted to all rifles of the regular Army that had the Model 1896 rifle sight; to all regular Army rifles after April 1903 and to National Guard rifles until 1905 when they were in turn replaced by the Model 1901 rear sight.

Rear Sight, Carbine, Model 1902

This rear sight was nearly identical to the Model 1902 rifle rear sight

Fig. 2-136. A cartridge rim or coin could be used to turn the binding screw knob (arrow) on the Type 4 Model 1902 rear sight.

except that the curve on the tangent base was 0.52 inch high at its highest point and it was marked "C" for carbine on the left side of the base. The four carbine versions of the Model 1902 rear sight underwent the same changes as the rifle rear sight and were fitted to all carbines issued to National Guard units after April 1903. It also replaced Model 1896 and Model 1898 carbine sights on the previous carbine models and was installed on the "U.S. Magazine Carbine, caliber .30, Model of 1899, altered for Knife Bayonet and Sling" manufactured at Springfield Armory and issued to military schools.

Rear Sight, Rifle, Board of Ordnance and Fortifications

This rifle rear sight was developed for the one hundred BOF rifles that were manufactured for testing in 1902. It was essentially the Model 1901 rear rifle sight with the leaf and base graduations changed to conform to the 26-inch barrel. The carbine style of leaf was used instead of the rifle leaf, which did not have the built-in drift correction of the standard Model 1901 rifle rear sight leaf. The base also lacked the steps at the front end of the rails, see Figure 2-137. Tests of the 26-

The American Krag Rifle and Carbine

Fig. 2-137. The rear sight used on the Board of Ordnance and Fortifications Rifle was a modified Model 1901. William R. Mook collection.

inch barrel showed less drift than either the service rifle or carbine. It led later to the adoption of the 24-inch barrel for the Model 1903 rifle.

REAR SIGHT, SCREWS

Rear sight screws varied in length depending on the rear sight used. Front screws also varied in length except those used with the Model 1898 and Model 1902 rear sights. All were flat head screws except the rear sight Model 1901 front screw, see Figure 2-138.

The **Model 1892** front screw was 0.382 inch high. The head was 0.220 inch in diameter and 0.09 inch thick. The screw was threaded for one half its length. The Model 1892 rear screw had a 0.20-inch-long shank and its head was 0.220 inch in diameter and 0.05 inch thick. The shank was threaded for its full

length. These screws were also often used to attach the Model 1896 rear sight to Model 1892 rifles during retrofitting. Two types of screws were used on the original early Model 1892 rifles: the **Type 1** screw had a slotted, flat head similar to the screws used on the .45-70 Springfield. The **Type 2** screws had a slotted flat head. The Type 1 screws are rarely seen.

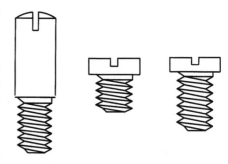

Fig. 2-138. Krag rear sight screws: l-r, Model 1901 front screw, M1892 rear and front.

174

The American Krag Rifle and Carbine

Model 1896 rear sight screws were slightly shorter than the Model 1892. The front screw was 0.380 inch high and the head diameter was 0.220 inch and 0.05 inch thick. The rear screw was the same as used on the Model 1892 rear sight with a 0.20-inch shank.

The **Model 1898** and **Model 1902** rear sight front and rear screws were the same height as the Model 1892/96 rear sight screws, 0.20-inch shank. Head diameter was 0.220 inch and 0.05 inch thick.

The **Model 1901** rear sight front screw was quite a bit different from the other rear sight front screws. The front screw hole was the pivot point for the upper base on the lower. The head of the front screw was therefore made longer so that the upper base would swivel around it.

The front screw was 0.452 inch long. Its rounded head was 0.195 inch in diameter and 0.220 inch high. The shank was threaded along its length.

The rear screw was 0.268 inch high. The head was 0.220 inch in diameter and 0.05 inch thick. The shank was threaded along its length.

NOTE: It is not unusual to see incorrect screws used to attach rear sights to rifles and carbines. The differences were so small in most cases, with the exception of the Model 1901 rear sight front screw, that they could be used interchangeably by armorers, hunters and collectors alike.

FRONT SIGHTS

The front sight blade was cut from sheet steel and pinned in a slot in the front sight base. Blade height varied according to the rear sight used, and also between carbines and rifles, see Figure 2-139.

Rifle Front Sight Blades

Four types of rifle front sight blades were used. The **Type 1** front sight blade was 0.05 inch thick at the base but stepped down to 0.035

The American Krag Rifle and Carbine

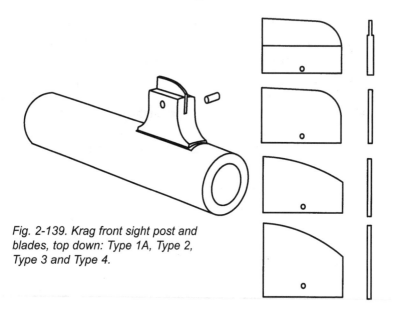

Fig. 2-139. Krag front sight post and blades, top down: Type 1A, Type 2, Type 3 and Type 4.

inch at the top. It had a pronounced forward curve and was used only on early Model 1892 rifles. There were apparently two variations of the Type 1 blade. The original **Type 1A** was 0.255 inch high. Its replacement with the **Type 1B,** which was 0.285 inch high, was approved June 20, 1894. The change from the Type 1A to the Type 1B occurred at Springfield Armory before the first Model 1892 service rifles were issued to the regular Army in October 1894. Those that may have been missed were mostly replaced during the Model 1892 to 1896 conversions in 1897 and 1900. The author's rifle, serial #1,178, still retains the Type 1B blade.

The **Type 2** blade was the same shape as the Type 1 blade but was taller than the Type 1A at 0.285 inch. The width was a uniform 0.05 inch thick. It was approved for use on the Model 1896 rifle and carbine. Blades installed on the carbine were slightly lower.

The American Krag Rifle and Carbine

Table 2-14 Front Sight Dimensions	
Rear Sight Model	**Blade Height**
1892 Rifle, Type 1A	0.255 (1)
1892 Rifle, Type 1B, 2	0.285 (2)
1896 Rifle	0.285
1896 Carbine	0.265
1898 Rifle	0.410
1898 Carbine	0.352
1901 Rifle	0.410
1901 Carbine	0.352
1902 Rifle	0.410
1902 Carbine	0.352
1. This front sight was used to circa serial #s 1,000-1,200. 2. The Type 1B front sight was used from circa serial #s 1,001-1,201 to the end of M1892 production.	

The **Type 3** front sight blade was also uniformly 0.05 inch thick, top to bottom. The front curve was increased so that there was a very gradual slope rear to front. This blade was 0.285 inch high.

The **Type 4** front sight blade was also uniformly 0.05 inch thick but taller at 0.410 inch. The blade had a gradual slope, rear to front. It appears to have been developed for use with the Model 1901 rear sight.

Table 2-14, above, presents front sight dimensions used with the various models. Keep in mind that rifles and carbines were still individually sighted at the Armory during Krag production, a practice that continued with the Model 1903 until 1909 when sufficient precision in rifling was achieved to allow bore sighting only. Range zeroing was often accomplished by increasing the height of the front sight blade to lower the bullet strike or inserting a slightly lower blade to raise the bullet strike.

Carbine Front Sight Blades

Carbine front sight blades were marked "C" on the lower left side, 0.10 inch in height. When installed, the "C" was usually below the top of the front sight stud and not visible except on Model 1899 front sight blades, which were marked higher.

Two types of carbine front sight blades were used. The **Type 1** carbine front sight blade was similar in design to the Type 3 rifle blade in that it had a gradual slope from rear to front. It was used on the Models 1896, 1898 and 1899 carbines with the Models 1896 or 1898 rear sights.

The **Type 2** carbine front sight blade was similar to the Type 4 rifle front sight blade in that it was taller than the Type 1 with a gradual slope rear to front. The "C" mark on the left side was usually visible as it was stamped higher on the blade. The Type 2 was used with the Model 1901 carbine rear sight.

Because front sight blades were not always changed when rear sights were, it is not uncommon to find Krag front blades reduced in height either by an armorer or the shooter to bring the sights into proper alignment.

Refer to Table 2-14 for the official front blade heights in relation to Krag model rear sight for which they were intended to be used. Keep in mind the earlier caution that each carbine was zeroed for range and windage before leaving the Springfield Armory. Blades were often

178

The American Krag Rifle and Carbine

Fig. 2-140. The Model 1905 front sight found on some Krag carbines and short rifles was not original equipment.

modified slightly to achieve range zero.

In 1906, the Springfield Armory made available front sight blades of different heights so that National Match competitors could fit the blade to the rear sight they were using and to the individual characteristics of their rifles. It does not appear that these blades were marked.

MODEL 1905 FRONT SIGHT

The Model 1905 front sight band, base and blade (Figure 2-140) installed on the .30-06 caliber Model 1903 Springfield was also used on Krag rifles cut down to carbine length by the Director of Civilian Marksmanship in the 1920s when the supply of original carbines ran out. They were also applied to rifle barrels shortened to make carbines or short rifles by a number of civilian entrepreneurs such as Bannerman, W. Stokes Kirk, etc. Many Model 1905 front sights were purchased on the surplus market before and after World War II and mounted on Krag rifles and carbines converted to hunting weapons by individuals and custom gunsmiths.

In short, these sights are not original equipment on Krag service rifles or carbines.

179

Chapter 3
Accessories

This chapter includes only the additional items of equipment issued to the regular soldier that related to his Krag rifle or carbine.

CLEANING RODS

Cleaning rods were an issue item with every rifle and carbine. The soldier was always expected to keep the bore of his issued weapons immaculate.

The ramrod had evolved into the cleaning rod with the advent of the Model 1865 Springfield Rifle and its self-contained metallic cartridge. The new .58-caliber rifle required a cleaning rod that could be used not only for cleaning the bore but for removing stuck cartridge cases, always a problem with the thin-walled copper and brass cases then in use. The Model 1865 rifles used the standard Model 1855 swelled ramrod taken from surplus percussion rifle-muskets as a cleaning rod. Even so, the Ordnance Department continued to refer to all one-piece cleaning rods as ramrods.

ONE-PIECE RAMROD

The Model 1892 Krag rifle carried a one-piece cleaning rod under the barrel, just as had its predecessor, the .45-70 Springfield. The Krag one-piece ramrod was made in four types.

The **Type 1** ramrod had a knurled brass head with a slight indentation at the tip and was 29.5 inches long. The knurling was parallel with the sides of the head. The brass head was brazed to the steel shank and was 0.259 inch in diameter and 1.165 inches long. The slot for the cleaning cloth was 0.120 inch wide and 0.430 inch long. The diameter of the rod was 0.196 inch and the end was rebated to 0.181 inch in diameter and thread for 0.475 inch with 26 threads to the inch, see Figure 3-1.

The American Krag Rifle and Carbine

Fig. 3-1. The Type 1 knurled, brass head cleaning rod may have been issued with the very earliest production Model 1892 rifles. Jonathan Peck collection, courtesy of Little John's Auction Services.

NOTE: The Type 1 knurled brass head ramrod was not issued on service rifles. It was considered "unsightly" and bent easily, according to Chief of Ordnance in the FY 1894 report to the Secretary of War. The Type 2, ramrod forged from steel bars, was substituted before the first issue of service rifles began in October 1894.

The **Type 2** ramrod was made entirely of steel and was adopted at circa serial #500. The head end was swelled around the cleaning cloth slot and had parallel sides. It was manufactured by forging to shape, then upsetting the end of a steel rod to form the head. Collectors often refer this as the "1st pattern solid head ramrod," see Figure 3-2. Three solid head ramrods were measured and all three were 29.437 inches long.

Fig. 3-2. Type 2 all-steel cleaning rod. Note that the sides of the head are parallel. North Cape Publications collection.

The *Description and Rules for the Management of the U.S. Magazine Rifle and Carbine, Calibre .30, 1894* gives the length of the solid head ramrod as 29.48

181

inches. The ramrod was said to have been reduced in length by 0.265 inch over the Type 1 and the head diameter reduced to 0.265 inch in diameter.

In fact, there are two lengths of the Type 2 ramrod, The **Type 2A** is 29.50 inches and the **Type 2B** is 29.25 inches long. The head diameter of the Type 2 rods measured was 0.267 inch in diameter, an increase of 0.002 inch, and was 0.950 inch long

The cleaning cloth slot was 0.110 inch wide and 0.410 inch long. The diameter of the rod was 0.20 inch at the front, tapering slightly to 0.189 inch at the rear ahead of the threads. The threaded area was rebated to 0.179 inch in diameter for 0.285 inch in length. It had 26 threads per inch.

The **Type 3** ramrod is often referred to as the "2nd pattern solid head" ramrod by collectors. It was also a steel rod with a swelled head like the Type 2. But the head on this rod had slightly rounded sides, see Figure 3-3. The diameter of the head was reduced to 0.25 inch in diameter at circa serial #20,000. The other dimensions remained the same as the Type 2B ramrod.

Fig. 3-3. Type 3 all-steel cleaning rod. Note that the sides of the head are slightly rounded. Scott Duff collection.

NOTE: The Type 3 ramrod was also supplied with the Model 1896 Cadet Rifle.

The American Krag Rifle and Carbine

One authority has speculated that the long Krag ramrods were made from unserviceable .45-70 ramrods. It seems unlikely as the diameter of the .45-70 ramrod at the bottom end is smaller in diameter than the Krag rod end. In fact, the one-piece ramrods were made from cast steel bars 0.28 inch in diameter that went through twenty-five manufacturing steps including rust browning. After forging, rods were ground to a uniform diameter, then the end was heated and upset to form the head, reheated and swaged to shape, ground, cut, annealed, straightened, drilled, punched, polished three times and browned.

The **Type 4** ramrod was used on the Model 1892 Carbine. It appears that its dimensions were the same as the Type 2 ramrod except it was shorter at 21.48 inches.

SECTIONAL CLEANING RODS

The **Type 5** cleaning rod was a three-piece sectional rod that was carried in the buttstock of the rifle and carbine stocks. It was accessed through a trapdoor in the butt plate. The three pieces of the cleaning rod were each 8.281 inches long and the diameter of the rods proper varied from 0.191 to 0.197 inch. The Type 5 cleaning rod was issued beginning with the Model 1896 carbine and rifle to the end of produc-

Fig. 3-4. Type 5 sectional cleaning rod, stored in the buttstock. Three segments were issued for rifles, two for carbines. North Cape Publications collection.

tion, see Figure 3-4. The first section's top end swelled into a barrel head 0.25 inch in diameter. It had a cleaning cloth slot 0.095 inch

The American Krag Rifle and Carbine

wide by 0.408 inch long. Sections two and three also had swelled ends at the front that varied from 0.25 to 0.255 inch in diameter. The front end of sections two and three were drilled and tapped to take the threaded end of the next section. All three sections were rebated at the bottom end to 0.150 inch and threaded.

By regulation, infantry troops carrying rifles were issued the first, second and third sections of the cleaning rod. Mounted troops carrying carbines were issued only the first and second sections.

All cleaning rods made for the Krag rifle and carbine were tempered. The one-piece cleaning rods were polished and blued. The jointed or sectional rods were not highly polished. The tempering process colored them gray and they were blued over that, giving them a dull, dark coloration. Cleaning rods were not marked.

To use the jointed cleaning rod, the sections were screwed together to make a rifle rod from three sections 24.25 inches long or a carbine rod from two sections 16.25 inches long. Since either the one-piece or jointed rods were obviously not long enough to pass through the barrel, they were inserted from the breech end after first removing the bolt, then from the muzzle end.

NOTE: The exact dimensions of the four types of cleaning rods will vary slightly due to the non-automated manufacturing techniques in use at the time.

BARRACKS CLEANING ROD

The barracks cleaning rod was made of brass rod 0.25 inch in diameter, see Figure 3-5. The handle was shaped into a ring. One rod was issued for every five rifles in a company. The end of the rod was upset into a button tip to hold the cleaning cloth. Two variations of the barracks cleaning rod were issued. The rifle rod was 32 inches long and the carbine rod was 26 inches long.

The American Krag Rifle and Carbine

OILERS

Two kinds of oilers were issued with the Krag rifle and carbine.

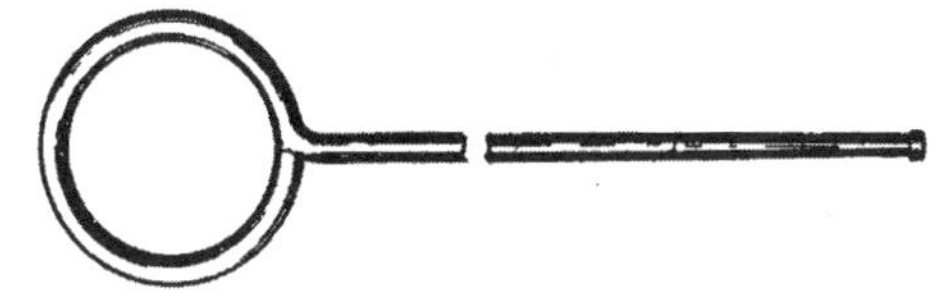

Fig. 3-5. Barracks cleaning rod. The rifle rod was 32 inches long, the carbine rod, 26 inches long.

BUTT TRAP OILER

The oiler was a nickel-plated hollow brass cylinder closed at one end with a screw cap. The cap held a steel wire with a flattened tip and was sealed with a leather washer. The flattened tip applied oil one drop at a time, an excellent procedure in view of the fact that the natural tendency was, and still is, to over-oil firearms. The oiler was developed and issued at circa serial #69,000 to the end of production for both rifles and carbines. The oiler was carried in the buttstock of the rifle and carbine in a slot just below the cleaning rods. Until the butt traps in Model 1892 rifles and Model 1896 carbines and rifles without the oiler slot were recut for the oiler, the soldier carried it in his pocket or in a loop of the cartridge belt or McKeever cartridge pouch.

NOTE: Do not try and insert an oiler into a Mills 100-round .30-40 cartridge belt if it is dry or aged. If you do, you will break the threads.

Two Types of oilers were issued. The **Type 1** oiler was 0.459 inch in diameter and 3.246 inches long, including the cap. The diameter of the Type 1 cap was 0.563 inch in diameter and knurled around the edges. The diameter of the hole in the neck was 0.258 inch,

Fig. 3-6A. Type 1 Krag oiler.

The American Krag Rifle and Carbine

see Figure 3-6A.

The **Type 2** oiler had the same dimensions as the Type 1 oiler but the hole in the body was smaller in diameter at 0.175 inch. By making the hole smaller, the size of the gasket could be increased to keep the cap from leaking. The knurling

Fig. 3-6B. Type 2 Krag oiler (left). Note the smaller-diameter hole in the Type 2 oiler.

on the edge of the cap was also finer than on the Type 1 cap. It is not known when the Type 2 oiler superseded the Type 1, see Figure 3-6B.

At least eight combinations of knurling, small- and large-diameter holes and threads have been observed.

Pocket Oiler

Fig. 3-7. Pocket oiler for Krag with refill can. William R. Mook collection.

A round oil can intended to be carried in the soldier's pocket was issued starting in 1901 to troops in tropical areas, in addition to the oiler carried in the buttstock. It held two ounces of sperm oil. The can was two inches in diameter and 0.5 inch thick. It was made of nickel-plated brass and had a screw top with a leather washer and a wire dipper flattened on the end, see Figure 3-7.

Screwdriver

In 1897, a special screwdriver was issued for the Krag rifle and carbine. It somewhat resembled the Model 1879 screwdriver issued for

The American Krag Rifle and Carbine

the .45-70 Springfield in that it had two blades. It did not have the clamp ground into the end of the longer blade for the mainspring, see Figure 3-8. The large blade had a small pin punch to drift out the pins in the butt plate cap, trigger and lower band. The screwdriver was carried in

Fig. 3-8. Model 1897 Krag screwdriver (center) compared to the Model 1879 .45-70 Springfield (left) and the Model 1903 (right). North Cape Publications collection.

the McKeever cartridge pouch or the soldier's pocket or pack.

CARBINE BOOTS

The scabbard for cavalry carbines was introduced in 1884. In actuality, it was a half scabbard and referred to as a boot. It was a sheath of leather that covered the receiver area of the carbine. It fastened to the saddle with three leather attaching straps and was mounted on the right side. The carbine was clipped to a sling or shoulder belt that looped over the trooper's left shoulder. When the trooper was on foot, the carbine dangled at his side or was carried in one or both hands; when mounted, it rode in the boot.

The Model 1887 carbine boot was the general-issue boot during the Krag period but because many cavalry troops already had both the Model 1885 (without the brass reinforcement) as well as the Model 1887, they were probably both in use by cavalry troops armed with the Krag carbine, see Figure 3-9.

The Model 1885 carbine boot was 11.75 inches high. It had three attaching straps, one that attached to the saddle bag stud on the cantle,

187

The American Krag Rifle and Carbine

Fig. 3-9. Rare photo showing a cavalry trooper with a Krag Model 1896 Carbine, Model 1885 Carbine Sling and Model 1887 Carbine Boot.

one that wrapped around the girth strap and one that attached to the cinch ring. The strap that attached to the cinch ring encircled the bottom of the boot. The front top of the boot was not reinforced.

The Model 1887 carbine boot was similar but was 13.5 inches high and had a brass reinforcing plate at the front of the throat. Also, the strap that fastened it to the saddle's cinch ring was mounted four inches above the bottom of the boot, see Figure 3-10.

Anyone who has any experience riding horses can immediately see the dangers of the sling and boot. If the trooper was thrown, the carbine

The American Krag Rifle and Carbine

had a tendency to stay in the scabbard until torn loose. If he was thrown cleanly, the carbine on the end of the sling often whipped back to strike him as he fell. Either way, severe injuries could and did result. Not only that, but the barrel, with the sensitive muzzle area, as well as the stock was fully exposed in the boot and subject to damage if the horse fell. Troopers riding through severe weather and, in the dusty Southwest, complained that their carbines were stripped of finish and lubrication after a few weeks in the saddle.

Figure 3-10. L-r, Models 1885 and 1887 Carbine Boots. P.B. Hayward, Jr., collection.

CARBINE SCABBARDS

The full-length scabbard attached to either side of the saddle, tipped so that the butt was easy to hand, was the answer. The scabbard had long been used by hunters, cowboys, trappers, ranchers and farmers to carry rifles and carbines when mounted. But not until 1895 did the Army adopt the full-length scabbard for the Cavalry arm. The scabbard was made of heavy black leather with enameled black iron buckles.

The **Type 1** scabbard was a leather sleeve that covered all but a few inches of the buttstock and was closed at the bottom end, see Figure 3-11. The scabbard was 30 inches long and 2.375 inches wide at the top with a small drain hole at the bottom. The edges of the scabbard were

The American Krag Rifle and Carbine

Fig. 3-11. Cavalry trooper with the Krag Type 1 scabbard and Krag carbine circa late 1890s.

sewn together with heavy waxed linen thread. Two leather straps fastened it to the saddle; the top strap attached to the ring on the front side of the saddle and the lower strap attached to the rear ring, depending on the model saddle being used. The straps could be adjusted to raise or lower the angle at which the scabbard hung. A single rivet reinforced the tab of leather that held the attaching ring. The top strap passed through a leather loop riveted to the left side of the scabbard behind and just below the mouth, see Figure 3-12.

The American Krag Rifle and Carbine

The Type 1 scabbard narrowed at the end of the forearm to hold the barrel tightly when at a gallop. It was manufactured at Rock Island Arsenal starting in December 1896 of black-dyed leather. All metal parts were painted with black enamel. Two metal strips form-

Fig. 3-12. Type 1 scabbard for the Krag carbine made of black leather before 1902. Craig Riesch collection.

ed a drain hole at the bottom. The scabbards were marked: Rock Island Arsenal/Inspector's Initials (usually "E.H.S.," "H.E.K." or "T.C."). Various company markings may also be noted on many, see Figure 3-13.

Fig. 3-13. Typical markings on the Krag carbine scabbard—"Rock Island Arsenal/E.H.S."

The **Type 2** scabbard was identical to the Type 1 scabbard but it was manufactured by J.M. Rosenfeld, Rock Island, Illinois, and so marked. Only about three thousand scabbards were made in 1898 and early 1899.

The **Type 3** scabbard was similar in construction to the Type 1 but had a brass reinforcing plate riveted to the front of the throat (arrow) to hold it open and make it easier to insert the carbine, see Figure 3-14.

The American Krag Rifle and Carbine

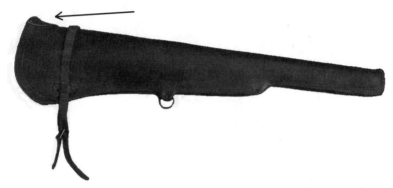

*Fig. 3-14. Type 3 scabbard for the Krag carbine (without the lower strap).
Note the brass reinforcement at the throat and the indentation for the barrel.
Scabbards were made of russet leather after 1901. Ed Cote collection.*

The scabbard was form-fitting around the barrel. Experience had shown that the leather tended to harden and shrink somewhat with age and this often made it difficult to remove the carbine. Also, the carbine's front sight cut the inside of the scabbard if the front sight cover was not used. It was long enough to allow the extended forearm of the Model 1899 carbine to be inserted.

The attaching straps were also changed on the Type 3 scabbard. The upper strap was the same and the lower strap was lengthened to encircle the scabbard. It was guided through two leather loops on either side of the iron ring as added reinforcement. The top strap passed through a leather loop riveted to the left side of the scabbard behind and just below the brass reinforcing plate at the mouth. Snaffle hooks, called German hooks at the time, were added to make it easier to mount and dismount the scabbard. Metal strips formed a drain hole at the bottom.

The Type 3 scabbard was issued in mid-1902. All were manufactured at Rock Island Arsenal of russet leather. All metal parts were painted with either black or brown enamel according to the period of manufac-

The American Krag Rifle and Carbine

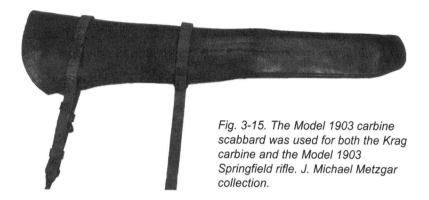

Fig. 3-15. The Model 1903 carbine scabbard was used for both the Krag carbine and the Model 1903 Springfield rifle. J. Michael Metzgar collection.

ture. The Type 3 scabbard was marked "Rock Island Arsenal/ Inspector's Initials." Later production was often marked with the year of manufacture. The earliest observed to date was "1903."

The **Model 1903** scabbard was issued in 1904 and was used with both the Krag carbine and the Model 1903 Springfield rifle. It was similar to the Type 1 scabbard in that it lacked both the indentation for the barrel and the brass reinforcing plate at the throat, see Figure 3-15.

GUN SLINGS

The official U.S. Army Ordnance Department nomenclature for the rifle sling was "gun sling." The sling for the Krag-Jørgensen rifle, like that for the .45-70 Springfield and the rifles and rifle muskets that preceded it, was not designed to be used as an aid to aiming, but strictly for carrying the rifle. Not until 1907 was such a rifle sling, designed for use as both a carrying strap and an aiming aid, adopted.

Three basic types were employed, nearly all manufactured at Rock Island Arsenal. During the Spanish-American War, contracts were let to four outside companies identified by Frank Mallory of the Springfield Research Service as J.J. Warren Company, Worcester, MA; Stender Saddlery Company; Harbison & Gathwright, Louisville, KY; and S. Scheuer & Sons, New York, NY. Krag slings are quite rare as many

The American Krag Rifle and Carbine

appear to have been converted to the Model 1907 pattern. One experimental model was tested in the Philippines and not adopted.

The **Type 1** sling was the Pattern of 1887. It was a leather strap 66.5 inches long by 1.25 inches wide with two leather loops or keepers, and a double brass claw at one end.

Fig. 3-16. Type 1 Krag Rifle Sling, Pattern of 1887. Craig Riesch collection.

The other end was folded over the rear sling swivel and a double-headed brass stud was inserted through slits to secure it. The double brass claw was threaded through the upper sling swivel and its hooks inserted into holes punched in the sling. The slings were made originally of russet leather, see Figure 3-16.

The **Type 2** sling was nearly identical to the Type 1 except that it was made up from two pieces of leather sewn together. The pieces came from Pattern 1855 or later slings that were "surveyed" and then salvaged for reasons of economy. Most of these slings appear black but only from years of oil and dirt.

Fig. 3-17. Type 2 Krag Rifle Sling made by salvaging "surveyed" slings and sewing two good pieces of leather together.

They were russet in color originally, see Figure 3-17.

The American Krag Rifle and Carbine

The **Type 3** was the first to be accorded a "model" designation, "Gunsling, U.S. Magazine Rifle, Model of 1898." It was 48 inches long and 1.25 inches wide. The sling was made of russet leather and was essentially a strap with a double brass claw at one end and a round tongue or tail at the other which was se-cured with a double-headed brass stud. Two sets of adjusting holes were used, four on the tail and ten above. Two leather loops were used to secure the sling, see Figure 3-18.

It was as-sembled to the rifle by passing the tail through a loop, with the loop

Fig. 3-18. Model 1898 sling for the Krag rifle. North Cape Publications collection.

turned so that its seam was next to the rough (flesh) side of the sling. With the smooth side of the sling against the stock, the tail was pulled through the upper sling swivel and back through the first loop, then down toward the butt plate.

The tail was now pulled through the second loop, then through the lower sling swivel, then passed back through the loop. The tail was adjusted so that the slits for the stud were opposite one another, then the stud was pushed through both slits to secure it. The sling was adjusted by hooking the brass claw into the one of the four sets of holes on the tail above the slit.

Two variations of the Model 1898 sling were used: the Krag version had four holes in the tail for adjusting; the Model 1903 Springfield sling had three. The earliest dated were made at Rock Island Arsenal, dated "1903," the first year RIA began to date leather goods.

The American Krag Rifle and Carbine

NOTE: According to General Order 81, July 17, 1902, the Army changed its leather gear from black to russet. This did not affect rifle slings as they had always been russet to prevent dye from staining uniform coats. Many leather slings used on previous models had been oiled so much that they often appeared black.

Fig. 3-19. Mills & Orndorff woven sling tested in the Philippines as a combination rifle sling, canteen and haversack sling. Craig Riesch collection.

The **Type 4** sling was designated as the "haversack, canteen and gun sling." It was a web sling woven of cotton 61 inches long by 1.25 inches wide, see Figure 3-19. The material looked very much like that found in the 100-round Mills web cartridge belt as it was manufactured by the Mills & Orndorff Company. It was intended for tropical use where the leather sling tended to rot and fall apart quickly. As reported by the Chief of Ordnance in the Fiscal Year 1902, several thousand of these Mills slings were procured for testing in the Philippines, but they were heartily detested by the troops. When wet, they tended to roll vertically and became a narrow cord that cut into the shoulder.

The British Army, however, liked the pattern and in 1901 adopted a Mills web sling for the Lee-Enfield rifle that was 48 inches long. A similar pattern sling is still in use today by the British Army.

The other sling associated with the Krag rifle was the Kerr "NobuckL" Adjustable Sling, used after the U.S. entered World War I when the

The American Krag Rifle and Carbine

Krag was issued to some Army troops and for training purposes. As such it was not considered to be an issue sling for the Krag rifle.

CARBINE SLING

The first carbine sling issued to mounted troops was the Model 1833. It was a 2.5-inch-wide buff leather belt that was 55.5 inches long with a brass belt buckle with two prongs. The end of the belt was protected by a "V"-shaped brass tip. The Model 1833 was superseded by the Model 1885 Carbine Sling, see Figure 3-20. It was 1.5 inch wide and 60.75 inches long and made from bridle leather dyed black. The brass buckle had a single prong. Both belts had a narrow welt rolled into each edge of the belt and both were made from harness leather.

The carbine was attached to the sling with a snap hook attached to a chain link which in turn was attached to a swivel which was riveted to a "U"-shaped frame. The top of the "U" was closed with a round steel dowel.

Fig. 3-20. M1885 Carbine Sling and M1896 Carbine. Don Moore collection.

The carbine sling was worn over the left shoulder with the buckle on the chest and the swivel on the right side about waist height. The carbine was clipped to the snap hook using the swivel plate and ring on the carbine's left side. The barrel and forearm of the carbine rested in the carbine boot attached to the saddle's quarter strap ring. When the Model 1895 scabbard replaced the Model 1887 carbine boot, it also eliminated the need for the Model 1885 carbine sling. After 1897, use

The American Krag Rifle and Carbine

of the carbine sling and boot was confined to those units that had not yet received the scabbard. The sling continued to be used for another two years by mounted troopers for carrying the carbine when dismounted. It was withdrawn from service after December 1898.

MODEL 1900 FRONT SIGHT COVER

One sight protector combined with a muzzle cover or tompion was developed for the Krag rifle. It was designated the "Model 1900 Front Sight Cover" and was based on a redesign of the Danish Krag-Jørgensen sight cover by Lt. Tracy Dickson, U.S. Army. Made of brass in two parts, it slipped over the front sight. A hinged cover dropped over the muzzle, see Figure 3-21. The forward part of the sight cover half was knurled. The sight cover was not marked in any way. The major drawback to this design was that the sight cover had to be removed before the gun was fired; otherwise, damage to the muzzle could result, and possibly to the shooter or those around him as bits of brass sprayed in every direction. To prevent this, supposedly, the shooter would see the bulky brass cover over the sight and be warned. In fact, when viewed through the rear sight aperture, it would be very easy to overlook the fact that the sight cover was still covering the muzzle.

Fig. 3-21. Krag front sight cover for the rifle. North Cape Publications collection.

To use, the shooter aligned the muzzle protector portion with the muzzle and pressed his thumb down on the knurling while pushing the device back and over the front sight. To remove, the knurling was pressed down at the same time that the device was pulled forward off the muzzle.

The American Krag Rifle and Carbine

MODEL 1901 FRONT SIGHT COVER

The "Model 1901 Front Sight Cover" was designed by Springfield

Fig. 3-22. Krag carbine front sight protector. Craig Riesch collection.

employee Charles Candrian, and patented for use on the carbine, see Figure 3-22. It was similar to the .45-70 Springfield Second Issue Sight Cover in that a piece of spring steel was formed into a double bow, open at the bottom and connected by two straight walls. The smaller upper bow was closed and surrounded the front sight blade. The Model 1901 Front Sight Cover snapped over the barrel and was designed to protect the inside of the scabbard from the sharp front sight blade as well as the sight blade itself. The Model 1901 Front Sight Cover was marked "C" for carbine on the left wall in serif type 0.1 inch high.

BREECH COVER

The breech cover for the Krag is an example of an item that was rejected by the U.S. Army's Ordnance Department yet so in demand by the men and officers in the field that it continued to be manufactured and distributed.

First authorized by General Order No. 23, 1897, the Ordnance Department initially manufactured 15,000 for field testing. Reports labeled it a nuisance and the order was rescinded in June 1899. But demand from the field for the breech cover, particularly in the north during the winter and spring and from the Philippines all year round, caused the Ordnance Department to manufacture another 17,000 before their use was again officially ended in 1903.

199

The American Krag Rifle and Carbine

Even so, while the Krag was in the field, they continued to be used. A similar cover was issued for the Model 1903 Springfield.

The breech cover was made of canvas with two leather ties at either end, see Figure 3-23. The cover was 11.6 inches wide by 10.9 inches long and was gusseted at the breech end to conform to the shape of the receiver and magazine.

The breech cover was positioned so that the back of the receiver and the bolt handle fit into the gusset, and the leather thongs were wrapped around the receiver and tied together. The soldier was told

Fig. 3-23. Canvas breech cover for the Krag rifle and carbine. North Cape Publications collection.

not to use a square knot so that one end could be yanked to free the knot and whip the cover off in an emergency.

Breech covers were stenciled on the inside in India ink, "PLACE OVER COCKING PIECE" and "ROCK ISLAND ARSENAL." The words "Rock Island" formed a bow over "Arsenal."

A similar cover was developed for the Model of 1917 Enfield and was also issued for use with the Model 1903 Springfield. It had a single thong on the forward end and four Carr snap fasteners.

BAYONETS AND SCABBARDS
The bayonet adopted for the Krag rifle was based on the Swiss Pattern of 1889 and designated the Bayonet Model 1892.

The American Krag Rifle and Carbine

Bayonets

Ten types of bayonet were used for the Krag rifle. The most common Krag bayonet was the Type 1 Model 1892 issued with the service rifle in eight variations.

The **Type 1** bayonet blade was 1.01 inch wide, 11.75 inches long, 0.218 inch thick and 16.3 inches long overall. The true edge was 10.6 inches long and the false edge was 4.375 inches long. A fuller ran down the center of the blade on either side and was 0.375 inch wide and 8 inches long. The bayonet had a spear point, being evenly curved top and bottom, see Figure 3-24.

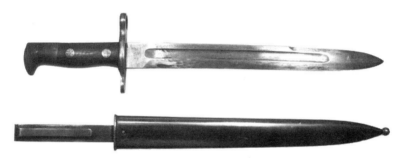

Fig. 3-24. Type 1 Krag rifle bayonet with Type 1 scabbard. North Cape Publications collection.

The grips were made of American Walnut and fastened with two rivets and washers. The pommel had a slight birds-head grip and was slotted at the top for the bayonet stud. Following the Swiss practice, the same Mauser-style catch was used.

The obverse of the ricasso was marked "U S" and the reverse was marked with the year of manufacture, "1894" through "1903."

The guard was perpendicular to the blade and was 3.435 inches high, 0.278 inch thick except at the bottom where it was rebated at the back to 0.179 inch thick for 0.910 inch. The bore in the guard which slid over the barrel was 0.625 inch in diameter.

The American Krag Rifle and Carbine

A total of eight variations of the Model 1892 bayonet were manufactured for the Krag, all at the Springfield National Armory.

On the **1st Variation** bayonet, the rivets were ground flush with the wooden grips (also called scales) and the washers that held their upset heads, see Figure 3-25. The walnut grips were sanded smooth and flush with the surrounding metal parts. The grips were then oiled. The metal parts of the bayonet, except the blade, were polished. Blades only were blued until April 1, 1895. At that time, the bluing was discontinued as it was found that the heat

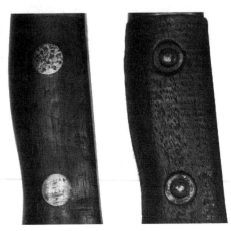

Fig. 3-25. Type 1, 1st and 4th Variation M1892 Krag Bayonets showing flush and rounded rivets and smooth and ridged grip scales. North Cape Publications collection.

of the bluing solutions drew the temper from the steel.

The **2nd Variation** bayonet was identical to the 1st Variation but the blade was polished bright.

The **3rd Variation** bayonet was identical to the 2nd Variation bayonet except that the walnut grips were no longer sanded flush with the surrounding metal but allowed to remain "proud." Also, the horizontal ridges produced by the milling machine were no longer sanded out, refer to Figure 3-25.

The American Krag Rifle and Carbine

The **4th Variation** bayonet was identical to the 3rd Variation bayonet except that the rivets holding the walnut grips or scales onto the tang were no longer polished flush, refer to Figure 3-25. Instead they were rounded slightly above the retaining washers. The change was authorized on November 9, 1899.

NOTE: Earlier bayonets may show the features enumerated in Types 2, 3 and 4 as many were refurbished over the years.

The **5th Variation** bayonet was manufactured for the Krag Cadet Rifle, Model 1896. They were identical to the 2nd Variation bayonet except that the blades were 8.687 inches long. The fuller was 6.125 inches long and the true edge was 7.75 inches long. The 5th Variation bayonet was made to a separate design and was not merely a cutdown infantry bayonet. The 5th Variation bayonets issued to the U.S. Military Academy at West Point were all dated either 1895 or 1900 and the blades and metal parts were polished bright. A total of 1,372 were manufactured, 404 in 1895 and 968 in 1900. The first group issued in 1895 had flush rivet heads while the 1900 group had protruding rivet heads. These bayonets were used until 1904 when the new Model 1903 Springfield (.30-03) with rod bayonet was issued at West Point. When the cadets later received the Model 1903 Springfield (.30-06), instead of the Model 1905 Knife Bayonet, standard infantry length Krag service bayonets (Type 1, 4th Variation) were issued as the shorter bayonet was thought to look better with the '03 rifle. These last were replaced in 1963 with the M6 bayonet for the M14 rifle.

The **6th Variation** bayonet was a standard 4th Variation infantry bayonet issued to the U.S. Military Academy at West Point as replacements for the Type 5 bayonet. They were neither nickel nor chrome plated.

The **7th Variation** bayonet was a standard Krag bayonet with the bore enlarged to 0.655 inch. This was done at the Manila Arsenal to fit these bayonets to the early "U.S. Magazine Carbine, caliber .30, Model

The American Krag Rifle and Carbine

of 1899, altered for Knife Bayonet and Sling," also manufactured at the Manila Arsenal. Most of these rifles had the barrels turned down to 0.620 inch ahead of the front sight base to allow the standard Krag bayonet to be used. But a few of the early models did not have the turned-down muzzle as it was judged more efficient and cheaper to enlarge the bayonet's bore. But enlarging the bore weakened the mounting around the muzzle and the practice of turning down the rifle's muzzle was adopted instead, see Figure 3-26.

Fig. 3-26. Krag Bayonet with the bore enlarged (left) at the Manila Arsenal for use on the "Philippine Constabulary Rifle" compared to the standard Model 1892 bayonet bore. Sam Shacks collection.

NOTE: Very few of the rifles issued to the Philippine Constabulary have survived and likewise, few bayonets. The majority of production of the "U.S. Magazine Carbine, caliber .30, Model of 1899, altered for Knife Bayonet and Sling" had the turned-down rifle muzzle. Beware of fakes.

The **8th Variation** bayonet also had its bore enlarged, to 0.645 inch to fit the one hundred Board of Ordnance and Fortifications rifles with 26-inch barrels that were produced for field testing. These bayonets were marked "26" on the upper rear of the guard. The survival rate of these bayonets is not known and, of course, they are quite easy to fake.

The **Type 2** bayonet was the "Combination Intrenching Knife and Bayonet." The design was tested as a way to provide both items in one form attachable to the rifle. The original Type 1 Model 1892 bayonet

The American Krag Rifle and Carbine

had been selected partly because it could also be used as a knife, or to dig with and to cut brush. But the straight blade did not make a good general-purpose knife and it was too light to cut brush or scoop out a firing pit quickly.

On June 8, 1900, an allotment of $2,900.17 allowed the manufacture of a new design, a combined bowie knife and bayonet using the Krag Model 1892 grip and mounting system. The new design was not intended to serve as a machete to cut away jungle growth, but as an all-purpose knife and bayonet. Of course, it was used as a machete by the troops, failed miserably at that task and was roundly condemned. All were dated "1900," see Figure 3-27.

Fig. 3-27. Combination Intrenching Knife-Bayonet for the U.S. Krag Rifle, Jonathan Peck collection, courtesy of Little John's Auction Service.

The blade was 9.1 inches long, 1.75 inches wide and 0.125 inch thick. The point was clipped into the standard bowie knife configuration and the false edge was 2.75 inches long. It had two ground fullers on either side, which produced a thin diamond cross section to the blade. The metal parts were finished bright, the rivets were rounded, the wood grips were proud of the metal, showed slight milling marks and were oil finished. The bayonet weighed 0.92 pound.

The American Krag Rifle and Carbine

The **Type 3** "Bolo Bayonet" grew out of the troops' experience in the Philippines with the heavy jungle-like undergrowth. It was designed to serve both as a weapon and to cut through heavy undergrowth as a hand-held bolo knife. The blade had a slightly curved back and a deep belly on the cutting edge. It was 10.375 inches long, 2.1 inches wide and 0.218 inch thick. The false edge was 3.25 inches long and the true edge was 10.125 inches long. The point was a modified spear point, see Figure 3-28.

Fig. 3-28. Bolo Bayonet for the U.S. Krag Rifle. Watch for fakes which may have screws instead of rivets attaching the grips.

The bayonet was manufactured in one piece and marked according to the year of manufacture on the obverse, either "1902" or "1903," and "U.S." on the reverse. Neither the blade nor the scabbards were marked with a serial number as were the later Model 1909 and 1910 non-bayonet bolo knives. The standard Krag hilt and attaching method was used. The guard was polished bright but all other metal parts were blued. The wood grips were proud of the metal, the rivets were rounded and the wood was oiled. The bayonet weighed 1.4 pounds.

A total of fifty-six Bolo Bayonets and scabbards were manufactured, fifty in May 1902 and six the following year. Interestingly

The American Krag Rifle and Carbine

enough, all are dated "1902." Forty-eight of the first fifty were issued for field trials in the Philippines, one per company to several infantry regiments. The reports were favorable but the project was dropped when the Model 1903 Springfield Rifle was adopted.

NOTE: The Bolo Bayonet is probably one of the rarest, if not the rarest, of American bayonets. Collectors should beware of fakes. Forty-eight were reported to have been tested in the Philippines and the disposition of those forty-eight is not known with certainty. Insist on unimpeachable provenance.

Scabbards

The scabbard developed for the Krag bayonet was made of steel and blued. It was 12.687 inches long, 1.282 inches wide and 0.545 inch thick. The tip of the scabbard was formed into a ball and pierced to allow moisture to seep out. The separate throat was riveted to the mouth of the scabbard and three types of belt attachments were used to attach the bayonet and scabbard to the leather garrison belt and the various types of web cartridge belts, see Figure 3-29.

Fig. 3-29. Overall view of the Model 1892 Krag bayonet and scabbard. North Cape Publications collection.

The **Type 1** scabbard belt attaching device was a simple piece of spring steel attached to the back of the scabbard with a rivet to form a hook. The attaching arm was slipped over the top of the Mills web cartridge belt and between two cartridge loops and was free to revolve 360 degrees on the rivet. The back of the arm was 5.550 inches long and the

The American Krag Rifle and Carbine

front was 3.55 inches long. The mouth was shaped so that the bayonet could only enter one way. This scabbard was manufactured from the start of production in 1894 to April 1897 and referred to as the Model 1892 scabbard, see Figure 3-30.

The **Type 2** (Model 1896) scabbard was identical to the Type 1 except that the movement or oscillation of the scabbard was limited by a pin to 100 degrees, fifty to either side in April 1897, see Figure 3-31 (arrow). The Types 1 and 2 scabbard hooks had a habit of working loose from the belt when the soldier was moving quickly in the bent-over position, lying down or when it caught on undergrowth. It also frayed the belt rather badly.

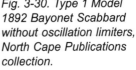

Fig. 3-30. Type 1 Model 1892 Bayonet Scabbard without oscillation limiters, North Cape Publications collection.

Fig. 3-31. Type 2 Model 1892 Bayonet Scabbard showing oscillation limiters. North Cape Publications collection.

The **Type 3** (Model 1899) scabbard had a positive belt attachment developed by Captain Rogers Birnie of the Ordnance Department. A wire spring was bent so that two arms formed a two-part keeper. The bottom of the wire keeper ran through a partial tube on the bottom of the attaching arm, and the ends were bent into half hooks that were captured in another tube at the top of the attaching arm. The two spring arms were 0.75 inch apart and could be pulled apart and folded down, see Figure 3-32, arrow. The belt was placed against the attaching arm and the

The American Krag Rifle and Carbine

spring arms folded up around a cartridge loop and hooked into the tube at the top. This bayonet scabbard was issued at West Point after 1907 to replace the Type 5 bayonet scabbard for the shorter Type 1, 4th Variation Krag bayonet in use to that time. Some 65,000 Type 1 and Type 2 scabbards were converted to this configuration.

The **Type 4** bayonet scabbard (Model 1903) was identical to the Type 3 with the Birnie belt attachment device with the single exception that the spring arms were bent inward so that they were only 0.5 inch apart, see Figure 3-33, arrow. The Type 4 scabbard was issued after the adoption of the Model 1903 nine-pocket infantry cartridge belts which used pockets rather than loops to hold the cartridges. Approximately 40,000 Model 1899 scabbards were altered to this configuration in and after 1905.

Fig. 3-32. Type 3 Model 1892 Bayonet Scabbard with the Birnie wire keeper attachment. North Cape Publications collection.

Fig. 3-33. Type 4 Model 1892 Bayonet Scabbard with the Birnie wire keeper attachment for the Model 1903 (and later) cartridge belts with pouches. Craig Riesch collection.

The **Type 5** scabbard was made for the short Cadet bayonet. It was 9.687 inches long and 1.25 inches wide. Three differ-

The American Krag Rifle and Carbine

ent belt attachments were used on the cadet bayonet scabbard. The **1st Variation** used the Type 2 limited swivel hook; the **2nd Variation** used the Birnie keeper and the **3rd Variation** used the Hoffman Attachment leather belt loop which was attached with two brass rivets to the swiveling arm, see Figure 3-34. The belt loop was doubled over so that it would slide over the waist belt worn by the cadets. The belt attachment was also limited in its swivel to 100 degrees. The leather was marked "Rock Island Arsenal/E.H.S."

Fig. 3-34. (L-r) USMA Cadet scabbards, Type 5, in 1, 2 and 3 variations. Craig Riesch collection.

The **Type 6** bayonet scabbard was shaped to fit the Combination Intrenching Knife-Bayonet and was made of blued steel. It was fitted with the Model 1899 Birnie belt attachment device, refer to Figure 3-27.

The **Type 7** bayonet scabbard was developed for the Bolo Bayonet. Again, it was made of steel and shaped to receive the heavy blade. The scabbard was also blued. It was fitted with the Model 1899 Birnie belt attachment device, refer to Figure 3-28.

Leather Adaptor for the Garrison and Other Leather Belts

The troops always had problems attaching the Krag bayonet scabbard to garrison and/or dress belts. A leather adaptor was developed and manufactured at Rock Island Arsenal between 1906 and 1909. The adaptor was made in two variations for the Model 1899 and the Model 1903 belt attachments. Both were russet in color, see Figure 3-35A.

The **Type 1** leather adaptor was 4.5 inches long and 2.75 inches wide with two wide rectangular cuts, each 0.375 inch from the top for the tubular fixtures on the attaching device, and two vertical slits for the

The American Krag Rifle and Carbine

belt. The first variation used with the Type 3 scabbard was unmarked.

The **Type 2** was 4.75 inches long and 2.75 inches wide and used with the Type 4 scabbard. The bottom slot was 0.5 inch lower than on the 1st Variation. These were marked "Rock Island/Arsenal/Year/Inspector's Initials." The most commonly seen inspector is "H.E.K."

Ammunition Carriers
McKeever Cartridge Box

In garrison or dress uniform, soldiers under arms wore the McKeever cartridge box on their garrison belts. The McKeever cartridge box was developed by First Lieutenant Samuel McKeever in the early 1870s. It was adopted by the Army in 1874 for the .50-70 and .45-70 cartridge used

Fig. 3-35A. Leather adaptor for garrison belt. Craig Riesch collection.

with the Models 1866, 1868, 1869, 1870 .50-70 and the Model 1873 .45-70 Springfield rifles. If use by cadets at the U.S. Military Academy at West Point is included, it is probably the longest-issued accoutrement in the U.S. Army, see Figure 3-35B.

Fig. 3-35B. McKeever Cartridge Box. Craig Riesch collection.

The McKeever cartridge box was made of heavy collar leather and opened like a clamshell. Two rows of 10 cartridges each were held in each half of the box by leather-backed loops that later gave way to linen, and then cotton loops. The loops were mounted on a bellows arrangement that allowed them to incline forward when the

The American Krag Rifle and Carbine

box was opened, see Figure 3-36. The McKeever cartridge boxes were made for the .50-70, .45-70, .30-40 and .30-03/.30-06 cartridges. The left side of the box (when worn) was bulged to provide a compartment for the screwdriver. The box was fastened closed at the top with a slit in a leather tab that slipped over a brass stud. The McKeever box was suspended from the garrison belt on two leather straps that were sewn and riveted to the

Fig. 3-36. McKeever Cartridge Box, marked "6th Cavalry," open. North Cape Publications collection.

back of the box. McKeever boxes issed for the Army were black and the front of the box was embossed "U S" while National Guard issue McKeever boxes for the .30-40 Krag cartridge were russet brown. Other boxes were later made for the U.S. Navy and Marines (dyed black). The most common National Guard and militia marked McKeever cartridge boxes were Pennsylvania (NGP), Massachusetts (MASS), New Jersey (NJ), New York (SNY) and Rhode Island (RIM). Other states used them as well, embossed with the state's initials, or the initials "NG" for National Guard.

The McKeever cartridge box was used during the entire Krag era by U.S. Army soldiers, West Point cadets and most National Guard units. West Point .30-40 McKeever boxes were to be blancoed white by regulation, but most photos extant of West Point cadets where the McKeever box is visible show it to be either black or russet. In the mid-1920s, when the supply of McKeever cartridge boxes ran out, a solid, nonfunctional box that resembled the McKeever was substituted.

Cartridge Belts

The cartridge belt was issued to troops when in the field. The standard cartridge belt was manufactured by the Mills & Orndorff Company (after 1905, the Mills Woven Cartridge Belt Company) and held one hundred .30-40 Krag cartridges in superimposed rows of fifty. During the Spanish-American War, contracts were let to other companies to produce cartridge belts on the Mills pattern. Belts holding either one hundred or fifty cartridges were produced by three other companies, Hurlbert, Spaulding and Russell.

Pattern 1894

The first cartridge belt developed for the Krag was the Pattern 1894 for infantry use and was the result of U.S. Patent No. 399,924, dated March 19, 1889, by T.C. Orndorff. It was manufactured for the .30-40 caliber Krag cartridge and had one hundred loops woven integrally into the belt, see Figure 3-37. The ends of the belt were protected from fraying by sheet brass tips that were folded over the ends and riveted

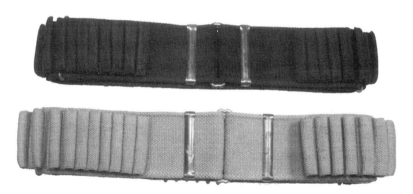

Fig. 3-37. Mills patent Pattern 1894 Infantry Cartridge Belt with 100 loops. Belts were dyed blue from 1894 to 1899. Craig Riesch collection.

The American Krag Rifle and Carbine

in place. Heavy brass wire retainers depended from the tips and clipped over the front of the belt between two cartridge loops. Their function was to prevent the weight of the ammunition from causing the belt to sag. The belt could be adjusted for length by folding the ends around and hooking the wire retainers between two appropriate cartridge loops. Sheet brass keepers were slipped over the folded ends and pushed as close to the "C" keeper as possible. Five brass grommets were mounted in the left side of the belt for attaching equipment.

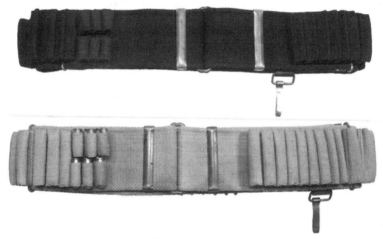

Fig. 3-38. Mills patent Pattern 1894 Mounted Cartridge Belt with six pistol cartridge loops added. Craig Riesch collection.

A variation of the Pattern 1894 belt was manufactured for mounted use, see Figure 3-38. It had one hundred rifle cartridge loops and two sets of three loops, one above the other, on the right-hand side of the belt for the .38 Long Colt revolver ammunition. A leather chape was fastened with two brass rivets to the bottom edge of the belt at the seventeenth cartridge loop (starting from the left side), which held a brass rectangle to which the Pattern 1881/1885 Stuart cavalry saber sling could be attached.

The American Krag Rifle and Carbine

Mills belts for the .30-40 Krag cartridge were marked on the brass sheet tips:

PAT. MILLS & ORNDORFF
AUG. 26,'67   MAR. 19,'89
JULY 31,'77   OCT. 31,'93
DEC. 28,'80   SEPT. 11,'94

Three types of keepers were used. The **Type 1** was the Pattern 1886 belt plate. It was cast from brass at the Watervliet Arsenal, New York, in late 1886. It was referred to as the "loose loop" or the "Whittemore Pattern," after the Watervliet commander who designed it. It was intended for use by Regulars but was also used by Volunteers during the Spanish-American War. Its sides were rolled so that they would hook over "C" keepers that were slipped over the folded ends, see Figure 3-39.

Figs. 3-39 & 3-40. (L-r) Pattern 1886 (Watervliet Arsenal) and Pattern 1887 (T.C. Orndorff Co.) Belt Plates. North Cape Publications collection.

The **Type 2** plate was stamped from sheet brass and manufactured by the T.C. Orndorff Company and designated the Pattern 1887. The initials "U S" were stamped within a borderless oval recessed into the face of the plate and the background around the letters was lightly stippled. The keeper had a semicircular recessed area for the tongue, see Figure 3-40.

The **Type 3** closure had a "hook and slide" fastener, which formed a rather rectangular "C" and was made of brass wire 0.180 inch in diameter. The back of the "C" or "hook" was caught in the bight of the left side of the belt where it was folded under so that its top

The American Krag Rifle and Carbine

and bottom curves enclosed the left side. The right side of the belt was squeezed together and slipped into the open front of the "C" or "hook." A brass keeper was pushed to within an inch or so of the belt end. The closure, patented in 1894 (the "Sept. 11, '94" date on the belt tip), was easy and cheap to make and rather efficient to use. And no separate keeper was needed, see Figure 3-41.

Hurlbert Cartridge Belt

During the Spanish-American War, the rapid in-

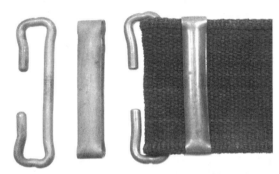

Fig. 3-41. The most common fastener for the 100-round .30-40 cartridge belt was the "C" closure.

crease in Regular and Volunteer forces far outdistanced the ability of the Mills Company to manufacture cartridge belts. At least three other companies received contracts to produce similar belts: Hurlbert, Spaulding and Russell. As the Mills Company held the patents for the integral weave of cartridge loop and belt, all three competitors produced belts with the cartridge loops sewn on. Hurlbert belts were probably the sturdiest and best constructed of the three competitive types. While the belts are not quite as thick, they were tightly woven and made of heavy cotton thread. Like the Mills belts, they had sheet brass keepers on each end with integral wire retainers. Hurlbert belts were tan and had three blue horizontal stripes running the length of the belt. They used the same type of fastenings as the Mills Pattern 1894.

Two types of Hurlbert cartridge belts were manufactured: The Type 1 belt had one hundred loops in two superimposed rows and the Type 2 had only one row of fifty cartridge loops. Hurlbert belts were marked in ink, "100 Loops/30 Caliber" or "50 Loops 45," see Figure 3-42.

The American Krag Rifle and Carbine

Fig. 3-42. Hurlbert 100-round double-row .30-40 cartridge belt. Craig Riesch collection.

Spaulding and Russell Cartridge Belts

Spaulding and Russell belts were similar but made of thinner material and are not as common as the Hurlbert belts. Spaulding belts were a tan-orange color with sixty khaki-colored loops, see Figure 3-43. Russell belts were tan. Spaulding belts were marked with India ink which quickly wore off. Russell belts were stamped on the brass tips.

Fig. 3-43. Spaulding 60-round single-row .30-40 cartridge belt for mounted troops. Craig Riesch collection.

NOTE: According to the 1916 Mills Catalog, the Mills Company produced a single-row .30-40 cartridge belt with three blue stripes woven into the light khaki-colored fabric. Examine the brass belt tips to determine if they were made by Mills or Hurlbert.

Parkhurst Belt

When rifles and carbines (100 of each) equipped with the Parkhurst clip-feeding device were manufactured for field testing in 1900, the

The American Krag Rifle and Carbine

order was given to manufacture four hundred cartridge belts with pockets to hold five .30-40 cartridges in a metal clip, two clips to a pocket. The Navy had issued a pocketed cartridge belt for the 6 mm Model 1895 Winchester-Lee rifles, but the Parkhurst belt was the Army's first, see Figure 3-44.

Fig. 3-44. U.S. Army trial cartridge belt with pouches (Type 1) for ammunition in the Parkhurst clip. This was the U.S. Army's first pocketed cartridge belt. Craig Riesch collection.

The Parkhurst belt was made by taking a standard Mills cartridge belt and removing loops and sewing on pockets. Two types were manufactured. The **Type 1** had only two pockets at either end of the belt and eighty cartridge loops. Ten loops at each end were removed and the pockets sewn to the belt in their place.

The **Type 2** Parkhurst belt had all one hundred cartridge loops removed from a Mills belt and ten pockets sewn onto the belt in their place. The pockets were fastened with plain brass snaps on both the Type 1 and Type 2.

The fastener for both types of belt was the standard "C" closure rather than a metal belt plate.

Mills Experimental Cartridge Belt

In 1901, an unknown number of experimental cartridge belts were acquired from the Mills & Orndorff Company. Because the woven cotton material of the belt and cartridge loop became both hard and

218

smooth with use, the cartridges had a propensity for working their way out of the loops. It was thought that by modifying standard infantry 100-round cartridge belts with flaps over every five sets of double-cartridge loops, the cartridges would not work loose and fall out. The flaps were made at Rock Island Arsenal but did not prove satisfactory and the design was not adopted, see Figure 3-45.

Fig. 3-45. Mills & Orndorff Experimental Cartridge Belt. The left flap is marked Rock Island Arsenal. Craig Riesch collection.

Model 1903 Mounted Cartridge Belt and Model 1903 Infantry Belt

The first pocketed cartridge belt to be adopted for general issue was the nine-pocket belt for mounted troops approved in 1903 (Report of the Chief of Ordnance to the Secretary of War). It was the forerunner of a long line of cartridge belts that are still in use today. An 80-round belt had been developed by Mills & Orndorff Company but was rejected. A nine-pocket belt submitted by Russell was accepted as the Model 1903. The nine pockets held two clips of five .30-03 cartridges for the New Model 1903 Springfield Rifle. The mounted belts had a leather-reinforced chape between the second and third pockets on the left for the saber hanger, see Figure 3-46.

The infantry variation had nine pockets and no chape, see Figure 3-47. Both variations of the Russell-manufactured belt were not marked. These belts were also used to hold loose M1898 cartridges.

219

The American Krag Rifle and Carbine

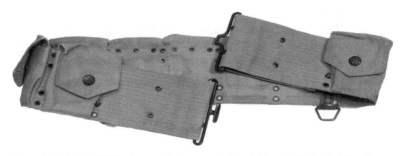

Fig. 3-46. Model 1903 nine-pocket mounted cartridge belt. Craig Riesch collection.

No doubt, both variations were used from 1903 to 1907 by doughboys and troopers to hold Krag cartridges loose in the pockets as the issue of the Model 1903 Springfield was delayed by a series of changes until 1907.

Fig. 3-47. Model 1903 nine-pocket Infantry cartridge belt. Craig Riesch collection.

NOTE: Many collectors mistakenly refer to these belts as the Model 1904 Mills belt. In fact, they were manufactured by Russell. The belts had no markings of any kind but were officially adopted in 1903.

The American Krag Rifle and Carbine

Wristlet

To increase the ammunition-carrying capacity of the individual soldier, T.C. Orndorff developed a webbing band with cartridge loops to be worn around one or both wrists. U.S. Patent #635,145 was granted on October 17, 1899; in 1900, the Mills & Orndorff Company manufactured 5,000 "wristlets" for trial by the U.S. Army. The wristlets proved both cumbersome and heavy and very unpopular with the troops; at the conclusion of testing, the idea was dropped, see Figure 3-48.

Bandoliers

In the same vein, a bandolier to be looped over the left shoulder crosswise about the body was developed. The inspiration came from British mounted troops in South Africa during the Boer War who wore their heavy leather ammunition belts in this manner because they were more comfortable. The Mills bandolier was issued primarily to mounted troops, see Figure 3-49.

Frankford Arsenal produced the cloth bandolier with six pockets holding ten cartridges each. The bandolier was made of light cotton with a close weave and was dyed tan. Each pocket was sewn closed at the top with a pull-strip

Fig. 3-48. The Mills-Orndorff wristlets with cartridge loops. The troops found them to be uncomfortable and cumbersome and they were never adopted. This catalog photo shows a soldier wearing both the wristlets and the 100-round bandolier.

to open it. Since the cartridges were loose in cardboard packets, the pockets had to be fastened closed until use, see Figure 3-50.

The American Krag Rifle and Carbine

Fig. 3-49. Mills & Orndorff 100-round bandolier for mounted troops. Craig Riesch collection.

In 1917 as the Krag rifle was being reissued for service during the Great War to Railroad Engineer troops and for training, a contract was given to the Remington Arms-UMC company to manufacture .30-40 ammunition. The ammunition was packaged in cloth bandoliers that held sixty cartridges in six pockets. The bandoliers are marked "60 Ball Cartridges, Cal. .30, Model of 1898, Remington Arms-U.M.C. Co. Muzzle Velocity at 53 1966 feet, Year date." Dates observed are 1917, 1918 and 1919.

Fig. 3-50. Frankford Arsenal bandolier holding sixty cartridges in six pockets.

The American Krag Rifle and Carbine

Ammunition Crates

The .30-40 Krag ammunition manufactured at either the Frankford Arsenal or by outside contractors was packed in wooden crates of 1,000 rounds (Frankford Arsenal) or 1,200 rounds (Remington-UMC, Winchester and others) for distribution. The Frankford Arsenal 1,000-cartridge crates contained fifty cardboard packets each holding twenty loose cartridges. The later 1,200-round crates contained twenty bandoliers holding sixty cartridges in six pockets. Each pocket held ten cartridges in cardboard packets.

The wooden ammunition crates manufactured at Frankford Arsenal during the period of Krag-Jørgensen service were made of 0.75-inch-thick pine boards, see Figure 3-51. The top was made of 0.50-inch-thick pine. The crate was 13 inches wide by 17.85 inches long by

Fig. 3-51. Frankford Arsenal shipping crate for the U.S. .30-40 cartridge. North Cape Publications collection.

The American Krag Rifle and Carbine

7.75 inches high. The crate had a strip of wood on either end for a handle. The top was held on by eight "J" bolts and wing nuts. The crate was sealed at Frankford Arsenal with wire seals on the front and rear of the crate before shipping.

The top of a specimen crate was marked "U.S. NO. 1501 2 WT. 75 LBS INV. FEBRUARY–20–1900."

The front and rear sides were marked "1000 BALL CAR-TRIDGES/MODEL 1898 RIFLE/CAL. .30. L. & R. POWDER/ ..FRANKFORD ARSENAL.."

The side panels were marked "MODEL 1898 RIFLE/CAL. .30." Above the handle was stamped into the wood the actual date of manufacture.

Fig. 3-52. Remington UMC shipping crate for the U.S. .30-40 cartridge in bandoliers. Ed Cote collection.

Before and during the Great War, contracts were let to other ammunition companies to produce .30-40 Krag ammunition for distribution to the regular Army until 1907 and to the National Guard and various military schools, see Figure 3-52. Between 1917 and 1919 when the Krag was used to equip combat support units such as Railroad Engineer troops as well as used for training, ammunition was packaged in both 20-round cardboard boxes and 60-round bandoliers,

The American Krag Rifle and Carbine

as described above, and shipped in wood ammunition crates. The crate held 1,200 cartridges in 60-round bandoliers. The end panels were removable and each was fastened with six "J" bolts and wing nuts. The crate was wire sealed at the factory before shipping. The crate was marked "1200 BALL CARTRIDGES CAL. 30/MODEL 1898/THE REMINGTON ARMS UNION METALLIC CAR-TRIDGE CO. INC./ U.M.C. BRIDGEPORT WORKS – BRIDGE-PORT, CONN. U.S.A."

Appendix A
Exploded View and Parts List
U.S. Krag Rifle and Carbine

1. Butt Plate Screw (lower)
2. Butt Plate Screw (Tang)
3. Butt Trap Cap
4. Butt Trap Cap Pin
5. Butt Plate
6. Stock (carbine)
7. Stock (rifle)
8. Lower Band Swivel
9. Guard Screw (rear)
10. Guard Screw (front)
11. Guard (trigger)
12. Band Spring
13. Handguard (carbine)
14. Barrel Band (carbine)
15. Lower Band Sling Swivel
16. Lower Band (rifle)
17. Stacking Swivel
18. Upper Barrel Band (rifle)
19. Bayonet Mount
20. Finger Groove
21. Receiver Bed
22. Bolt Handle Seat
23. Lightening (Air) Channels
24. Barrel (carbine-22 inches)
25. Barrel (rifle-30 inches)
26. Handguard (rifle)
27. Receiver
28. Ejector
29. Ejector Pin
30. Cutoff
31. Trigger
32. Trigger Pin
33. Sear
34. Sear Spring
35. Carrier & Follower
36. Gate
37. Magazine Spring
38. Hinge Bar
39. Side Plate
40. Striker
41. Firing Pin/Cocking Piece
42. Mainspring
43. Bolt Body
44. Extractor Pin
45. Extractor
46. Bolt Sleeve
47. Extractor Rivet
48. Safety Lock
49. Rear Sight
50. Front Sight Stud
51. Front Sight Blade
52. Front Sight Pin
53. Rear Sight Screw Holes
54. Rear Sight Screw (rear)
55. Rear Sight Screw (front)

Detailed exploded views are shown in Chapter 2 for the Stock (Figure 2-10), Barrel, Receiver, Trigger Assembly, and Bolt.

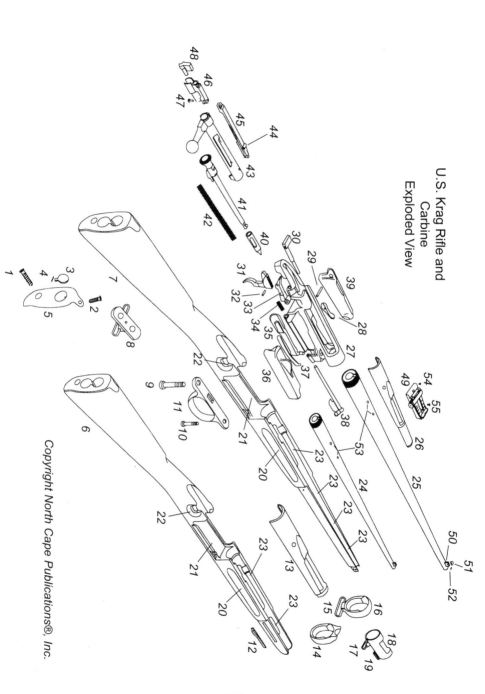

U.S. Krag Rifle and
Carbine
Exploded View

227

Appendix B
Krag Rifle and Carbine Serial Numbers

Unfortunately for collectors, no exact list of serial numbers of the Krag rifle and carbine was ever kept by the Ordnance Department. The commander of the Springfield Armory made quarterly reports to the Chief of Ordnance which included totals of rifles and carbines manufactured during the previous quarter. The Chief of Ordnance then made annual reports which included totals of rifles and carbines to the Secretary of War. But it is not known exactly how information was gathered for those reports, analyzed and verified. For instance, were the rifles and carbines reported as completed actually in various stages of assembly or were they arms which had been completed and forwarded to stores? Enough inconsistencies between the various reports and store keepers records exist to prevent an exact accounting at the remove of 100 to 110 years.

The methods used to gather data were not consistent and varied with the different commanding officers and Chiefs of Ordnance. Keep in mind that there were no mechanical adding machines, let alone computers, in the 1890s and early 1900s. All figures were entered into day books or production records, in pencil, by hand. When a report was called for, the data was compiled from these records and added, again by hand. The possibility of errors creeping in was high.

The primary sources for the *suggested* chart of "U.S. Krag Rifle and Carbine Serial Numbers" shown in Table B-1 are the "Report of Principal Operations at Springfield Armory for the Fiscal Years 1894 through 1900" and "Annual Report, Fiscal Year Ending . . ." from 1901 through 1904." To the author's knowledge, this is the first *published* attempt at a monthly serial number chart for the American Krag.

These reports contain a great deal of data that can be used to construct a chart of serial numbers produced over time. They contain statements regarding the average number of arms produced daily for the previous fiscal year as well as occasional daily figures for various

228

The American Krag Rifle and Carbine

periods. We also know that the Springfield Armory worked a 5.5- or 6-day work week (Monday through Saturday noon) in eight-hour shifts. Employees were given six holidays off (New Year's Day, Washington's Birthday, Decoration Day, Independence Day, Labor Day and Christmas). The plant also shut down for ten working days annually at the beginning of July. The result is a work year of approximately 290 days.

Two questions exist with quantifying total Krag production: 1) what was the total number of Model 1892 rifles produced, and 2) what was the total number of all Krags produced?

The Annual Reports of the Chief of Ordnance state that 2,951 Model 1892 rifles were produced in FY 1894 and 14,491 in FY 1895, plus four prototype carbines, plus the 404 Cadet Rifles made the following year which total 17,850. We also know that the Springfield Armory was producing 40 rifles per day to the end of August 1894 and 60 finished rifles per day afterward on a 5.5- or 6-day work week.

If the production rate of 60 per day continued to the end of Calendar Year 1895 (first half of FY 1896), another 7,920 Model 1892 rifles would have been produced, bringing the total to 25,770 Model 1892 arms, which runs over into the serial number range ascribed to the Model 1896 carbines and even some Model 1896 rifles, the earliest of which observed with any degree of reliability to date is serial number 24,460.

Regarding the total number of Krag rifles and carbines manufactured, the numbers vary widely according to various writers and researchers from a low of 476,045 (January 1904) to a high of 499,036, the latter listed in the Springfield Research's "Serial Numbers of Known U.S. Krags." But the U.S. Government's officially reported number of total service rifles and carbines is 474,693 with Krag manufacturing ending in November 1903 as reported in the "Annual Report of the Chief of Ordnance to the Secretary of War, Vol. 10," for Fiscal Year 1904.

This figure is very important as the U.S. Government paid royalties to the Norwegian government on all service rifles manufactured. Service rifles did not include experimental arms, Cadet rifles,

The American Krag Rifle and Carbine

26-inch barrel rifles or rifles remanufactured from existing arms such as the short rifles used by the Philippine Constabulary and by school military programs, or .22 Caliber Gallery Rifles. The total for these brings the number manufactured to 477,580 (excluding the Constabulary and School short rifles which were converted service carbines). Subtracting the total number of non-service rifles manufactured from new parts leaves a figure of 475,516 which is only 823 more arms for which royalties were paid.

But we know that the majority of the .22 Caliber Gallery Rifles manufactured in 1905–1906 had serial numbers in the 476,000–478,400 range. Other rifles with serial numbers in the 499,000 range have been reported. There might be several explanations: 1) recording errors; 2) rifles assembled from spare parts, including receivers, at a later date; 3) rifles rebuilt using new receivers taken from inventory after official production ceased in November 1903; 4) more rifles were built than were reported until the inventory of spare parts was depleted. Until a satisfactory answer is found, the author prefers to take the Government at their word (in this matter only) and offers the following monthly chart of serial numbers as a reasonable *approximation,* based on a total of 474,693 arms produced, plus an additional 2,064 non-royalty arms.

When using B-1 to identify a change in a part, keep in mind that approval given on a particular date did not mean that it was introduced to the production line immediately. Weeks or months might be needed to complete drawings and tooling before the change was put into production. Also, parts already in inventory were used up first before new parts were introduced unless it was a question of safety.

Finally, it is emphasized again that the term "circa" means "on or about," and it is applied throughout this book to serial numbers in exactly that way.

The American Krag Rifle and Carbine

Table B-1 U.S. Krag Rifle and Carbine Serial Numbers (Calendar Year — End of Month)	
1894	
January 1	1 and 2
April	160
May	250
June	911 Production reported as 40 per day
July	1,814
August	2,504 1,600 rifles reported finished and ready for issue
September	2,934 2,037 rifles reported completed April 28, 1894 Daily production of 60 per day reported to end of FY 1895
October	5,254
November	6,678
December	7,894
1895	
January	9,211
February	10,531
March	11,851
April	13,171
May	14,491
June	15,811
July	17,329 69 per day to end of FY 1896 (10,535 rifles, 7,111 carbines and 404 Cadet rifles) in 264 working days
August	18,847

Table B-1, cont. U.S. Krag Rifle and Carbine Serial Numbers (Calendar Year— End of Month)	
1895, cont.	
September	20,365
October	21,883
November	23,401
December	24,919 Model 1892 production ends, Model 1896 begins
1896	
January	26,437
February	
March	27,196 Mid-February to May 1, no arms assembled due to barrel shortage
April	
May	31,596 Assembly resumed at 200 per day
June	35,996
July	38,196 Assembly reaches 300 per day
August	40,836 Resumed 120 per day to end of FY 1897
September	43,476
October	46,116
November	48,756
December	51,396
1897	
January	54,036
February	56,676

The American Krag Rifle and Carbine

Table B-1, cont. U.S. Krag Rifle and Carbine Serial Numbers (Calendar Year— End of Month)	
1897, cont.	
March	59,316
April	61,966
May	64,596
June	67,236
July	69,876 29,566 M1896 Rifles & 12,022 carbines mfg'd to date.
August	72,156
September	75,156
October	77,796
November	80,436
December	83,076
1898	
January	85,716
February	88,356 U.S.S. Maine sunk in Havana Harbor
March	91,436 Daily production increased to 140
April	94,516 War decalred on Spain, April 21
May	97,776 Daily production increased to 160, May 26. Commodore Dewey defeats Spanish fleet at Manila Bay (May 1)
June	101,396 Daily production increased to 200 per day, June 13; 240 June 20, and 280, June 26; Model 1898 production begins; U.S. V Corps lands in Cuba, June 20; First U.S. troops land in Philippines, June 30.
July	115,024 Daily production increased to 300, July 11; 340 July 20. First Model 1898 completed July 8, circa 109,000. Battle of San Juan and Kettle Hills, July 1–2.

The American Krag Rifle and Carbine

Table B-1, cont. U.S. Krag Rifle and Carbine Serial Numbers (Calendar Year— End of Month)	
1898, cont.	
August	124,421 Daily production increased to 363, August 13; Daily production to 405 to end of FY 1899; Peace accord signed between Spain and the United States, August 13.
September	133,331
October	142,421
November	151,151
December	160,061 Philippines ceded by Spain to the United States
1899	
January	168,971
February	177,881 Philippine insurgency begins
March	186,791
April	195,681
May	204,591
June	213,501
July	217,901 Daily production reduced to 200 to end of FY 1900
August	222,301
September	226,701 Model 1899 carbine production begins
October	231,101
November	239,901 Issue of rifles to U.S. Navy/Marine Corps begins
December	240,101

The American Krag Rifle and Carbine

Table B-1, cont. **U.S. Krag Rifle and Carbine Serial Numbers** **(Calendar Year— End of Month)**	
1900	
January	244,301
February	248,701
March	253,501
April	257,901
May	262,301
June	266,701 Boxers murder German Ambassador in Peking, June 20. Siege of foreign legations begins
July	272,201 Daily production increased to 250 through FY 1901; 9th U.S. Infantry and Marine Battalion lands in China
August	277,701 August 12-14, siege of foreign legations in Peking ends
September	283,201
October	288,701 Parkhurst rifle and carbine production
November	294,201
December	299,701
1901	
January	305,201
February	310,701
March	316,201
April	321,701 Board of Ordnance and Fortifications rifle production; Philippine insurrection deemed under control
May	327,201
June	332,701

The American Krag Rifle and Carbine

Table B-1, cont. U.S. Krag Rifle and Carbine Serial Numbers (Calendar Year — End of Month)	
1901	
July	338,201 U.S. military rule ends in Philippines
August	343,710
September	349,201 President McKinley shot, T.R. becomes President
October	354,701
November	360,201 U.S. Army War College founded
December	365,701
1902	
January	371,201
February	376,701
March	382,201
April	387,701 Moro insurgents defeated in Philippines
May	393,201 American military occupation of Cuba ends.
June	398,701
July	404,201 61,638 rifles and 1 carbine mfg'd in FY 1903
August	409,451
September	414,451 U.S. Marines land in Panama to safeguard railways
October	419,576
November	424,701 Panamanian civil war ends, U.S. forces withdrawn
December	429,826

The American Krag Rifle and Carbine

Table B-1, cont. U.S. Krag Rifle and Carbine Serial Numbers (Calendar Year — End of Month)	
1903	
January	434,951
February	440,076
March	445,201
April	450,326
May	455,451
June	460,576
July	463,475 17,424 rifles mfg'd in 1st half of FY 1904
August	466,374
September	469,273
October	472,172
November	474,693 Production officially ends
Production of the Model 1898 Krag ended in November 1903. How much longer the Krag rifle continued to be manufactured and assembled is a matter of conjecture. If in fact 499,036 were built, production would have continued into June 1904 at the same rate as in 1903, interfering with the start of Model 1903 production.	

The American Krag Rifle and Carbine

U.S. KRAG RIFLE AND CARBINE MODELS, SERIAL NUMBER RANGES

Krag rifle and carbine models were manufactured in eleven different models. Their approximate serial number ranges are shown in Table B-2.

Again, it must be emphasized that the ranges shown are estimated based on observation, various Ordnance Department reports, and work done by previous authorities. Particularly confusing are the serial number ranges for the Model 1898 and 1899 carbines. As the same receiver was used for both rifle and carbine, they were drawn from inventory according to production needs and so are indistiguishable. The ranges presented are the result of observation, records kept by others, and serial numbers reported in the "Serial Numbers of Known U.S. Krags," *Serial Numbers of U.S. Martial Arms.*

An overlap will be noted between the end of the Model 1892 rifle and the start of Model 1896 carbine/rifle production. M1896 carbines with the lightening hole have been observed in the 21,500 serial number range with receivers marked "1895." Model 1896 rifles in the 24,200 serial number range have also been observed.

Table B-2 U.S. Krag Rifle and Carbine Serial Number Ranges	
Model	**Serial Number Range**
M1892 Rifle	1 through 24,500 (1)
M1892 Carbine	1,015-1,575
M1896 Cadet Rifle	Circa serial #s 24,200 through 35,200 (2)
M1896 Carbine (2, 3)	21,500 through 39,500 (4) 61,000 through 75,000 82,472 through 87,498
M1896 Rifle	24,460 through 109,000
M1898 Rifle	109,100 through 476,045 (4)
M1898 Carbine	113,600 through 139,000 (2, 4, 5)
M1899 Carbine (2)	223,371 through 230,739 244,218 through 268,055 279,531 through 291,529 301,418 through 316,722 341,602 through 362,433 420,710 through 420,810
Board of Ordnance and Fortifications Rifles	385,120 through 387,869
Model 1898 .22 Caliber Gallery Rifles	475,650 through 478,067 (2, 4)
Parkhurst Loading Device Rifles and Carbines	288,273 thrugh 289,154

1. Approximate range.
2. Observed range. Arms within these ranges are not necessarily consecutive.
3. M1896 carbines with serial numbers in the 5-digit range have been recorded. They may have been used in ammunition testing in 1895.
4. Serial numbers reported in *Serial Numbers of Known U.S. Krags,* F. Mallory, Springfield Research Service.
5. M1898 carbines in the mid-150,000 to 160,300 range have been observed.

Appendix C
Ammunition for the U.S. Krag Rifle
and Carbine
BY ED FURLER, JR.

For several hundred years, black powder had been the only available propellant for use in the early firearms. However, black powder, due to its chemical nature, left much to be desired. When it is ignited, not all of its components are converted into gas, and the resulting incomplete combustion forms a thick cloud of smoke and heavy barrel fouling. Also, black powder was unable to produce the high velocities and flat trajectories needed for accurate shooting at longer ranges.

Then in 1885 came a discovery which would open up a whole new world in ammunition development when a French chemist, Paul Marie Eugene Vieille, invented the first true smokeless powder. There had been smokeless type powders developed prior to that, but they had all used a nitroglycerine base and were neither totally smokeless, nor truly a powder. One good example of this is the Cordite used by the British in their .303 Enfield cartridge.

The invention of a true smokeless powder by Monsieur Vieille had opened the way worldwide for the adoption of small caliber high velocity rifles. France completed the design of a new small bore (8 mm) smokeless powder rifle, the Lebel, in three months in 1886. Switzerland, Germany, Great Britain were not far behind. By 1891 almost all of the major nations, except the United States, had adopted smokeless powder cartridges.

However, the United States military, which was still armed with the single-shot "Trapdoor" Springfield and its black powder .45-70 cartridge, had investigated the adoption of a small bore smokeless powder cartridge. Tests were conducted in 1889 and 1890 at Springfield Armory with a .30-caliber cartridge and different types of black and smokeless powders. The selection of the .30 caliber was more or

The American Krag Rifle and Carbine

less made at random with Col. A. R. Buffington stating in his October 7, 1890 report to the Chief of Ordnance: "The even .30 caliber was chosen as being the smallest admissable, all things considered, not for any special principle involved. . ."

A board of officers met on December 16, 1890, at the Army Building in New York City to select a repeating rifle. The date of July 1, 1892 had been chosen by the Secretary of War as the cutoff date for the submission of arms to be considered. In the meantime, Frankford Arsenal had been hard at work developing a .30-caliber cartridge for use in the new rifle.

This cartridge had a 220-grain metal-jacketed round-nose bullet originally backed by 35 to 40 grains of Belgian Wettern powder to give a muzzle velocity of 2,000 fps from the 30-inch barrel. The Belgian powder was replaced in May 1894 by the American-made Peyton Powder as well as Leonard, DuPont and Laflin & Rand W. A. (the W. A. standing for Whistler and Aspinwall). These latter four powders had a nitroglycerine base and while producing good ballistics, their nitroglycerine base tended to cause excessive bore erosion.

The case itself was rimmed, bottle-necked and made originally from a thin brass blank, but this made for a weak case and it was replaced with a case made from a thicker blank and became the Model 1895 cartridge. In the early years of production the primer was corrosive and mercuric, a factor which prevented the reloading of the case as the mercury weakened the brass case. This problem led to the development, and, in February 1898, the adoption of the non-mercuric and corrosive Frankford Arsenal H48 primer compound. Also, in an effort to protect the brass case from the effects of the corrosive powder, Frankford Arsenal continued tin plating the cases, a practice which continued until 1900.

As adopted in 1892, the bullet for the Krag cartridge weighed 220 grains, and had a round nose. A variety of materials were used for the bullet jacket. The original jacket was made of German silver, but that proved unsatisfactory and was replaced with a jacket consisting of a layer of low-carbon Swedish steel encased in cupronickel. Some jacket

Fig. C-1. Cartridge, Ball, Caliber .30, Model of 1898 as manufactured by Remington-UMC Company. Roy Marcot collection.

material omitted the Swedish steel and used only the cupronickel, a copper-based alloy with a 10 to 30 percent nickel content. This alloy would be used until the Frankford Arsenal ended production of the .30-40 Krag cartridge around 1914. These bullets, when originally adopted, had a smooth jacket and were not lubricated; however in 1896 a single-cannelured bullet was adopted, followed by a three-cannelured bullet in July 1900.

The American Krag Rifle and Carbine

In an effort to improve accuracy, Frankford Arsenal in 1903 adopted the Cole bullet. This was a 220-grain bullet with a more stream-lined shape than the standard service round. It was not cannelured but retained the cupronickel jacket of the previous bullets. Frankford also issued a new service round with an increased muzzle velocity of 2,200 fps as opposed to the 2,000 fps of the original cartridge. The powder used in it originally was Peyton powder, but this was replaced with Laflin & Rand W. A. which produced lower chamber pressures. This new load was issued to the troops beginning in October 1899, but within a year its usage was discontinued due to reports coming in about broken locking lugs. Its manufacture was ended in March 1900 and in August of that same year the Ordnance Department ordered the 3,500,000 rounds reloaded to the older specifications.

In addition to the service, guard, gallery and blank cartridges, Frankford Arsenal also produced a multiball round in 1902 for the Krag in an attempt to increase the lethality of the

Fig. C-2. A Frankford Arsenal package of 20 empty, primed shells, ready for reloading.

round. They also produced empty cartridge cases (Figure C-2), bullets and primers which were packaged and shipped to various National Guard units. This allowed armorers to reload cartridges, particularly gallery cartridges, at some savings, primarily in transportation costs. The Regular Army did not reload service cartridges.

One of the final cartridge types to be produced at Frankford was the handloaded Palma Match round. The arsenal loaded 10,000 rounds in 1907 for use by the U. S. Palma Trophy Team, but the National Rifle Association decided to use a commercially loaded round from the Union Metallic Cartridge Company. This round used a 203-grain pointed bullet which had a better trajectory than the round-nose government bullet.

The American Krag Rifle and Carbine

During the Spanish-American War, Frankford Arsenal was unable to keep up with the demand for ammunition. Contracts were issued to the Union Metallic Cartridge Company, U.S. Cartridge Company, Winchester and Kynoch. Kynoch used Cordite powder and their cases have a "C" on the head stamp and are dated either "1898" or "1899." Cordite did not burn completely in the Krag case and was withdrawn. The other companies had their troubles as well. After several apparently spontaneous eruptions of Winchester ammunition in cartridge belts, that ammunition was withdrawn from service. And U.S. Cartridge Company ammunition earned a reputation for misfires.

Again, in the years leading up to, and during World War I, contracts were issued by the Ordnance Department to various American commercial ammunition companies to produce both service and blank rounds. The companies included Remington-UMC, Winchester, Peters and U.S. Cartridge Company. This time the commercial ammunition seemed to perform better and none of it appears to have been withdrawn for reasons of unsuitability.

The .30-40 Krag went through a whole range of so-called speciality loads, as has every cartridge ever adopted by the United States military. These will be covered in detail in the following listing. With the adoption of the .30-Model 1906 cartridge, the .30-40 Krag fell into disuse by the military, but was quickly picked up by the hunting public. A wide variety of hunting loads soon followed as did the number of hunting rifles chambered for this fine cartridge. It was found that the .30-40 Krag was suitable for use on most large game in North America and became a very popular cartridge which is still loaded and used to this day.

To this day, the largest elk taken in North America is listed in the Boone & Crockett register as having been downed with a .30-40 Krag round.

The following photographs are from the cartridge collection of Craig Riesch.

The American Krag Rifle and Carbine

U.S. Krag Rifle and Carbine Service Cartridges

Cartridge, Ball, Caliber .30, Model of 1892
Round-nose bullet, German silver or cupronickel steel jacket.
35 to 42 grains Wettern, Peyton or Leonard powder.
Muzzle velocity 2,000 fps.
Corrosive and mercuric primer, tinned case.

Cartridge, Ball, Caliber .30, Model of 1895
Round-nose bullet, cupronickel or cupronickel steel jacket.
34 to 42 grains Peyton, Leonard, Laflin & Rand W. A., and
DuPont powder.
Muzzle velocity 2,000 fps.
Single cannelured bullet, tinned case. Figure C-3.

Fig. C-3. Cartridge, Ball, Caliber .30, Model of 1895.

Cartridge, Ball, Caliber .30, Model of 1898
Round-nose bullet, cupronickel or cupronickel steel jacket.
30.5 to 42 grains Peyton, Laflin & Rand W. A., Leonard and
DuPont powder.
Muzzle velocity 2,000 fps.
Non-mercuric Frankford Arsenal H48 primer adopted. Figure C-4.

Fig. C-4. Cartridge, Ball, Caliber .30, Model of 1898.

Blank Cartridge, Whole Case, Caliber .30, Model of 1893
No bullet, extended case.
65 grains of black powder.
Full-length case, crimped mouth, untinned.

The American Krag Rifle and Carbine

Paper Bullet, Blank Cartridge, Caliber .30, Model of 1896
Paper bullet.
5 grains E. C. smokeless powder.
Tinned case, later brass.
Figures C-5 and C-6.

Fig. C-5. Blank Cartridge, Paper bullet, tinned cases, Caliber .30, Model of 1896.

Cartridge, Dummy, Caliber .30, Model of 1896
Standard round-nose service bullet. Three knurled rings at base, inert primer.

Cartridge, Dummy, Caliber .30, Model of 1899*
Standard round-nose service bullet. Four holes equally spaced at case base, inert primer.

Cartridge, Dummy, Caliber .30
Standard round-nose service bullet. Corrugated body, inert primer.

Fig. C-6. Blank Cartridge, Paper bullet, Caliber .30, Model of 1896. Made from fired brass cases.

Cartridge, Proof, Caliber .30, Type 1
Round-nose lead bullet.
Wetteren smokeless powder.
Straight tapered case.

Cartridge, Proof, Caliber .30, Model of 1897
Standard round-nose service bullet.
49 grains compressed Wetteren or DuPont smokeless powder.
Bullet was special 0.294-inch diameter.

Cartridge, Reduced Range, Caliber .30, Model of 1901
Standard round-nose service bullet.

246

The American Krag Rifle and Carbine

Smokeless powder.
Muzzle velocity 900 fps.
Front of case nickeled.

Cartridge, Reduced Range, Caliber .30, Model of 1903
218-grain lead bullet.
Smokeless powder.
Muzzle velocity 900 fps.
Case blackened, cannelured at neck.

Cartridge, Gallery, Caliber .30, Model of 1895*
Round lead ball.
5.2 grains DuPont Revolver Ball Powder
Muzzle velocity 700 fps.
Case manufactured from brass rod.
Figure C-7.

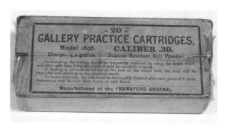

Fig. C-7. Cartridge, Gallery, Caliber .30, Model of 1895.

Cartridge, Gallery, Caliber .30, Model of 1896*
Round lead ball.
5 grains black powder or 2.5 grains Bullseye smokeless.
Muzzle velocity 700 fps.
Case cannelured 0.25 inch from mouth.
Figure C-8.

Cartridge, Gallery, Caliber .30, Model of 1904
107-grain semi-pointed lead bullet.
3 grains Bullseye smokeless powder.

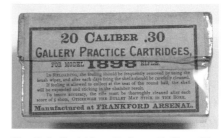

Fig. C-8. Cartridge, Gallery, Caliber .30, Model of 1896.

The American Krag Rifle and Carbine

Muzzle velocity 750 fps.
Case cannelured 0.35 inch from mouth.

Cartridge, Gallery, Sub-Caliber, Caliber .30
107-grain round-nose lead bullet.
2.5 to 3 grains Bullseye smokeless powder.
Muzzle velocity 700 fps.
Case cannelured 0.36 inch from mouth.

Cartridge, Guard, Caliber .30, Model of 1904
156-grain round-nose lead bul-
let.
DuPont No. 1 smokeless
powder.
Muzzle velocity 1,160 fps.
Case cannelured 0.13 inch
from mouth.

**Cartridge, Guard, Caliber
.30, Model of 1905***
177-grain round-nose lead bullet. 7.3 grains Bullseye smokeless powder.

*Fig. C-9. Cartridge, Guard, Caliber
.30, Model of 1905.*

Muzzle velocity 1,150 fps.
Case cannelured 0.21 inch from mouth. Figure C-9.

Cartridge, Sub-Caliber, Caliber .30, Model of 1902
Standard round-nose service bullet.
Smokeless powder.
Muzzle velocity 2,000 fps.
Cannon primer, Berdan, 0.317-inch diameter.

Cartridge, Sub-Caliber, Caliber .30, Model of 1903
Standard round-nose service bullet.
Smokeless powder.

The American Krag Rifle and Carbine

Muzzle velocity 2,000 fps.
Berdan 0.25 inch diameter primer.

Cartridge, Sub-Caliber, Caliber .30, Model of 1925
172-grain jacketed pointed boat tail bullet.
Smokeless powder.
Muzzle velocity 2,000 fps.
Boxer 0.210-inch-diameter primer, Monel primer cup.
Figure C-10.

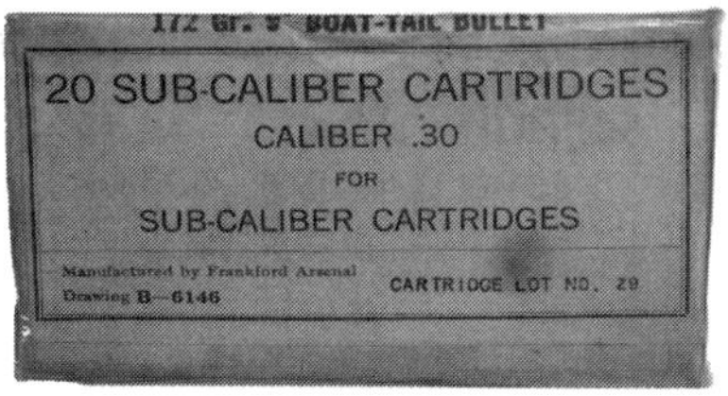

Fig. C-10. Cartridge, Sub-Caliber, Caliber .30, Model of 1925.

Cartridge, Multiball, Caliber .30, Model of 1902
Two round lead balls.
Smokeless powder.
Reduced range for guard use.
Boxer primer.

.30-40 Primed Shells, Model 1898
For field reloading.
Refer to Figure C-2.

Blank Cartridges with Cardboard Wads, Crimped
No bullet (M1898) M3 Pre–World War I.
Figure C-11.

Fig. C-11. (1898) M3 pre–World War I blank cartridges. This example was manufactured by Remington Arms Company.

* Note: Model years shown on cartons refer to the Model of rifle or carbine, not to the cartridge model.

249

Fig. C-12. Top, Model 1892 and below, Model 1895 cartridges.

Fig. C-13. Sectioned cartridges show how the walls of the Model 1895 case were thickened and the primer pocket deepened and reinforced after August 1895. Sectioned cartridges are from the Scott Duff collection.

Appendix D
U.S. Krag Rifle and Carbine Models

The collector of the American Krag rifle and carbine should keep two things in mind: 1) the Krag rifle was the first production repeating rifle manufactured at the Springfield Armory. Tolerances were closer and different steels with different machining characteristics were being used for the first time. 2) The American Krag was not a duplicate of the Danish Krag, and six months for finalizing and testing the changes that had been made were simply not enough to work out all the bugs. Yet, the majority of the changes made to the Krag during its production life, with the exception of those to rear sights, were made to reduce the cost of and the time to manufacture, not to improve its reliability, ease of use and the accuracy, which was quite good from the beginning. Of the more than 140 changes made to the Krag (not including rear sights) only about six concerned reliability, safety or accuracy. The Krag's perceived inaccuracy was due to the rear sight and variations in powder from manufacturer to manufacturer (and even lot to lot in the beginning) and not to the rifle's design.

The Model 1892 was the first small-caliber rifle, and it was the last carbine to be issued to mounted troops in the U.S. Army. It was not issued to the U.S. Navy and Marine Corps, who had adopted the Model 1895 Winchester-Lee Magazine Repeating rifle in 6 mm (.276 caliber) until November 1899 when they, too, adopted the Krag.

MODEL 1892 SERVICE RIFLE

Many collectors have divided the Model 1892 into two variations based primarily on the use of two different types of front barrel bands, one solid, the other of the double strap variation. Neither the U.S. Army nor the Ordnance Department made any such distinction. Since more than fifty changes were made to the Krag rifle in the first two years of its production, twenty-four of them in the bolt assembly alone, it doesn't

The American Krag Rifle and Carbine

Fig. D-1. The Model 1892 Krag Rifle. This example is serial number 1,178. North Cape Publications collection.

make sense to assign such a distinction to one part.

The introduction of the Model 1892 rifle into the U.S. Army was not a smooth process. A series of problems interrupted the planned distribution of Krags to the regulars. The first had to do with punctured cartridge primers, which allowed combustion gases to erode the bolt face. The problem was traced to both the firing pin and primer. The primer was made of soft copper and the firing pin had a squarish tip. New primers made of harder brass and a change in the shape of the pin's tip from flat to round in late 1895 eased, but never completely eliminated, the problem.

The second problem was the rear sight. Initial firing tests were carried out during the winter of 1893–94 to develop the ballistics tables for the .30-40 cartridge from which the rear sight graduations were calculated. But that winter in New England was one of the coldest in years. Cold air is denser than warm air and tends to slow a bullet, causing its trajectory to vary significantly when the temperature climbs to 80 degrees Fahrenheit and above.

The mean high and low temperatures that winter were recorded at the Framingham, Massachusetts, meteorological station as 21 to 31 degrees Fahrenheit with the lowest temperature at 11 degrees. Twelve inches of rain, snow and ice also fell in December, complicating the shooting schedule further. The intensely cold conditions made it difficult to produce a usable ballistics table. As a result, during most of the year, the Krag shot above its sights. The bullet also drifted left beyond two hundred yards, complicating aiming even more as the rear sight did not compensate for bullet drift as had the Model 1884 rear sight on the .45-70 Springfield.

Springfield Armory also encountered difficulty engraving the sight leaves, and a new machine had to be developed to do so. Other problems plagued the start of production but were sufficiently solved, it was thought, for production to begin in earnest in the spring of 1894 and distribution to the regular Army to start in October of that year.

The rifle manual, known as the "Description and Rules for the Management of . . .," had been printed for every arm since the Model 1863 Springfield, but was not published until early in 1895, after most of the troops had been issued the new rifle. An earlier issue might have avoided many of the problems the troops encountered.

When field complaints were collated and analyzed in late 1895, the appropriate changes were ordered. New cartridge cases were fabricated with thicker walls and new primers and the rear sight was recalibrated.

But the Ordnance Department, in the person of its chief, Colonel Alfred Mordecai, did not believe that a complicated rear sight would be of any use in battle when the soldier was too nervous, frightened and preoccupied to make fine adjustments. He may have been right in that assumption, but in the mid-1890s, American soldiers were only shooting at paper targets.

A more practical problem troubled the soldiers. When carried at trail arms (rifle in the shooting hand, hanging at the side), the heel of the hand closed over the front of the receiver ring, which could become very hot from shooting or exposure to intense summer sun. The handguard was lengthened to the rear to cover the top of the receiver ring and eliminate the problem.

A better cutoff device was also designed and the safety was improved. The one-piece ramrod made it difficult to mount the bayonet quickly, was always snagging on brush and other impediments during exercises, and the long, thin steel rod bent and wore against the

The American Krag Rifle and Carbine

rifling. It was redesigned into a three-piece rod (two pieces for carbines) and stored in a compartment in the buttstock, out of the way.

When all of the changes made to the Model 1892 were added up, it became clear to the Ordnance Department in late 1895 that the design had undergone enough changes that a new model designation was in order.

In brief then, the Model 1892 rifle can be identified by the following characteristics: 1) one-piece ramrod in a ramrod channel under the forend. 2) No lightening grooves in the forend or buttstock. Solid butt plate without a trap. Thin butt plates; the earliest straight, later with the toe curved forward. 3) "High" comb and thin wrist stock. 4) Short handguard that does not cover the receiver ring. 5) Receiver dated "1894." 6) Stock cartouches of Samuel W. Porter (S.W.P.) dated 1894 on the left to circa serial #1,177 and on the right from #1,178 to circa serial #1,932. After, J.S. Adams (J.S.A.) dated 1894, 1895 or 1896. The cartouches were all in script letters.

Before leaving the Model 1892, it is interesting to note that all Model 1892 receivers carry a date of 1894. Very early Model 1896 carbines and Model 1896 rifles without the ramrod and ramrod channel and a thicker wrist were dated 1895 and were manufactured in the last half of Calendar Year (CY) 1895. It had been the stated intention of the Ordnance Department to stamp the date of manufacture on the receivers (changed to Model year in 1896), yet in the case of the Model 1892, this seems not to have been done.

Craig Riesch has suggested that all receivers used on the Model 1892 and dated "1894" may have been manufactured in Calendar Year 1894. Three pieces of data support this theory. 1) Reports by the Chief of Ordnance to the Secretary of War for FY 1895 contain no analytical acceptance tests for receiver steel lots, although they are listed for barrel steel lots. 2) Payroll reports of the period do not show payments made for receivers during the last half of FY 1895 (first half of CY 1895). 3) Various inventory reports show that up to 15,000 receivers were at various stages in the manufacturing process and inventory. Unfortunately, records observed to date are too fragmentary for the author to draw any firm conclusions.

The American Krag Rifle and Carbine

Mitigating against this theory is the fact that at least two changes were made to the Model 1892 receiver during CY 1895. The head of the Type 1 ejector pin was redesigned to eliminate the "tail." The original ejector pin had required that a slot be milled in the receiver wall. This appears as early as circa serial #7,400 (December 1894). It would have been impossible to eliminate the slot in the receiver wall if all receivers had already been manufactured.

The author and editor welcome any comments.

MODEL 1892 CARBINE

The Model 1892 Krag carbine was actually a prototype developed for testing. Two were produced in 1894 and one was sent to the Board on Cavalry and Drill Regulations at Ft. Riley, Kansas, and the second to Rock Island for design studies (serial numbers were 1,015 and 1,575). When the results of the Ft. Riley test arrived, they included three recommendations: 1) crown the muzzle, 2) eliminate the cleaning rod to make it easier to insert into the carbine boot and 3) reduce the carbine's weight by reducing the length of the stock and adding lightening grooves wherever possible.

Springfield Armory submitted two more carbines in line with Ft. Riley's recommendations with shortened forearms rounded to the now-familiar shape. Two lightening holes had also been drilled into each buttstock. Where the original two Model 1892 carbines had used clamping barrel bands, band springs were substituted and a barrel band similar to that used on the Model 1896 Carbine was substituted but with a shallow sighting groove. The forward barrel band was eliminated as was the cleaning rod and its channel. The muzzle was also crowned, which eased wear and tear on the carbine boot tip. These last two carbines were the prototypes of the Model 1896 carbine.

MODEL 1896 KRAG CADET RIFLE

In spite of the fact that the Krag Cadet rifles were actually of Model 1892 derivation in virtually every respect, Brigadier General D. W. Flagler, then Chief of Ordnance, ordered that the Cadet rifles and the

The American Krag Rifle and Carbine

new carbines be designated as the Model of 1896. The Cadet rifles included many of the changes made to transform the Model 1892 rifle into the Model 1896 rifle.

The 404 Cadet rifles that were manufactured starting in late 1895 and shipped to the U.S. Military Academy at West Point for use by the cadets in 1896 did not have sling swivels as West Point cadets did not parade with slung rifles. The rear of the buttstock was not cut for the sling swivel plate, and the upper rear barrel band was a solid oval of the type that was used on the Model 1899 carbines.

The Cadet rifles did not have the lightening grooves in the forend nor the butt trap for the cleaning rod and oiler. Instead, they retained the one-piece cleaning rod carried in the forend under the barrel. The other major point of difference between the Model 1896 Cadet and Model 1896 service rifle, and all Krag service rifles, lay in the fact that the rear barrel band was retained with barrel band spring of the same type used on the Model .45-70 Springfield Rifle and Carbine and the Models 1896, 1898 and 1899 Krag Carbines.

Over the years, Cadet rifles are reported to have been nickel-plated. No evidence for this practice exists in any official records so far uncovered. The same applies to the short bayonets with which these rifles were equipped. The receivers of all Cadet rifles were dated 1895 or 1896 and the stock cartouche was either J.S.A./1895 or J.S.A./1896. Four hundred rifles were shipped to West Point in March 1896 without their rear sights. These followed three weeks later (with the balance of the rifles) and were installed at the Military Academy.

The Model 1896 Cadet rifles were used by the cadets at West Point until 1900 when they were recalled, rebuilt and reissued as standard service rifles. New Model 1898 rifles with Model 1896 rear sights were issued to the cadets in their stead. These "second-issue" cadet rifles were standard service rifles. The short Cadet bayonets were recalled and the standard-length bayonets were issued in their place. These had a much longer service life as they were used not only with the Krags but with the Model 1903 and M1 Garand rifles which replaced them, until 1963 when the M14 rifle was adopted and they were exchanged for the M6 bayonet.

The American Krag Rifle and Carbine

Fig. D-2. Model 1896 Rifle. North Cape Publications collection.

The survival rate of the original Model 1896 Cadet rifles is not known with any accuracy. Records indicate that of the 404 manufactured, two were surveyed and one was destroyed. That leaves six unaccounted for if the figure of 395 returned to Springfield Armory is correct. Three Cadet rifles have been reported to the author in private collections, including serial #35,804 pictured in the late Colonel William Brophy's *The Krag Rifle*. A fourth Model 1896 Cadet rifle was donated to the West Point Museum by Franklin Mallory.

MODEL 1896 SERVICE RIFLE

The Model 1896 rifle (and carbine) underwent more changes than any other model of the Krag rifle. In summary, 1) the barrel was crowned, 2) the guide rib on the bolt was relieved to lighten the piece, and 3) the slot for the sleeve stud was eliminated. 4) The cocking piece received a notch so that the safety could be applied to lock the bolt closed when there wasn't a round in the breech and the bolt was not cocked. 5) The cocking piece lug was also beveled on the bottom. 6) The extractor was given a pin to drop into a notch in the receiver bridge to hold the bolt open 7) and a rivet replaced the screw that held the extractor to the cocking piece. 8) A new cutoff using a spring and spindle replaced the old one that used a flat spring. 9) The bolt sleeve was shortened and 10) the extractor arm was thinned slightly and 11) countersunk for the rivet head. 12) A groove was added for the safety lock spindle. 13) A new butt plate was curved at the

257

The American Krag Rifle and Carbine

toe, 14) made thicker, and 15) bored through for a butt cap and 16) the butt plate screw head was flattened. 17) The front sight blade was made thicker (0.05 inch) 18) and the curve more pronounced 19) and the width of the front sight slot remained unchanged. 20) The guide lip was changed in the magazine to make it thicker. 21) The handguard was lengthened to cover the front of the receiver ring 22) and the rivets were countersunk to prevent pinpoint burns. 23) The crimp in the handguard spring clips was also eliminated. 24) The stock wrist (small) was thickened, 25) the toe rounded 26) and holes for the cleaning rods and oiler were drilled. 27) Lightening cuts were added to the forend and forearm to reduce the weight of the stock. 28) The thickness of the side plate was increased 29) and the cartridge guide was lengthened. 30) The thumbpiece of the safety was increased in thickness and the spindle was made as a separate piece and press-fitted. 31) A spring and spindle were also added for a more positive hold. 32) A three-piece cleaning rod was substituted for the one-piece rod 33) and the cleaning rod stop was removed from the stock. 34) A new rear sight was developed with a thumbscrew instead of a spring-loaded catch 35) and recalibrated. 36) The rear sight screws were reduced slightly in length and the threads cut the length of the shaft. On the receiver, 37) a notch was added for the extractor pin to hold the bolt open when the rifle was tipped up or down for cleaning or inspection. Finally, 38) the mainspring was lengthened from 30.5 to 33.5 coils.

Model 1896 receivers were marked "MODEL 1896" except for early production which are marked only "1895" or "1896" without the word "MODEL."

All Model 1896 stock cartouches are "J.S.A./1896," "J.S.A./1897" or "J.S.A./1898" in script. Original Model 1896 rifles used the Model 1896 rear sight but during later refurbishing or repair, the Model 1898, Model 1901 or Model 1902 rear sight was substituted at various points in its service life.

The Model 1896, like the Model 1892, was widely used during the conflicts in Cuba and Puerto Rico. The regular Army was completely equipped with one or the other model. They also were

The American Krag Rifle and Carbine

Fig. D-3. Model 1896 Carbine. Don Moore collection.

widely issued to the regulars in the Philippines, although because this conflict started later and went on longer, the Model 1898 dominated.

MODEL 1896 CARBINE

The changes made to the last two Model 1892 carbines very closely described the new Model 1896 carbine, approved on May 17, 1895. Tooling up and production of receivers, which required weeks or months of lead time, was begun in June 1895. Those receivers manufactured through December of that year were marked "1895" on the left side of the receiver.

The Model 1896 Krag Carbine had a short, 22-inch barrel and a shortened stock reminiscent of that used on the Model 1884 .45-70 Springfield Carbine. Forty years of use (from the first Sharps Model 1853 carbines procured for testing, to the Model 1884) had convinced the Mounted Branches that this was the correct stock form for mounted use.

The Ordnance Department was under intense pressure to produce a carbine. The Model 1896 carbine may have been approved on May 17, 1895 but delays harassed the management at Springfield Armory. The failure of the contracting steel suppliers to deliver acceptable lots of barrel steel set production back somewhat during the period mid-February to early May and depleted inventories. Additional time was also required to complete the calibration of the rear sight for the carbine.

The American Krag Rifle and Carbine

Production of receivers and other parts may have begun as early as June of 1895. Receivers made in 1895 were marked "1895" without the word "MODEL" preceding it. Those made in January and early February of 1896 were marked "1896" on the receiver, again without the word "MODEL." Thereafter, the word "MODEL" was always used. The new carbines were placed into inventory as they came off the production line and in March 1896, issue to the troops began. Two months later, all Cavalry troops had exchanged their .45-70 Springfield carbines. After this initial production, carbines were always manufactured at the start of each Fiscal Year.

It should be noted the exact date production began on the Model 1896 carbine and rifle is not known for certain. It has generally been accepted that Model 1896 carbines were produced before rifles, but a glance at the list of serial numbers compiled by the Springfield Research Service suggests otherwise. The earliest Model 1896 reliably reported to the author at this writing is 22,062, a rifle. The earliest Model 1896 carbine reported with any degree of assurance, was 24,709.

The Model 1896 was a handsome carbine. Its short stock lent a certain grace to the arm and forward of the receiver it retained the lines of the .45-70 Springfield carbine. The Model 1896 rear sight as recalibrated for the carbine was mounted on the barrel. Those issued for use with the carbine were marked "C" on the base and leaf. Gradations on the leaf ranged from 700 to 2,000 yards. As originally manufactured, when equipped with the Model 1896 carbine rear sight, the rear sight was protected by a barrel band that had a raised hump on the top designed to protect the rear sight when the carbine was thrust into the carbine boot or scabbard.

In the mid-1890s, mounted troops of the Cavalry, Artillery and Signal Corps were still issued the 1885 Carbine Sling and the Carbine Boot first introduced in 1884. The Model 1896 carbine therefore had the cavalry swivel mounted on the left side of the stock, above the trigger assembly.

The carbine did have a few faults that needed to be corrected. The stock received the same modification that had been made to the rifle stock, i.e., the wrist was thickened and in 1897, a cut for the oiler

was made between the upper and lower lightening holes in the buttstock. The sharp edge of the extractor tended to cut the inside of the leather carbine boot as did the front sight blade. The sharp edges were rounded and work was begun on a front sight protector. Also, if the leaf on the rear sight was left in the raised position, it was knocked backward and sometimes jammed the carbine in the scabbard.

The Model 1896 was the primary carbine used by regular mounted troops in Cuba. As every Krag collector knows, Colonel Leonard Wood's and Lt. Colonel Theodore Roosevelt's 1st Volunteer Cavalry (Rough Riders), 1,041 officers and enlisted men, were equipped with the Model 1896 carbine. They were the only Volunteer Army unit equipped with Krags. They may not have had their cavalry horses at San Juan Hill and Kettle Hill, but they did have their Krag carbines during their eighty-five days in Cuba.

After 1900, Model 1896 carbines that underwent repair or refurbishment were often restocked with the Model 1899 "long forearm, short nose" carbine stock without the inletting for the cavalry swivel plate. At the same time, they were often equipped with either the Model 1901 or Model 1902 rear sights. If so, they received the appropriate Model 1901 handguard (no sight protector hump) or the Model 1902 handguard (sight protector hump).

MODEL 1898 RIFLE

The Model 1898 rifle solved the last niggling problems with the Krag rifle. It is almost indis-

The American Krag Rifle and Carbine

tinguishable from the Model 1896 externally except for the change in the shape of bolt handle recess cutout from a flared and recessed oval to square and the reversal of the magazine cutoff from the "up" position to "down" when off. If you remove the receiver from the stock, you see at once that it also lacks the "apron" below the bolt handle recess. For this reason, the Model 1892 or 1896 barreled action cannot be inserted into a Model 1898 stock, although the reverse is true. A number of other changes were introduced into the Model 1898 that primarily dealt with improved production techniques and these are enumerated in Chapter 2, U.S. Krag Rifle and Carbine Part-by-Part.

The Model 1898 production began at circa serial #109,000 and since it was the last rifle model, all rifle receivers were marked "MODEL 1898." The biggest change that occurred during the production of the Model 1898, other than the elimination of the apron in the bolt handle recess, was the change in rear sights. Because of the complexity of this issue, the rear sights are discussed in detail in Chapter 2, Rear Sights.

All other changes to the Model 1898 rifle were made to ease production. Only three of these changes are visible from the exterior. A new headless cocking piece was developed that was expected to be cheaper to produce than the flared cocking piece. It was used primarily on the Model 1899 carbine as it turned out. But besides proving to be more expensive to manufacture, it did not provide protection to the shooter's face in the case of a ruptured primer or burst case, and so was discontinued.

When American black walnut used in making stocks ran low, the firm of Louis Windmuller and Roelker, who furnished the wood, substituted Italian walnut. Whereas American black walnut developed a deep reddish-brown color when oiled, Italian walnut developed a lighter tan to yellow color. Some 13,000 stocks were made of Italian walnut in late 1899. The same wood was also used to make grips for the bayonet during this period.

The third externally visible change was a slot cut into the bottom of the forward barrel band and bayonet mount to allow it to be tightened more securely.

The American Krag Rifle and Carbine

Fig. D-5. Model 1898 Carbine. Craig Riesch collection.

The Model 1898 service rifle was produced from July 8, 1898 (circa serial #109,000) to November 1903 (circa serial #476,600) or possibly later. The Chief of Ordnance reported to the Secretary of War in 1904 that a total of 474,693 Krag rifles and carbines had been manufactured. Still, questions remain about the total number of Krags produced as serial numbers into the 499,000s have been encountered. See Appendix B for a discussion of this problem.

MODEL 1898 CARBINE

As with the Model 1896 rifle and carbine, no distinction was made in the Model 1898 receiver between rifle and carbine. Rifle serial numbers began at circa serial #109,000 and ran to the end of production, but only about 5,000 Model 1898 carbines were manufactured and it is generally accepted that their serial numbers fall into the range circa 113,000 through 139,000 (circa July–September 1898).

The Model 1898 carbine stock was a shortened version of the Model 1898 rifle stock. Like the rifle, the Model 1898 carbine cannot be seated in the Model 1896 carbine stock.

The Model 1898 carbine was widely used by cavalry troops in the Philippines during the pacification campaign. Like the Model 1898 service rifle, it underwent changes, primarily to the rear sight. A great number of Model 1898 carbines were restocked while in service with the Model 1899 carbine stock.

The American Krag Rifle and Carbine

THE NAVY ADOPTS THE KRAG

The Navy Department and the Marine Corps adopted the Krag-Jørgensen rifle in July 1899 (the start of Fiscal Year 1900). The issue of rifles to both services began in November 1899 in the circa serial #239,000 range. They were issued with the Model 1898 rear sight for the 2,200 fps Model 1898 cartridge. The Navy issue included many of the Italian walnut stocks.

After the recall of the 2,200 fps cartridge, Navy and Marine Corps Krags were called back in early 1900 to have the Model 1896 rear sight installed. In July 1902, they were called back again to have the Model 1902 rear sight substituted for the Model 1896. When the rear sights were changed, requiring new handguards, every attempt was made to match new light-colored handguards to the stocks. Because the Navy's ships and the Marines were stationed around the world, the changeover from the 6 mm Model 1895 Winchester-Lee rifles to the Krag Jørgensen was not completed until the end of 1902.

A few Model 1898 rifles had been issued to militia and volunteers during the Spanish-American War, but state militias did not begin to receive Krags until Fiscal Year 1903. The Krag lasted one year longer with the National Guard than with the regulars.

The Krag Jørgensen Model 1898 also had the distinction of serving in Cuba, Puerto Rico, the Philippines, Haiti and in France during World War I. Railway Engineer units marched down the Strand in London with their Krags in mid-1917 on their way to the English Channel and France. Six regiments of Railway Engineers, the 10th, 15th, 16th, 17th, 18th and 19th Engineers, were armed with between 7,500 and 10,000 Krags while overseas.

MODEL 1899 CARBINE

While there was no Model 1899 rifle, the Ordnance Department decreed a Model 1899 carbine by virtue of a new stock, handguard, barrel band and rear sight. Otherwise the Model 1898 and Model 1899 carbines are identical with a number of Model 1898 carbines having been converted to the Model 1899 by virtue of restocking during re-

The American Krag Rifle and Carbine

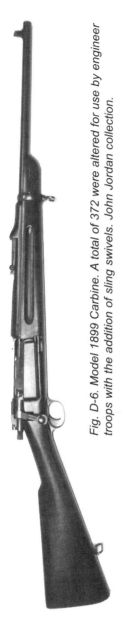

Fig. D-6. Model 1899 Carbine. A total of 372 were altered for use by engineer troops with the addition of sling swivels. John Jordan collection.

furbishment or repair. Model 1899 carbines are marked "MODEL 1899" on the left side of the receiver. Their serial number ranges can be found in Appendix B.

The Model 1899 carbine stock was developed to reduce the costs associated with producing two different stocks. The Model 1899, between the barrel band cut rearward to the stock butt, was made using the same tooling as for the rifle. This required that its forearm be lengthened and the nose shortened.

Many collectors have felt that the change was made to provide greater protection for the shooter's hand from overheated barrels. But the Ordnance reports are clear; cost savings were the deciding factor. Most of the same tooling and machines could be used to make the carbine stock as was used to make the rifle stock. Only the nose, forward of the barrel band, had to be cut differently.

A number of Model 1899 carbines received the "headless" cocking piece. For some time, this feature was assumed to be a characteristic of all Model 1899 carbines by many collectors. But in fact, the headless cocking piece was installed only for a short period between January and October 1900.

The Model 1899 carbine was issued with the Model 1898 carbine rear sight calibrated for the 2,200 fps Model 1898 cartridge for six months only, starting in January 1900. Almost immediately, the Model 1898 2,200 fps cartridge was withdrawn from service in favor of the Model 1898 2,000 fps cartridge. The majority

265

The American Krag Rifle and Carbine

of Model 1899 carbines, it is believed, were still in storage and the Model 1898 rear sight was exchanged for the Model 1896 carbine rear sight. Like its predecessors, the Models 1896 and 1898 carbine, the Model 1899 carbine was subjected to a series of rear sight changes that are fully described in Chapter 2, Rear Sights.

BOARD OF ORDNANCE AND FORTIFICATIONS RIFLE

In 1884, the Board on Cavalry Equipment submitted a request to the Chief of Ordnance for a carbine with a 24-inch barrel that would provide the range of a rifle yet still be light and short enough to be manageable by mounted troops. Some 1,000 24-inch carbines were built in 1886 (and few in succeeding years) for testing but the arm was never adopted.

Fig. D-7. Board of Ordnance and Fortifications rifle with the 26-inch barrel. Tests on this rifle influenced the selection of the 24-inch barrel for the Model 1903 rifle. Jonathan Peck collection, courtesy of Little John's Auction Service, Inc.

In 1900, a request for a short-barreled rifle was again submitted, this time to the Board of Ordnance and Fortifications for a rifle with 26-inch barrel that could be used by infantry and cavalry alike, thus reducing the costs involved in producing, storing and distributing two different arms. The BOF agreed and authorized the Ordnance Department to produce one hundred rifles with 26-inch barrels and

The American Krag Rifle and Carbine

send to them to Plattsburgh Barracks, New York, for testing.

To keep the costs as low as possible, Model 1898 barrels were simply reduced in length by four inches. Stock forends were turned down to fair evenly into the rifle front barrel band which was enlarged on a mandrel to fit the larger barrel diameter. A Model 1901 carbine rear sight was recalibrated and the graduations were stamped by hand onto the leaf.

Testing produced better-than-expected results. The short rifle was found to be just as accurate as the 30-inch service rifle. The amount of drift in the bullet from the 26-inch barrel was reduced by almost half which made it possible for the soldier to shoot far more accurately in crosswinds. While the 26-inch rifle was not adopted, the results of its tests undoubtedly played a major part in the decision to adopt a 24-inch barrel for the Model 1903 rifle over the 30-inch barrel being tested in the Model 1901 rifle. The decision was even more significant when you consider that virtually every major battle rifle then in use including the British Lee-Enfield Mark I series, Mauser Gew. 98, Italian Carcano, Austrian Mannlicher, French Lebel, Japanese Arisaka and Swiss Schmidt-Rubin had barrels of about 30 inches.

Philippine Constabulary Rifles

The Philippine Constabulary was first organized on July 18, 1901, as a police force composed of Philippine nationals, charged with keeping the peace throughout the islands. Although the Constabulary did not come under the command of the War Department, they were led by American Army officers and trained by American military regulars, long before the term "adviser" came into the military vocabulary. They were originally armed with obsolete American and Spanish weapons including the .45-70 Springfield, Remington single-shot shotguns, probably Model 1 or Model 4 Rolling Blocks, and 7 mm Spanish Mausers.

In 1906, Henry T. Allen, Chief of the Philippine Constabulary, requested that a rifle suitable to the short stature of his Constabulary troops be procured. Allen had ordered the purchase of 300 M1899 carbines with ammunition and cartridge belts and issued these to mem-

The American Krag Rifle and Carbine

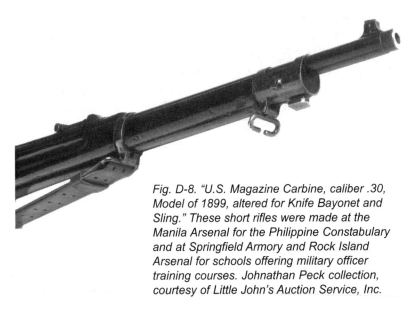

Fig. D-8. "U.S. Magazine Carbine, caliber .30,
Model of 1899, altered for Knife Bayonet and
Sling." These short rifles were made at the
Manila Arsenal for the Philippine Constabulary
and at Springfield Armory and Rock Island
Arsenal for schools offering military officer
training courses. Johnathan Peck collection,
courtesy of Little John's Auction Service, Inc.

bers of the Constabulary. He was pleased with their performance but
noted that the carbines could not accept a bayonet, a tool indispensable
to the type of policing activities performed by the Constabulary. He
suggested that they be refitted with Krag rifle stocks altered to fit the
carbine barreled-receiver, see Appendix G, Bibliography, for the ori-
gin of these reports.

At about the same time, a number of colleges and high schools
with officer training programs were requesting a shorter rifle suitable
for teenagers. The rifles were used not only for drill and parade purposes but for rifle practice and marksmanship training.

The result was the "U.S. Magazine Carbine, caliber .30, Model
of 1899, altered for Knife Bayonet and Sling," designed at the Springfield Armory.

The term "Philippine Constabulary rifle" is a collector's term
and not one ever used by the Philippine Constabulary or the U.S. Ordnance Department. The altered carbines used by the Philippine Constabulary all appear to have been made at the Manila Ordnance Depot.

The American Krag Rifle and Carbine

Many researchers and collectors would argue that these are the only true "Philippine Constabulary rifles."

In Fiscal Year 1907, Asa F. Fisk, Ordnance Officer for the Philippine Constabulary, reported that an additional 2,120 rifles (he was probably referring to carbines) were purchased to bring the total to 2,420, of which 1,615 had been "remodeled" (by shortening rifle stocks, turning down the carbine barrels for the knife bayonet and stretching rifle upper barrel bands).

In Fiscal Year 1908, Mark L. Hersey, Chief Supply Officer for the Philippine Constabulary, reported that "the remodeling of the carbine has been effected. There have been equipped 3,365 carbines during the past year." The total of "remodeled carbines" produced for the Constabulary during the three fiscal years then is 4,980.

In 1906, the Springfield Armory remanufactured 350 "U.S. Magazine Carbine, caliber .30, Model of 1899, altered for Knife Bayonet and Sling" from Model 1898 and Model 1899 carbines. The first of these were sold to Girard College in November. Further remanufacturing was accomplished between 1908 and 1915 until a total of 4,074 were completed. All were sold or lent to various academies, high schools and colleges.

The short rifles, whether used by the Philippine Constabulary or in a school training program, were made from Model 1898 and Model 1899 carbines. They were produced by reducing the length of a rifle forend by 8 inches to fit the carbine barrel. The lightening groove thus exposed in the bedding was cut square and filled with a rectangular piece of walnut, sanded smooth. The forward barrel band was stretched slightly on a mandrel to fit the larger-diameter carbine barrel.

The carbine barrel, which was 0.635 inch in diameter at the muzzle, was turned down for 0.75 inch to a diameter of 0.620 inch to accept the bore of the Krag bayonet. The new muzzle diameter was also the correct diameter to accept the Model 1905 bayonet adopted for the new Model 1903 rifle, but only the Krag bayonet appears to have been issued to the Constabulary.

269

The American Krag Rifle and Carbine

Original "U.S. Magazine Carbine, caliber .30, Model of 1899, altered for Knife Bayonet and Sling" produced at Springfield Armory for schools will show the cartouches of J.F. Coyle as "J.F.C." or Charles Valentine, "C.V.," in script or C.C.V. in block letters inside a rectangular box with rounded corners.

In addition to the 4,074 "U.S. Magazine Carbine, caliber .30, Model of 1899, altered for Knife Bayonet and Sling" produced by the Springfield Armory and the 4,980 at the Manila Arsenal, a total of 613 were produced at Rock Island between 1911 and 1914 for a grand total of 9,667 produced at U.S. Government armories.

The collector should also be aware that in the 1930s, an unknown number of "Krag short rifles" were sold by several dealers and wholesalers, most notably W. Stokes Kirk. These were standard Model 1898 rifles with shortened rifle barrels and stocks. They can be identified by the Model 1905 front sight assembly used instead of the Krag front sight base and blade. It was quicker and easier to apply the banded Model 1905 front sight than the Krag front sight that required that a seat be milled for the base, and then the barrel be repolished and reblued. One W. Stokes Kirk advertisement noted that the knife bayonet could be attached to the rifle, "which gives great protection to the big-game hunter at close range when the ammunition is exhausted." Apparently that ad writer never hunted "big game."

The fate of the short rifles used by the Constabulary is uncertain. They apparently remained in service until 1917 when they were replaced by the Model 1903 .30-caliber rifle. One unverified report states that all Krags left in the islands in 1925 were loaded onto a barge and sunk in the Mindanao Deep. That would have been a cheaper course than returning them to the United States for disposal.

Parkhurst-Equipped Rifles and Carbines

The Krag rifle had been selected in 1892 over the clip-loading Mauser, Lee-Enfield, Lebel, Mannlicher and other systems because the Ordnance Department wanted a rifle that could be fired as a single loader with a magazine full of cartridges held in reserve. The Krag-Jørgensen

The American Krag Rifle and Carbine

rifle was the only design that met this qualification. Many Ordnance officials felt that a magazine without a cutoff would cause the soldiers to waste ammunition in combat.

The action before Santiago in Cuba during the Spanish-American War prompted many field officers to call for a clip-loading device for the Krag, despite the fact that after-action reports showed that the Krag had been used in the campaigns in Cuba primarily as a single loader. But many officers, among

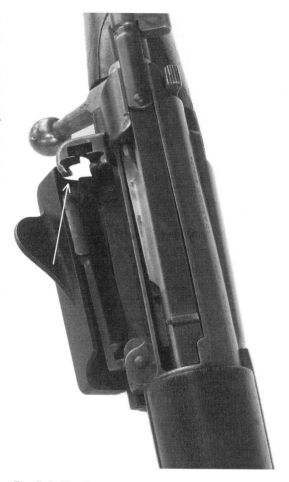

Fig. D-9. The Parkhurst clip-loading device (arrow) was developed by for the Krag rifle and carbine to permit faster loading from a clip. Craig Riesch collection.

them Lieutenant Colonel Theodore Roosevelt, pointed out that during the attack up San Juan Hill, thousands of cartridges had been dropped by the troops struggling to reload their weapons.

The American Krag Rifle and Carbine

Edward G. Parkhurst of Hartford, Connecticut, a well-known design engineer of the time, and Lyman E. Warren of New York, N.Y., had designed and patented a device that allowed the Krag to be loaded from a clip. Parkhurst also designed and patented the clip. The device and a new magazine guide lip were attached to the receiver wall at the rear and bottom of the magazine. When the gate was opened, a brass clip containing five cartridges was inserted into the guide lips and pushed down with the thumb. The gate was then flipped closed and the bolt worked to load the first round. Extensive testing was carried out on his system using a modified Model 1892 rifle. Parkhurst submitted the modified rifle to the Board of Ordnance in February 1899.

Among the tests conducted by Board of Ordnance officers was a firing test using four soldiers ranging from an experienced marksman to a new recruit. They each fired the rifle with the clip-loading device, then with cartridges taken from a belt and then from a pants pocket, in both magazine and single-loading modes. The savings in time for the clip-loading device was only few seconds. Interestingly enough, the clerk, the recorder of the board, managed to shoot his twenty rounds in each category at least one second faster than the experienced marksman. But then they were not under the pressure of combat.

By November of that year, testing was completed and a favorable report was submitted recommending that one hundred rifles and one hundred carbines be modified for field testing. When Colonel Alfred E. Mordecai, then Chief of Ordnance, decided not to pursue the field tests, he was overruled by Lt. General Nelson Miles, President of the Board of Ordnance and Fortifications. In May 1900, orders were given to manufacture the rifles and carbines with the Parkhurst clip-loading device and on July 6 of the same year, $1,178.57 was allotted for the task. Two thousand clips were also manufactured and two hundred cartridge belts were produced with pockets for the clips. The last order was subsequently modified to produce two hundred cartridge belts with ten pockets and two hundred with two pockets. Both types were

The American Krag Rifle and Carbine

manufactured at Rock Island Arsenal. The clip-loading devices and clips were manufactured at Springfield Armory between July and October 1900 under the supervision of Parkhurst himself.

The rifles and carbines were shipped the following month to the Philippines for field trial under combat conditions. The reports from men and officers were distinctly favorable when they were received and collated in June 1902, nearly a year later. But by this time, Springfield Armory was already working with the Ordnance Department on the clip-loading Model 1901 Springfield which was based on the Mauser 1898 design and further work on the Parkhurst design was discontinued. There is some indication that some of the Parkhurst-equipped rifles and carbines did not make their way back from the Philippines to Springfield until at least 1907, or later.

Other clip-loading devices were submitted but none were considered superior to the Parkhurst-Warren design and none were submitted to actual trials.

Gallery Rifles

Between 1880 and 1900, the population of the United States grew by more than a third to 75,995,000 people. The introduction of the electric trolley and the spread of interurban rail lines encouraged the growth of suburbs. Land values rose quickly as farm land turned into homes and vacant land into farm land.

The rise of the suburb had a significant effect on military training. By the turn of the century, fewer and fewer National Guard units had access to nearby rifle ranges. Those in the cities were closing both from the twin pressures of new construction and increasing urbanization. Those in nearby suburbs were being pushed ever farther out. A .22-caliber rifle could be used in the close confines of a pistol range and even indoors with the proper precautions. Thus more time could be devoted to rifle handling and marksmanship training at a much lower cost.

The U.S. Navy had been the first of the services to institute a .22-caliber training program. The Winchester Repeating Arms Com-

The American Krag Rifle and Carbine

pany converted 100 of the 12,000 Model 1870 .50-caliber Rolling Block rifles manufactured at Springfield Armory in 1870 for the Navy to fire a .22-caliber rimfire cartridge.

In 1901, Harry M. Pope and the J. Stevens Arms Company produced .22-caliber rifle and carbine barrels for the Krag. The Stevens-Pope barrel was rifled one turn in eight and the barrels were drilled so that the bore was offset breech to muzzle with the high end at the breech and the low end at the bore. The .22 barrels were to be installed by turning out the .30-caliber barrels and screwing in the new .22-caliber barrel. The threads were indexed so precisely that the barrel bottomed against the receiver ring at exactly the proper 90-degree angle for the front sight. By "tipping" the bore from back to front, the standard .30-caliber service extractor could be used to withdraw the spent cartridge. Users were advised that in order to keep the spent cases from falling down inside the magazine well and jamming the action, they should keep a dummy .30-40 cartridge in the magazine or

Fig. D-10. A total of 841 Krag Model 1898 rifles were converted to .22-caliber rimfire "Gallery" rifles at Springfield Armory for indoor and short range practice, primarily by the National Guard and schools. Jonathan Peck collection, courtesy of Little John's Auction Service, Inc.

else remove the side plate so that the cases could fall out.

The Stevens-Pope .22-caliber barrels were purchased by the National Guards of New Jersey, Ohio, Pennsylvania and Washington State. But in 1905, the Chief of Ordnance declared that the barrels were not an authorized item of equipment and they were withdrawn.

Enough interest had been expressed by the various National Guards in the .22 Stevens-Pope system that the Ordnance Department developed a .22-caliber version of the Krag service rifle using standard Krag service receivers, most of which are in the serial number range 475,000 or above, although a few earlier serial numbers have also been observed. The right, rear edge of the receiver ring was relieved to allow a shooter to insert the .22-caliber cartridge into the chamber. The barrel was drilled so that the bore was offset breech to muzzle as with the Stevens-Pope barrels, but Springfield Armory chose to place the start of the bore at the bottom of the barrel so that it ended at the top of the muzzle. This overcame some of the aiming problems inherent in the earlier Stevens-Pope barrels.

The extractor system was modified to handle the smaller cartridge case below the line of the bore. An auxiliary extractor was installed by drilling two holes on either side of the receiver ring and inserting the spring-loaded legs. A ring with a slot cut out for the extractor was placed over the auxiliary extractor against the rear of the barrel and pinned in place. When the bolt was retracted, the service extractor gripped the auxiliary extractor which in turn held the .22-caliber rimfire case. When the bolt was withdrawn past an extractor trip a little more than halfway back down the bolt race, the service extractor was forced up, releasing the auxiliary extractor which in turn released the fired case.

The receivers were marked "CAL./.22" behind the serial number on the left side of the receiver. They can also be identified by the small hole drilled through the left side of the receiver wall for the extractor trip between the words "SPRINGFIELD ARMORY." Stocks will show a standard "J.S.A." cartouche on the left side of the stock over the year 1905 or 1906 but will not show a "P" proof mark as they were not proof fired. Those initial 124 barreled receivers which were later put into replacement stocks may or may not show a cartouche and a "P" proof mark, depending on whether or not they were taken from service rifles and refinished.

The intent had originally been to provide .22-caliber barreled actions to be interchanged with standard .30-caliber service stocks to save the cost of producing an entire rifle. It was a fine, money-saving idea but reckoned without the reluctance of soldiers and armorers alike to dismount their rifles more often than necessary. A great part of a rifle's accuracy is in its bedding, i.e., the tight fit of barreled action to stock. The process of removing and replacing barreled actions was sure to destroy the rifle's accuracy. Consequently, only 124 .22-caliber barreled actions were produced for shipment to the field and these were later placed in spare stocks. In his Fiscal Year 1905 report, the Chief of Ordnance stated that "500 .22 caliber Barrels and receivers, Model 1898" were 50% complete. The balance were completed in Fiscal Year 1906 but in Fiscal Year 1907, the process of withdrawal began as the Model 1903 Springfield using the Hoffer-Thompson .22-caliber cartridge holder had been perfected. The Hoffer-Thompson system used with the Model 1903 Springfield had the advantage over the Model 1898 .22 Caliber Rifle of allowing the soldier to practice loading and firing the rifle with ammunition in clips.

All in all, a total of 841 .22-caliber Model 1898 rifles were manufactured and all appear to have been issued to the National Guard rather than to the regular Army. By 1910, the Hoffer-Thompson system had completely replaced the Model 1898 .22-caliber rifles. In 1912, the Director of Civilian Marksmanship was authorized to sell off the Model 1898 .22-caliber rifles at $7.50 each.

STAR-GAUGED KRAG RIFLES AND CARBINES

Star-gauging refers to an apparatus developed to measure the diameter of the bore of rifle and carbine barrels at several points to determine the degree of deviation within the bore. In short, it was a measure of how true the bore had been drilled and reamed. Pads extending from

The American Krag Rifle and Carbine

the end of the gauge could be made to expand against the bore to provide the measurements.

The first Krag barrels were star-gauged in August 1906 and used in the National Matches of that year. Model 1898 rifles with Model 1901 rear sights and star-gauged barrels were also made available for sale through the then new Civilian Marksmanship Program for use in target matches. The rifles were furnished with a certificate but were not marked in any way. Without the certificate, it is impossible to know which barrels were star-gauged and which were not.

THE U.S. KRAG BAYONET

The Board of Officers convened in November 1890 to select a new magazine loading rifle was also responsible for selecting a bayonet.

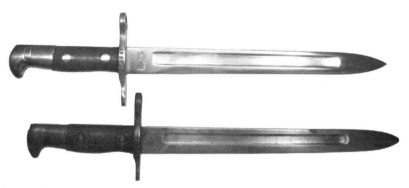

Fig. D-11. Top, Model 1889 Bayonet for the Swiss Schmidt-Rubin Rifle. Below, Model 1892 Krag Bayonet. North Cape Publications collection.

Accordingly, the Board examined bayonets from Austria, Belgium, Denmark, Great Britain, Japan and Switzerland before selecting the Swiss pattern. The September 27, 1892 report to the Chief of Ordnance ". . . recommends for use with the trial arm [Krag] a knife bayonet similar to that on the Swiss magazine rifle [Model 1889], and provided with a metal scabbard . . . ."

277

The American Krag Rifle and Carbine

Their report, on August 15, 1892 suggested that ". . . the Swiss knife is fully as good a bayonet as any of the others described. As a knife, used as a weapon, its double guard and the shape of the handle give it an advantage over the others used. For cutting brush or for breaking up when held in the hand the surface of the ground, it is also thought to be superior . . . it has one of the best forms of attachment to the rifle."

The form of attachment was, of course, the Mauser system by which a slot in the upper surface of the bayonet's grip slid over a stud mounted on the rifle's upper band. A ring at the top of the guard slid over the barrel to form a secure mounting directly along the line of the bore.

A total of eight variations of the Model 1892 bayonet were manufactured for the Krag, all at the Springfield National Armory, including a shortened version for the cadets at the U.S. Military Academy at West Point. The bayonets were marked "U S " on the ricasso (without periods) and stamped with the year of manufacture on the reverse. Dates ran from 1894 through 1903.

SUB-CALIBER RIFLES

The Krag rifle served a final use with both the Navy and the Army as a sub-caliber rifle which could be attached to the barrel of a naval gun or fitted into the breech of an artillery piece. This allowed soldiers to be trained without the expense of expending actual gun or artillery rounds.

An unknown quantity of rifles with stocks removed were used. Naval sub-caliber rifles were attached to the cannon's barrel and fired by an electric solenoid or by manually pulling the trigger. Army sub-caliber rifles were fitted into the breeches of 3.2-inch siege guns and 4.2-inch cannon. The receiver protruded from the breech and the rifle was fired by manually pulling the trigger.

Sub-caliber rifles were used for training purposes at least into the 1920s.

Appendix E
Dismounting and Assembling by Soldier

(These are the actual instructions given to the soldier for dismounting and reassembling the Krag rifle or carbine. They have been annotated where necessary. Refer to the exploded view in Appendix A.—Ed.)

The bolt and magazine mechanism can be dismounted without removing the stock. The latter should never be done except for making repairs, and then only by some selected and instructed man.

To Dismount Bolt Mechanism

1. Draw the bolt fully to the rear, then place the piece across of the left arm.

2. Lift the front end of hook of extractor off bolt with left thumb and at the same time turn bolt handle to left with right hand (Fig. 118). The bolt can then be drawn from the receiver.

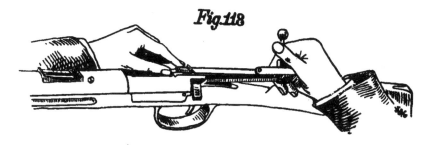

Fig.118

3. Take the bolt handle in left hand, back of hand down, bolt upside down. Grasp the cocking piece with right hand (Fig. 119).

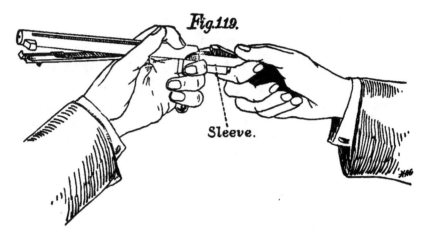

4. Slightly draw back cocking piece and turn it towards the operator until the firing pin can be removed from the bolt.

5. Take firing pin in left hand and bear down on point of striker with right thumb until it leaves the firing pin; remove main spring from firing pin and the latter from sleeve.

To Assemble Bolt Mechanism

1. Observe that the safety lock is turned to the left. Reverse the order of the steps of fifth operation in dismounting.

2. Grasp the bolt handle in left hand as in third operation in dismounting, and the firing pin in the right hand, extractor uppermost. Insert firing pin in bolt.

3. Grasp handle of bolt with fingers of both hands, bolt directed downward, and with both thumbs on the rear of safety lock (Fig. 120), push strongly forward and turn to right with thumbs until the arm of the sleeve engages the collar of the bolt.

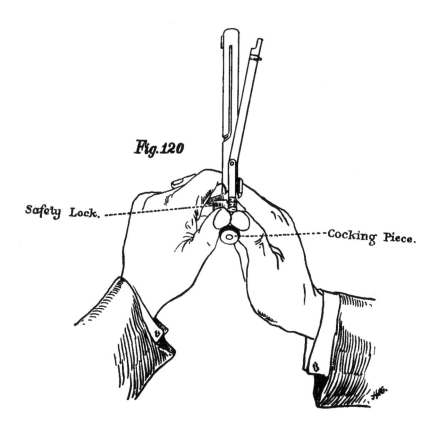

Fig.120

Safety Lock. ---- ---- Cocking Piece.

4. Grasp bolt and cocking piece as in third operation for dismounting. Draw back and turn cocking piece from the operator until its nose enters the notch on the rear end of the bolt (Fig 119).

5. Take bolt in the right hand and introduce it into the receiver, keeping the extractor lifted with the right thumb (Fig. 121). Turn bolt to right and at the same time press strongly with the first finger against right side of extractor.

The American Krag Rifle and Carbine

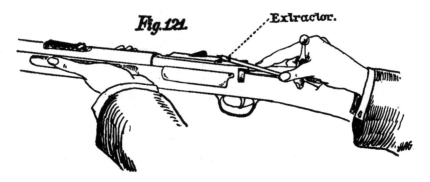

Fig.121. Extractor.

To Dismount Magazine Mechanism

1. The gate being closed, engage the flanged head of a cartridge case under the lug on the front end of the hinge bar head and turn the latter toward the gate, out of its seat; then bear heavily on the gate with the palm of the right hand, to overcome the pressure of the magazine spring, and, with the left, press forward against the lug, drawing the hinge bar pin from the receiver.

2. Remove the gate, magazine spring, and carrier and follower.

To Assemble Magazine Mechanism

1. Hold the piece with the right side uppermost. Insert arbor of carrier into its hole in receiver and place end of left thumb across magazine to prevent carrier swinging into place.

2. Place magazine spring in its channel, convex side up, rounded end to the rear, particularly observing that the lip at its front end rests in the notch on the heel of the carrier.

3. Place gate in its seat, lug entering between carrier and magazine spring. Remove left thumb and at the same time press gate against magazine spring with right hand.

282

The American Krag Rifle and Carbine

4. Insert hinge bar pin in front hinge hole in receiver with left hand, and press gate down strongly until the pin can be pushed through gate into rear hinge hole.

5. After the hinge bar pin is fully home, turn the head into its seat by opening the gate.

To Complete Dismounting
Not to be done by Soldier

The bolt and magazine mechanisms having been dismounted, proceed as follows:

1. Remove upper band screw and slip band forward off barrel.

(The upper barrel band cannot be removed from those rifles and carbines with certain "high front sights," most notably the 0.410-inch-high front sight used with the Model 1901 rear sight. It is not a good idea to remove the front sight blade. Slide the barrel band as far forward as possible and work around it.—Ed.)

2. Loosen lower band screw, remove band.
3. To remove the hand guard, raise the leaf of the rear sight to its vertical position and move the slide to top of leaf, force hand guard springs off barrel by screw driver blades inserted between guard and stock, then turn guard across barrel and remove it over the top of sight leaf.

(Following the Government instructions may well crack the handguard. To avoid doing so, carefully remove the rear sight and slide the handguard forward on the barrel until you can lift it straight off.—Ed.)

4. Remove guard screws and guard.
5. Remove receiver and barrel from stock.

The American Krag Rifle and Carbine

(If the barreled receiver will not release from the stock, swab the junction of metal and wood with lemon oil and let soak for several hours. Hold the rifle upside down, the stock wrist in both hands, and gently ([!]) tap the muzzle on a carpeted floor. If the stock does not release, swab with more lemon oil and repeat. Do not force or you will splinter the stock wood.—Ed.)

6. Remove side plate screw, then side plate by pushing out the rear end, until free from the receiver, and draw to the rear.

7. Remove ejector pin by means of its knob, and then ejector.

8. Press trigger forward until nose of sear is withdrawn from its slot in receiver; then bearing against right side of sear, push it out of its seat.

9. Turn cut-off until point of spring spindle rests on ridge in spring spindle seat of receiver. A light tap on front edge of thumb-piece will remove cut-off. The point of the spring spindle will rest on the ridge when the spring will not turn the cut-off up or down.

10. To remove safety lock, turn it vertical and strike front face of its thumb-piece a light blow.

The rear sight leaf should never be removed from the base nor the base from the barrel except for making repairs.

(Ordnance Department instructions to the soldier.—Ed.)

The barrel should never be unscrewed from the receiver.

To Assemble after Dismounting

1. Safety Lock. Introduce the point of the tang of a small file, or any tool of similar size and shape, between the thumb-piece and the spring spindle, thus compressing the spring and forcing the spring spindle into the thumb-piece; insert the safety lock spindle in its hole in the sleeve, the thumb-piece being held vertical, push the safety lock forward, gradually withdrawing the tool.

The American Krag Rifle and Carbine

2. Cut-Off. Insert its spindle, the thumb-piece turned down into the cut-off hole in the receiver, until the spring spindle strikes the receiver; then with the blade of a screw-driver, force the spring spindle into its hole in the thumb-piece and push the cut-off into place. Care must be taken that the flattened and not the straight sides of the spring spindle bear on the curved surface of the recesses in the receiver.

3. Sear and trigger. Insert the spring in its hole in the sear, start the hinge of the sear into the seat in the receiver, and with the blade of the screw-driver, compress the spring in its hole until the sear can be pushed into place.

(This step requires a great deal of patience.—Ed.)

Reverse and follow in inverse order the other operations of dismounting.

Appendix F
Glossary

Air Chamber	Early Ordnance Department designation for lightening grooves in the rifle forend or carbine forearm.
Aperture	Opening in the rear sight.
Bight	Bend in the sling.
Bluing	A chemical or heat process by which the top layers or iron or steel are oxidized to a blue-black color.
Bore	The hollow interior of a gun barrel.
Braze	Process by which two metal parts are joined together by allowing a mixture of melted brass and silver to flow between two joints when heated.
Breech	The rear end of a gun barrel or forward end of the receiver that holds the cartridge to be fired.
Browning	A chemical process by which a steel or iron part is given an even coat of rust to prevent reflections. The term "browning" was used by the Ordnance Department and is synonymous with the modern term "bluing."
Butt	The rear end of a gun stock that is held against the shoulder.
Butt Plate	Metal cap that covers the end of the buttstock to prevent splintering.
Cannelure	Ordnance Department term for rimless cartridge case. Also one or more grooves around the circumference of the bullet into which the case mouth is crimped.
Carburize	To force particles of carbon into soft steel to harden the surface.
Cartouche	A stamp impressed into wood or metal. This final armory inspector's mark is found on the left side of the Krag rifle or carbine stock, above the trigger assembly except for a short time between circa serial #s 1,178 and 1,932 when it appeared on the right side behind and below the bolt handle.

The American Krag Rifle and Carbine

Case-Harden	A process in which iron or low-carbon steel is heated to red hot in the presence of a source of carbon, then cooled quickly without exposure to air to form a thin surface layer of hard metal over a softer, less brittle core. If the metal is cooled in water, it produces mottled blues, reds, and yellows. If cooled in oil, a black color is imparted to the metal.
Chamfer	To remove a sharp metal edge by beveling.
Cleaning Rod	One-piece or jointed wood or metal rod used to clean the barrel's bore. Ordnance called the one-piece rod a ramrod.
Comb	The top ridge of the buttstock.
Crown	The rounded end of the muzzle that protects the rifling.
Doughboy	Nickname for an infantry soldier, predecessor of G.I.
Drift	Flight to right or left of line of sight caused by spin imparted by rifling.
Fillet	Concave filling at the junction of two surfaces.
Flanged Case	Rimmed cartridge case.
Forearm	Part of the carbine stock forward of the receiver, under the barrel.
Forend	Longest part of a rifle stock forward of the receiver, under the barrel.
Forge	To form metal by hammering it after it has been heated to a plastic condition.
Lands	Raised spirals inside a barrel which engrave the bullet and impart spin.
Left Side	Side opposite the magazine gate; that side of the rifle or carbine to your left when held in the firing position.
Lug	Earlike projection which acts as a support, or to which a support can be fastened.
Milled	To shape or dress metal by using a rotary cutter.
Model	Designation applied to weapons. Until the 1930s, the year in which the arm was adopted as the Model designation, i.e., Model 1892 Krag Rifle.
Muzzle	Front of the barrel.

Niter Blue

To impart a bright blue color to steel or iron parts by immersing them in molten potassium nitrate.

Pattern

Designation usually appied to items of equipment. Until 1902, the Pattern designation was the year of adoption, i.e., Pattern 1887 Cartridge Belt Buckle.

Proof

Signature initial or number stamped on wood or metal signifying that the arm has been test-fired with a high-pressure cartridge and meets established specifications.

Ramrod

Wood or steel rod used to seat a ball and powder charge in muzzleloading rifles. Also used by the Ordnance Department to denote one-piece cleaning rods.

Receiver

That part of the firearm to which are attached the stock, barrel, bolt assembly and magazine.

Refurbish

To rebuild or otherwise restore to full service a military firearm.

Right Side

Side with the magazine: that side to the shooter's right when the rifle or carbine is held in the firing position.

Russet

Reddish-brown color; U.S. Army leather equipment was dyed russet brown after 1901.

Sans Serif

A type face in which letters or numbers are without lines or short strokes depending at an angle from a number or letter. This text is an example of a sans serif type face.

Serif

A type face in which the letters have short lines or strokes projecting, usually at an angle from a number or letter. This sentence is an example of a serif type face.

Small

Stock wrist behind the receiver grasped by the shooting hand.

Stamp

A process of forming metal with a power-driven hammer against a die.

Stud

A projection from a surface to which another part is attached.

Survey

To remove an item of equipment from U.S. Army service due to obsolescence or damage.

Temper

To change the physical properties of a metal by heating.

Tenon

The end of a barrel which fits into the front of the receiver.

Zero

To adjust the sights of a firearm so that the bullet strikes the center of a target at a given distance.

Appendix G
Bibliography

Books and Periodicals

Ball, Robert W. *Springfield Armory, Shoulder Weapons 1795-1968*, Antique Trader Books, Dubuque, IA 52004, 1997.

Batha, Thomas D. *U.S. Martial .22 RF Rifles*, Excalibur Publications, Tucson, AZ 85740-5369.

Brophy, Lt. Col. William S., USAR, ret. *The Krag Rifle*, Beinfeld Publishing, Inc., North Hollywood, CA, 1980.

Brophy, Lt. Col. William S., USAR, ret. *Arsenal of Freedom: The Springfield Armory 1890-1948*, Andrew Mowbray, Inc. Publishers, Lincoln, RI, 1991.

Catalog of the Stevens-Pope Rifle Barrels and Specialties, J. Stevens Arms & Tool Co., Chicopee Falls, Mass., 1902.

Cunningham, Gary M. *American Military Bayonets of the 20th Century*, Scott A. Duff Publications, Export, PA 15632, 1998.

The Development of the Mills Woven Cartridge Belt, 1877-1956, The Mills Equipment Company Ltd, London, 1956.

Duguld, Col. A.F. CMG. *A Question of Confidence*, Service Publications, Ottawa K2C 3Y9, 1999.

Frasca, A. J., and R. H. Hill. *The .45-70 Springfield*, Springfield Publishing Company, Northridge, CA, 1980.

The American Krag Rifle and Carbine

Frasca, A. J. *The .45-70 Springfield, Book II, Springfield Caliber .58, .50, .45 and .30 Breech Loaders in the U.S. Service, 1865–1893*, Frasca Publishing, Springfield, Ohio, 1997.

Hardin, Albert N. Jr. *The American Bayonet 1776–1964*, Albert N. Hardin Jr., New Jersey, 1977.

Langellier, John P. *Uncle Sam's Little Wars: The Spanish-American War, Philippine Insurrection and Boxer Rebellion, 1898–1902*, Chelsea House Publishers, Philadelphia, PA, 2002.

M. C. Lilley & Company. *Regulation United States Army Uniforms and Equipments for National Guard Officers*, Catalogue No. 24, Columbus, Ohio, 1914.

MacCarthy, D.E. "The United States Armory at Springfield, Mass. – 1," *American Machinist Magazine*, March 22, 1900.

MacCarthy, D.E. "The United States Armory at Springfield, Mass. – 2," *American Machinist Magazine*, March 29, 1900.

MacCarthy, D.E. "The United States Armory at Springfield, Mass. – 3," *American Machinist Magazine*, April 5, 1900.

Mallory, Franklin B., and Ludwig Olson. *The Krag Rifle Story*, Springfield Research Service, Silver Spring, MD 20914, 2nd edition, 2001.

Musicant, Ivan. *The Banana Wars: A History of United States Military Intervention in Latin America from the Spanish-American War to the Invasion of Panama*, Macmillan Publishing Company, New York, 1990.

O'Donnell, Michael J., and J. Duncan Campbell. *American Military Belt Plates*, O'Donnell Publications, Arlington, VA, 1966.

The American Krag Rifle and Carbine

Parkhurst, E.G. "The Manufacture of Military Rifle Barrels," *American Machinist Magazine*, April 26, 1900.

Phillips, William. "The Evolution of the Pocket-Type Rifle Cartridge Belt in the United States Service," *Journal of the Company of Military Historians*, Vol. XXII, Spring, 1970.

Poyer, Joe. *The Model 1903 Springfield Rifle and Its Variations*, 2nd Edition, North Cape Publications, Inc., Tustin, CA 92781, 2004.

Poyer, Joe, and Steve Kehaya. *The Swedish Mauser Rifles*, 2nd Edition, North Cape Publications, Inc., Tustin, CA 92781, 2003.

Poyer, Joe, and Craig Riesch. *The .45-70 Springfield*, North Cape Publications, Inc., Tustin, CA 92781, 4th Edition, 2006.

"Serial Numbers of Known U.S. Krags," *Serial Numbers of U.S. Martial Arms*, Volumes 1, 2, and 3, Springfield Research Service, Silver Spring, MD 20914. 1990.

Shields, Joseph W. *From Flintlock to Ml*, Coward-McCann, Inc., New York, 1954.

Shockley, Col. Philip M. *The Krag-Jørgensen Rifle in Service*, World-Wide Gun Report, Inc., Aledo, IL 1960.

Stubbs, Mary Lee, and Stanley Russell Connor. "Armor-Cavalry, Part 1, Regular Army and Army Reserve," *Army Lineage Series*, Office of the Chief of Military History, United States Army, U.S. Government Printing Office, Washington, D.C., 1969.

Waite, M.D., and B.D. Ernst. *Trapdoor Springfield: The United States Springfield Single Shot Rifle, 1865–1893*, Beinfeld Publishing, North Hollywood, CA, 1980.

The American Krag Rifle and Carbine

Wallace, W. B., Captain. *Text Book of Small Arms*, His Majesty's Stationery Office, London, 1904.

U.S. and Philippine Government Publications
"Annual Reports of the Chief of Ordnance to the Secretary of War for the Fiscal Year ended June 30, 1894, 1895, 1896, 1897," Government Printing Office, Washington.

"Annual Reports of the War Department for the Fiscal Year ended June 30, 1898, 1899, 1900, 1901, 1902, 1903 and 1904, Report of the Chief of Ordnance," Government Printing Office, Washington.

Description and Rules for the Management of the U.S. Magazine Rifle and Carbine, Calibre .30, Government Printing Office, Washington, 1894.

Description and Rules for the Management of the U.S. Magazine Rifle and Carbine, Calibre .30, Government Printing Office, Washington, 1898.

Description and Rules for the Management of the U.S. Magazine Rifle and Carbine, Calibre .30, Government Printing Office, Washington, 1917.

Hersey, Mark L. "Report of the Philippine Commission, Report of the Director of Constabulary, Appendix 6, Report of the Chief Supply Officer, Ordnance Division, FY 1906," Bureau of Constabulary, Manila, P.I., August 1, 1906.

Annual Report, Report to the Secretary of Commerce and Police, Bureau of the Constabulary, War Department, U.S.A., 1907.

Fisk, Asa F. "Report of the Chief Supply Officer, Office of the Ordnance Officer, Bureau of Constabulary, Report for FY 1907," Manila, P.I., July 29, 1907.

The American Krag Rifle and Carbine

Fisk, Asa F. "Report for Fiscal Year Ending June 30, 1908, Bureau of Constabulary, Office of the Property Officer," Manila, August 10, 1908.

Hersey, Mark L. "Report of the Chief Supply Officer, Headquarters, Philippine Constabulary, Officer of the Chief Supply Officer," Manila, P.I., August 17, 1908.

Official Register of the United States Containing a List of the Officers and Employees in the Civil, Military, and Naval Service together with a List of Vessels Belonging to the United States, July 1, 1903, Volume 1, Legislative, Executive, and Judicial, Government Printing Office, Washington, 1903.

"1890–1900 Mean Winter Temperature," Framingham, MA, U.S. Historical Climatology Network Data Set, National Archives, Washington, D.C.

The American Krag Rifle and Carbine

ABOUT THE AUTHOR

Joe Poyer is the author of more than 400 magazine articles on firearms, the modern military, military history and personal security. He has written and published twelve novels with worldwide sales exceeding five million copies and authored or coauthored nine nonfiction books on the modern military from other publishers.

He is the editorial director and publisher of North Cape Publications®, Inc., which publishes the "For Collectors Only®" and "A Shooter's and Collector's Guide" series of books for firearms collectors and shooters. In these series, he has written or coauthored: *The .45-70 Springfield*; *U.S. Winchester Trench and Riot Guns, and Other U.S. Combat Shotguns*; *The M1 Garand, 1936 to 1957*; *The SKS Carbine*; *The M14-Type Rifle*; *The SAFN-49 Battle Rifle*; *The Swedish Mauser Rifles*; *The M16/AR15 Rifle*; *The Model 1903 Springfield Rifle and Its Variations*; *The American Krag Rifle and Carbine*; *Swiss Magazine Loading Rifles, 1869 to 1958;* and *The AK-47 and AK-74 Kalashnikov Rifles and Their Variations*.

Mr. Poyer has served as editor of the following magazines: *Safe & Secure Living*; *International Military Review*; *International Naval Review* and as field editor for *International Combat Arms*. He is currently at work on a new book in the "For Collectors Only" series, *The Model 1911 and 1911A1 Military and Commercial Pistols*.

Mr. Poyer was the on-camera Military Affairs Analyst and Reporter for a major television station in Los Angeles, California. He also imported the very fine L1A1A inch pattern FAL rifles from Australia in the late 1980s.

ABOUT THE EDITOR

Craig Riesch is a well-known collector and scholar of U.S. military small arms. He is the author of *U.S. M1 Carbines, Wartime Production* and is the coauthor of *The .45-70 Springfield* and *The M1 Garand, 1936 to 1957*. He also edited *The American Krag Rifle and Carbine* and *Swiss Magazine Loading Rifles, 1869 to 1958*, all in the "For Collectors Only" series plus *The AK-47 and AK-74 Kalashnikov Rifles* in the "Shooter's and Collector's" series. Both series are guides to antique and collectible modern firearms identification and verification.

Mr. Riesch has spent a great deal of time studying U.S. military firearms and is consulted by many collectors for authentication of military and civilian arms. He has been a collector himself for over forty years. Mr. Riesch is a U.S. Army combat veteran and served in Vietnam during the period of the Tet Offensive. He worked for 33 years as a product operations manager for a major defense company.

The American Krag Rifle and Carbine

BOOKS FROM

NORTH CAPE PUBLICATIONS®, INC.

The books in the "For Collectors Only®" and "A Shooter's and Collector's Guide" series are designed to provide the firearms collector with an accurate record of the markings, dimensions and finish found on an original firearm as it was shipped from the factory.

FOR COLLECTORS ONLY® SERIES

The .58- and .50-Caliber Rifles and Carbines of the Springfield Armory, 1865–1872, by Richard A. Hosmer ($19.95). This book describes the .58- and .50-caliber rifles and carbines that were developed at the Springfield Armory between 1865 and 1872 and which led ultimately to the selection of the famed Allin "trapdoor."

Serbian and Yugoslav Mauser Rifles, by Branko Bogdanovic ($19.95). Thousands of Yugoslav Mauser rifles have been imported into North America in the last two decades and Mr. Bogdanovic's book will help the collector and shooter determine which model he or she has, and its antecedents. Every Mauser that found its way into military service in Serbia/Yugoslavia is listed and described.

Swiss Magazine Loading Rifles, 1869 to 1958, by Joe Poyer ($19.95). A complete part-by-part description for the Vetterli, Schmidt-Rubin, and K-31 rifles in all their variations by serial number range, plus a history of their development and use, their cleaning, maintenance, and how to shoot them safely and accurately.

The American Krag Rifle and Carbine (2nd edition, revised), by Joe Poyer, edited by Craig Riesch ($19.95). A part-by-part description of the first magazine repeating arm adopted for general service in American military history.

The Model 1903 Springfield Rifle and Its Variations (2nd edition, revised and expanded), by Joe Poyer ($22.95). Includes every model of the Model 1903 from the ramrod bayonet to the Model 1903A4 Sniper rifle. Every part is described by serial number range, markings and finish.

The American Krag Rifle and Carbine

The .45-70 Springfield (4th edition, revised and expanded), by Joe Poyer and Craig Riesch ($19.95), covers the entire range of .45-caliber "trapdoor" Springfield arms, including bayonets, tools and accoutrements.

U.S. Winchester Trench and Riot Guns and Other U.S. Combat Shotguns (2nd edition, revised), by Joe Poyer ($16.95). Describes the elusive and little-known "Trench Shotgun" and all other combat shotguns used by U.S. military forces.

U.S. M1 Carbines, Wartime Production (5th edition, revised and expanded), by Craig Riesch ($19.95), describes the four models of M1 Carbines from all ten manufacturers. Complete with codes for every part by serial number range.

The M1 Garand, 1936 to 1957 (4th edition, revised and expanded), by Joe Poyer and Craig Riesch ($19.95). This book covers such important identification factors as manufacturer's markings, proof marks, final acceptance cartouches stampings and heat treatment lot numbers plus detailed breakdowns of every part in minute detail.

Winchester Lever Action Repeating Firearms, by Arthur Pirkle
    Volume 1, The Models of 1866, 1873 & 1876 ($19.95)
    Volume 2, The Models of 1886 and 1892 ($19.95)
    Volume 3, The Models of 1894 and 1895 ($19.95)
These famous lever action repeaters are completely analyzed part-by-part by serial number range in this first new series on these fine weapons in twenty years.

The SKS Carbine (3rd revised and expanded edition), by Steve Kehaya and Joe Poyer ($16.95). The SKS Carbine "is profusely illustrated, articulately researched and covers all aspects of its development as well as . . . other combat guns used by the USSR and other Communist bloc nations." Glen Voorhees, Jr., *Gun Week.*

British Enfield Rifles, by Charles R. Stratton (each volume, $16.95)
    Volume 1, SMLE (No. 1) Mk I and Mk III
    Volume 2, Lee-Enfield No. 4 and No. 5 Rifles
    Volume 4, Pattern 1914 and U.S. Model of 1917 Rifles

The American Krag Rifle and Carbine

The British Army's famed rifles are analyzed in detail on a part-by-part basis, complete with all inspector's and military markings. Each volume above now in 2nd edition, revised.

The Mosin-Nagant Rifle (4th revised and expanded edition), by Terence W. Lapin ($19.95). A comprehensive volume covering all aspects and models from the Imperial Russian rifles to the Finnish, American, Polish, Chinese, Romanian and North Korean variations. Includes part-by-part descriptions of all makers plus all variants such as carbines and sniper rifles.

The Swedish Mauser Rifles (2nd edition), by Steve Kehaya and Joe Poyer ($19.95). A complete history of the development and use of the Swedish Mauser rifles is provided as well as a part-by-part description of each component. All 24 models are described and a complete description of the sniper rifles and their telescopic sights is included. All markings, codes, regimental and other military markings are charted and explained. A thorough and concise explanation of the Swedish Mauser rifle, both civilian and military.

A SHOOTER'S AND COLLECTOR'S GUIDE SERIES

The AK-47 and AK-74 Kalashnikov Rifles and Their Variations (2nd edition, revised and expanded), by Joe Poyer ($22.95). The AK-47 and its replacement, the AK-74, are examined on a part-by-part basis to show the differences between various types of receivers, other parts, and the AK and AKM models. Also contains a detailed survey of all models of the Kalashnikov rifle from the AK-47 to the AK-108.

The M16/AR15 Rifle (3rd edition, revised and expanded), by Joe Poyer ($22.95). This 155-page, profusely illustrated, large-format book examines the development, history, and current and future use of the M16/AR15. It describes in detail all civilian AR15 rifles and takes the reader step-by-step through the process of accurizing the AR15 into an extremely accurate target rifle.

The M14-Type Rifle (3rd edition, revised and expanded), by Joe Poyer ($19.95). A study of the U.S. Army's last and short-lived .30-caliber battle rifle. Also includes the National Match M14 rifle, the M21 and M25 sniper rifles, civilian semiautomatic match rifles, receivers, parts and accessories

The American Krag Rifle and Carbine

and the Chinese M14s. A guide to custom-building a service-type rifle or a match-grade, precision rifle.

The SAFN-49 Battle Rifle, by Joe Poyer ($14.95). This detailed study of the SAFN-49 provides a part-by-part examination of the four calibers in which the rifle was made, a description of the SAFN-49 Sniper Rifle and its telescopic sights, plus maintenance, assembly/disassembly, accurizing, restoration and shooting. A new exploded view and section view are included.

COLLECTOR'S GUIDE TO MILITARY UNIFORMS

Campaign Clothing: Field Uniforms of the Indian War Army
Volume 1, 1866–1871 ($12.95)
Volume 2, 1872–1886 ($14.95)
Lee A. Rutledge has produced a unique perspective on the uniforms of the Army of the United States during the late Indian War period following the Civil War. He discusses what the soldier really wore when on campaign. No white hats and yellow bandanas here.

A Guide Book to U.S. Army Dress Helmets, 1872–1904, by Mark Kasal and Don Moore ($16.95). From 1872 to 1904, the men and officers of the U.S. Army wore a fancy, plumed or spiked helmet on all dress occasions. As ubiquitous as they were in the late 19th century, they are extremely scarce today. Kasal and Moore have written a step-by-step, part-by-part analysis of both the Models 1872 and 1881 dress helmets and their history and use. Profusely illustrated with black-and-white and color photographs of actual helmets.

All of the above books can be obtained directly from North Cape Publications®, Inc., P.O. Box 1027, Tustin, CA 92781 or by calling Toll Free 1-800 745-9714. Orders may also be placed by Fax (714 832-5302) or via e-mail to ncape@ix.netcom.com. CA residents add 7.75% sales tax. Current rates are any two books: Media Mail (7-21 days) $3.95, add $0.95 for each additional book. Priority Mail: 1-2 books $5.95 or 3-10 books, $10.50. International Rates on request to E-mail address: ncape@ix.netcom.com. Visit our Internet Website at http://www.northcapepubs.com. Our complete, up-to-date book list can always be found there.

The American Krag Rifle and Carbine

NOTES